Lectures in Industrial Organization Theory

IB

Lectures in Industrial
Organization Theory

Kaushik Basu

BLACKWELL
Oxford UK & Cambridge USA

First published 1993

Blackwell Publishers
238 Main Street, Suite 501
Cambridge, Massachusetts 02142
USA

108 Cowley Road
Oxford OX4 1JF
UK

Library of Congress Cataloging-in-Publication Data
Basu, Kaushik.
  Lectures in industrial organization theory / by Kaushik Basu.
    p.   cm.
  Includes bibliographical references and index.
  ISBN 1-55786-111-0 (hb). — ISBN 1-55786-343-1 (pbk.)
  1. Industrial organization (Economic theory)   I. Title.
HD2326.B373   1993
338.6 — dc20   92-7707   CIP

British Library Cataloguing in Publication Data
A CIP catalogue record for this book is available from
the British Library.

Typeset in 10 on 12pt Times
by Colset Pte Ltd, Singapore
Printed in Great Britain by Biddles Ltd., Guildford

This book is printed on acid-free paper

Contents

Preface ix

1 **Introduction** 1
  1.1 Origins 1
  1.2 Prospectus 3

2 **Game Theory: Normal-Form Games** 5
  2.1 Introduction 5
  2.2 Nash equilibrium 8
  2.3 A refinement of Nash: perfection 13
  2.4 A coarsening of Nash: rationalizability 18

3 **The Standard Market Structures** 25
  3.1 Introduction 25
  3.2 Monopoly 25
  3.3 Competition 28
  3.4 Oligopoly 31
  3.5 Dominant firms and fringes 33

4 **Oligopoly and Some Non-Cournot Equilibria** 36
  4.1 Introduction 36
  4.2 Rationalizability and oligopoly 37
  4.3 Bertrand equilibrium and the Edgeworth indeterminacy 40

5 **Nonlinear Pricing** 44
  5.1 Introduction 44
  5.2 Two-part tariffs 45
  5.3 Monopoly and efficiency 48
  5.4 Nonlinear pricing 51
  5.5 Tie-ins, clusters and interlinkage 60

6 **Quality**   66
  6.1 Introduction   66
  6.2 Quality hierarchies   67
  6.3 Strategic substitutes and complements   69
  6.4 Quality, status and market disequilibria   71

7 **Durability**   80
  7.1 Introduction   80
  7.2 Durability under monopoly and competition   80
  7.3 Durable goods: renting and selling   88

8 **Location, Brands and Advertising**   93
  8.1 Introduction   93
  8.2 Location   93
  8.3 Brand proliferation   96
  8.4 Advertising   99

9 **Game Theory: Extensive-Form Games**   105
  9.1 Introduction   105
  9.2 The idea of perfection in extensive games   107
  9.3 Repeated games and trigger strategies   112
  9.4 Simple strategy profiles   117
  9.5 Critiques, refinements and extensions   120

10 **Oligopoly in the Extensive Form: Two Examples**   124
  10.1 Introduction   124
  10.2 The two fishermen   124
  10.3 Towards collusion   129

11 **Quantities and Prices**   133
  11.1 Introduction   133
  11.2 First quantity, then price   134
  11.3 Quick-response oligopoly   137
  11.4 Supply functions equilibria   141

12 **Collusion**   149
  12.1 Introduction   149
  12.2 Some legal issues   150
  12.3 Infinitely repeated oligopoly   152
  12.4 Finitely repeated oligopoly   156
  12.5 Extensions   159

13 **Entry Deterrence**   163
  13.1 Introduction   163
  13.2 Capacity, investment and deterrence   165
  13.3 Chain stores and reputations   177
  13.4 Sequential entry   182

14 **Managerial Incentives**   188
    14.1 Introduction   188
    14.2 The incentive equilibrium   189
    14.3 Extensions and critiques   193

15 **Switching Costs**   196
    15.1 Introduction   196
    15.2 A formal model   197
    15.3 Switching costs and rural credit   202
    15.4 Captive segment conditions and profit   204

16 **Government Intervention**   208
    16.1 Introduction   208
    16.2 Mixed oligopoly   209
    16.3 Partly state-owned firms and entry barriers   212
    16.4 Pigouvian interventions   215
    16.5 The state and the law: some open issues   216

References   219

Subject Index   230

Author Index   234

To my mother, Usha Basu

Preface

This book is based on a one-semester graduate course, which I taught at Princeton University's Department of Economics during 1989–91. After my return to the Delhi School of Economics I have worked extensively on the "lectures" to convert them into the present textbook. This subsequent work consisted mainly of elaborating on arguments, elucidating theorems and constructing diagrams which aid intuition – the main objective of the exercise being to expand the reach of the book. Given the rapidly rising literacy of economics students, I hope that by the time the book makes it to the stands it will be of some use even to senior undergraduates.

The idea of writing up my lectures as a book is not something that I pursued without apprehension. But I had a clear agenda. I wanted a book which would take the reader into modern industrial economics starting from the first principles of game theory, which would view the subject as one grounded in institutions and the law and, finally, which would be short and serve the purpose of a one-semester course, whether for self-education or as lecture material.

The last objective in a field as large and exciting as industrial organization theory implied that I had to confront the decision of what to include and what to omit. While I know of economists agonizing over this problem, I found, somewhat to my dismay, that in my case what came in really handy was my ignorance. It ensured that many of the themes that were omitted could not have been otherwise. Over and above this, I was guided by the principle that the book should enable the reader to *pose* questions of policy. It seems to me that the best drafted laws concerning monopoly and other industrial matters are often misconceived; and this is an area where *theoretical* economics has a lot to offer. I have therefore tried to select topics which draw the reader's attention to such matters. The two chapters on game theory are self-contained. They go somewhat beyond what is needed in the other chapters. It is hoped that having read this book the reader will be able to take up with ease topics which do not occur here but are in keeping with his or her interests.

The "his or her" reminds me that at one stage I did try to mix the genders of the agents in the book to signal my stand against sex discrimination. The strategy that I followed was to use male pronouns for all agents in the first eight chapters and female pronouns in the last eight. But it later struck me that this implied that men play normal-form games and women only extensive-form ones. I feared this would be playing into the hands of my detractors! I therefore abandoned such effort and maintain that "he" in scientific discourse means "he or she."

As far as my debts go, there are many. My students in Princeton not only bore the brunt of an emerging manuscript but their queries often stimulated me into new lines of thought. Some of the chapters or related papers were presented in seminars at Harvard, Princeton, Barcelona, Copenhagen, the Delhi School of Economics and the Indian Statistical Institute in New Delhi and I benefited immensely from these.

During my stay in Princeton, Abhijit Banerji, Jeroen Swinkels, Jorgen Weibull, and I ran a weekly game-theory workshop. It was supposed to be a give-and-take of knowledge from which I got away with a disproportionate amount of take.

Several people have read parts of the manuscript and discussed related matters with me and influenced my thinking. The list includes Yukiko Abe, Dilip Abreu, T.C.A. Anant, Alaka Basu, V. Bhaskar, the late Sukhamoy Chakravarty, David Cooper, Arup Daripa, Avinash Dixit, Harold Kuhn, Ivan Lengwiler, Ajit Mishra, Anjan Mukherji, Badal Mukherji, Andy Postlewaite, Anindya Sen, and Nirvikar Singh.

My secretaries in Princeton, Barbara Mains and Claire Cabelus, greatly eased my load by not only taking on the word-processing work but helping me with my research in more ways than I could have asked for.

I spent the summer of 1991 at the Indira Gandhi Institute in Bombay. The excellent research support and the congenial atmosphere of the Institute were very valuable to me during the last stages of my work. In Delhi, I have been fortunate to have, as in several other earlier ventures, the remarkably intelligent research assistance of Shobhana Chandra.

And, finally, the Delhi School of Economics, where I have met some of the best students anywhere, provided an intellectual atmosphere which handsomely made up for the more mundane things it lacks, such as filing cabinets and telephones that work.

Kaushik Basu

1

Introduction

1.1 ORIGINS

The increasing influence of a discipline is evident when it usurps the acronym of another. For a long time, a mention of "IO" in economics would automatically be taken to be a reference to input–output analysis. But input–output's claim to the acronym IO had to give way to the demands of industrial organization, in the same way that those writing on "almost ideal demand systems" have been forced to look for a new short form in order to make room for a more urgent syndrome of present times.

But industrial organization is not a new subject. Not only are its foundations traceable to the eighteenth century, but by 1838 we have a neat mathematical model for analyzing duopolies, thanks to the economic dabblings of a professor of mechanics at Lyon, in France. The reference is, of course, to Antoine Cournot. Cournot was a pioneer, and he made no effort to persuade his contemporaries. And neither were they persuaded. So Cournot's work was left to languish for a very long time, in fact to the end of the nineteenth century, when it was revived by the founders of marginalist analysis. Some interest in the work was also generated by a review article by Joseph Bertrand, a mathematician, in the *Journal des Savants*,[1] 1883. Bertrand's article itself had the germs of interesting ideas which would not be recognized as such until well into the twentieth century. In contemporary industrial organization theory, the "Bertrand equilibrium" is quite ubiquitous. Indeed this must be the only time when an equilibrium has been named after a person on the basis of a book review.

While Cournot laid the foundations for abstract theoretical work, the first full-fledged work on industrial organization, dwelling on analytical issues and evidence from the world of business, is probably *The Economics of Industry* by Alfred and Mary Paley Marshall published in 1879. This is not a very well-known book and one reason for this must be that Alfred Marshall never thought well of much of the book[2] and its better parts were absorbed in his *magnum opus*, *Principles of Economics*, 1890.

In this little book, the Marshalls delve into many "contemporary" themes. They talk about competition and monopoly. They point out that with free competition prices get pushed down to the cost of production. This is dubbed the "law of normal supply." In writing about monopoly, they point out how a monopoly outcome can be brought about by a group of firms acting collusively. Referring to a collusive industry as a "combination," they remark how combinations, even if they do not succeed in charging monopoly prices, can raise prices above the competitive level.

In the same chapter on monopolies and combinations, a very interesting discussion is conducted on how cartels can be policed and what kinds of entry-deterrent strategies can be used by cartels to prevent their power from being undermined. These are, of course, subjects close to the heart of contemporary industrial organization theory, and the book by Alfred and Mary Marshall can be thought of as a precursor to the works of Joe Bain and Paolo Sylos-Labini.

Although this is not always evident from Alfred Marshall's written work, he took great interest in the facts and statistics of industry. When he and his wife went to the Alps for their summer vacations, as holiday reading Alfred would carry books of "facts"![3] Behind most of his theoretical work on industry were reams of industrial statistics which he had collected and studied.

After the Marshallian period, the progress in theoretical and empirical research became somewhat divided. In the 1930s theoretical research on industry got impetus from the works of Edward Chamberlin and Joan Robinson.[4] But by the 1950s industrial economics had become synonymous with empirical studies of industries, the most prominent being the work of Joe Bain.

At one level the chasm between theory and empiricism seems to be growing, with the former having received a big boost in recent times as a consequence of advances in game theory. At last the dominance of marginalist analysis seems to be giving way to strategic models. And this new technique has made industrial organization a major industry among economists.

Somewhat curiously, these advances, by provoking new interest in industry, have also generated considerable empirical research in this area, so much so that the *Journal of Industrial Economics* celebrated this phenomenon in 1987 with a special issue entitled "Renaissance in empirical industrial economics."

Quite apart from such empirical work, there is another way in which modern industrial theory has moved closer to worldly matters. For a long time it was felt that economists had very little to say on matters of industrial legislation such as antitrust and other restrictive trade practices. It is increasingly clear that lawyers have even less to say on these matters, but they do. Here, therefore, is one area with scope for intellectual arbitrage. After all, which industrial practices can be considered restrictive or harmful to welfare can be very difficult to decide and the judgment will depend on intricate economic analysis. Though still in its nascency, research on the law and economics of industry is potentially a very important field and this book will touch upon the subject in more than one place.

1.2 PROSPECTUS

The present book is focused primarily on recent *theoretical* advances in the study of industrial organization. Yet I wish to keep it rooted in reality. I try to achieve this by my choice of topics and by making frequent digressions to comment on institutional matters in the light of the theoretical research discussed in the book.

Much of the work presented here is game-theoretic. Hence, it seemed useful to divide the book into two parts – one, where time does not enter the picture, that is, firms interact simultaneously and in a one-shot manner, and another, where the sequence of moves is germane. In the language of game theory, the first relates to normal- or strategic-form games and the second relates to extensive-form games. Accordingly, the next chapter is an introduction to normal-form game theory . The six chapters that follow it are all on industrial economics, where the behavior of and interaction between firms can be modeled as part of a normal-form game.

Chapter 9 is once again a game-theoretic interlude where the reader is introduced to extensive-form games and, in particular, repeated one-shot games. This is followed by six chapters on industrial organization, which make use of solution concepts from extensive-form game theory. The final chapter is devoted to a discussion of government intervention.

Because of the rapid advance in the pure *theory* of industrial organization, its methods are also of intrinsic interest and can be used in other areas of economics, such as development, agrarian structure and international debt. Digressions to illustrate such applications are made in several places.

NOTES

1 For an English translation see Daughety (1988).
2 He referred to it as a "popular book, which was necessarily superficial" (see Whitaker, 1975, p. 84).
3 See Marshall's letter to J.B. Clark, dated 24 March 1908 (Pigou, 1925, p. 417). For more discussion on Marshall's fastidiousness with facts, see O'Brien (1990).

4 Interesting evidence of this impetus is to be found in the seventh edition, published in 1956, of Chamberlin's book *The Theory of Monopolistic Competition.* In this he supplemented an earlier bibliography on works on monopolistic competition to cover the period May 1948 to May 1956. His search yielded 806 titles. The number of books and papers on this subject in these eight years was therefore "more than the entire period prior to 1948 and brought the total to 1497" (the quote is from the Preface to the Seventh Edition).

2

Game Theory: Normal-Form Games

2.1 INTRODUCTION

Chess, warfare, political skirmishes, and oligopolistic interactions are all kinds of games; and game theory is a method for analyzing such games, predicting outcomes, and prescribing strategies. In this section I shall give a very brief sketch of game theory, in particular that pertaining to non-cooperative normal-form games. Noncooperative extensive-form games will be taken up later. Since I shall not go into cooperative games at all, the adjective "noncooperative" will also be redundant for my purpose.

Before going into a formal discussion, let us consider a particular game: the Battle of the Sexes. Contrary to what one would expect from the title, the Battle is a tame story of a man and a woman planning an evening out. The possible alternatives are to go to a ballet and to watch Sumo wrestling. Both would hate to land up in different places. Should that happen, they get a utility of zero each. If they both go to the ballet the man gets 2 utils and the woman gets 4. If they both go to see Sumo wrestling, the man gets 4 utils and the woman gets 2. What will they do?

The first thing they should do is to write up the game as a *pay-off matrix* as shown below. This makes it easy to analyze.

			Man	
			Ballet	Sumo
G_1:	Woman	Ballet	4, 2	0, 0
		Sumo	0, 0	2, 4

In each cell in the pay-off matrix, the left-hand number is the pay-off of the player choosing between rows and the right-hand number is the pay-off of the column player.

Let us suppose that each player, in this case the man and the woman, has to decide where he or she will go; and the decision is taken simultaneously. These are usual features of a *normal-form* or *strategic-form* game. If they moved in a sequence, then we would have an *extensive-form* game. Let us for the time being restrict attention to the normal form.

A large body of the game-theory literature argues that the two possible outcomes are (Ballet, Ballet) and (Sumo, Sumo). This is because each of these configurations has the following interesting property: starting from such a configuration, no player can benefit through a unilateral change of plan. Consider the case of (Ballet, Ballet). Here the woman is getting 4 utils and the man 2 utils. If the woman changes her strategy from Ballet to Sumo, she will get 0 utils. Similarly if the man, instead of playing Ballet, unilaterally deviates and plays Sumo, he will get 0 utils. More formally, the strategy combinations of (Ballet, Ballet) and (Sumo, Sumo) are the two *Nash equilibria* of the Battle of the Sexes. It should be checked that for any other strategy combination, for example (Sumo, Ballet) – i.e. the woman chooses Sumo and the man chooses Ballet – at least one player expects to benefit from a unilateral deviation.

If the same game was played in a sequence, a pay-off matrix would no longer be a suitable representation. Suppose that the above game is played with the woman moving first. In that case, we would represent the extensive-form game as a *game tree*, as shown in figure 2.1. The first mover, in this case the woman, is referred to as player 1 and the other is referred to as player 2. The first element in each pay-off vector is player 1's pay-off. In labeling the branches, B is used for Ballet and S for Sumo.

A simple backward-induction argument suggests that the equilibrium outcome in this extensive-form game consists of player 1 playing B_1 and player

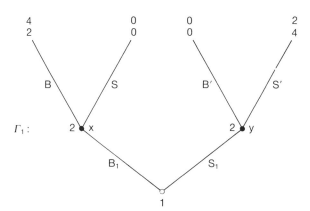

Figure 2.1

2 playing B. The argument goes as follows. Note that if node x is reached, 2 would play B instead of S since that way he gets 2 instead of 0. Similarly, at y, 2 would play S' instead of B'. Since 1 can clearly reason this out, 1 will know that if she plays B_1 she will end up getting 4 and if she plays S_1 she will get 2. Hence 1 will play B_1. Therefore, by this argument we would expect her to move B_1 and him to move B. In fact most *solution concepts* or *equilibrium concepts* will predict (B_1, B) as the outcome.

While a pay-off matrix cannot be used – at least in a straightforward way – to represent an extensive-form game, it is usually supposed that a game tree can be used to represent a normal-form game. This is done in the tree illustrated in figure 2.2.

The main difference between the game trees Γ_1 and Γ_2 is that in Γ_2 there is a broken line joining nodes x and y. This means that when 2 makes his move he does not know whether he is at x or y; that is, 2 has to make his move without knowing what 1 has done. It is in this sense that Γ_2 could be thought of as a simultaneous-move game. What Γ_2 actually represents is a game where

(a)   1 moves first; 1's move is kept secret from 2; and then 2 moves.

Whether we think of Γ_2 as a sufficiently good representation of a normal-form game or not depends on whether we feel that the outcome in a game like (a) would be the same as in a game where

(b)   1 and 2 move simultaneously.

There are some who treat (a) and (b) as indistinguishable in terms of expected outcomes. But it is possible to argue that in (a) player 1 would take advantage of being the first-mover and would necessarily move Ballet; 2

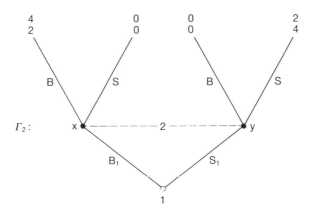

Figure 2.2

would anticipate this and move Ballet as well. Hence, it is possible to argue that, with a structure as in (a), (Ballet, Ballet) is the only possible outcome, whereas with (b), as we have already seen, (Ballet, Ballet) *and* (Sumo, Sumo) are possible. According to this view Γ_2 is not a sufficiently good representation of a normal-form game. So much for extensive forms for the time being. We shall return to them later. Let us now proceed to a formal analysis of normal-form games.

2.2 NASH EQUILIBRIUM

A (noncooperative, normal-form) game has three components. There is a set $N = \{1, \ldots, n\}$ of players. Each player $i \in N$ has a nonempty set S_i of strategies open to him. We shall use S to denote the Cartesian product $S_1 \times \ldots \times S_n$. Each player i has a pay-off function

$$P_i: S \to R$$

where R is the set of real numbers. We denote $(P_1, \ldots, P_n)$ by P. A *game* is simply an ordered triple (N, S, P).

A set S_i of strategies may be finite or infinite, but for simplicity we shall assume that S_i is a subset of the m-dimensional Euclidean space R^m.

It is now easy to see why the Battle of the Sexes is a game. In the Battle, $N = \{\text{woman, man}\}$. Pick any two arbitrary points x and y from R^m. If we think of x as denoting Ballet and y as denoting Sumo, then for all $i \in N$, $S_i = \{x, y\}$. Finally, P_1 and P_2 are as described by the pay-off matrix G_1 above. For example, $P_1(x, x) = 4$, where player 1 is the woman.

Given a game $G = (N, S, P)$, and given $s \in S$ and $t_i \in S_i$, we use (s/t_i) to denote the following strategy combination:

$$(s_1, \ldots, s_{i-1}, t_i, s_{i+1}, \ldots, s_n)$$

In the game G, the strategy combination s^* is a *Nash equilibrium* if and only if, for all $i \in N$,

$$P_i(s^*) \geqslant P_i(s^*/s_i) \qquad \text{for all } s_i \in S_i$$

It is easy to construct games in which no Nash equilibrium exists. This raises the obvious question whether we can isolate a class of games for which a Nash equilibrium always exists. The following theorem answers this question.

Theorem 2.1 If $G = (N, S, P)$ is a game such that for all $i \in N$

(a) S_i is compact and convex
(b) P_i is continuous and

(c) $P_i(s/t_i)$ is quasi-concave with respect to $t_i \in S_i$, for all $s \in S$,

then G has at least one Nash equilibrium.

The proof of this theorem entails the use of Kakutani's fixed point theorem. I shall not give a proof here. For proofs of similar theorems the reader can consult Nash (1951), Rosen (1965), or Friedman (1986). I shall prove instead an important corollary of the above proposition, the proof of which entails an argument similar to that used to prove theorem 2.1 but is less laborious. Before venturing into that, note that since S_i is a subset of a Euclidean space, S_i is *compact* if and only if it is closed and bounded. Note also that a real-valued function f defined on R^m is *quasi-concave* if, for all $x, y \in R^m$ and $\lambda \in (0, 1)$, $f(\lambda x + (1-\lambda)y) \geq \min\{f(x), f(y)\}$. For *strict quasi-concavity* we simply have to change the weak inequality sign, $\geq$, to strict inequality, $>$, in the previous sentence.

Corollary 2.1 If $G = (N, S, P)$ is a game such that (a) and (b), as in theorem 2.1, are satisfied and, in addition, for all $i \in N$, $P_i(s/t_i)$ is strictly quasi-concave with respect to $t_i \in S_i$, for all $s \in S$, then G has at least one Nash equilibrium.

PROOF Suppose the hypothesis of corollary 2.1 is valid. For each player $i \in N$, define the *best response function for i*, $r_i: S \to S_i$, as follows: for all $s \in S$, $r_i(s) = \text{argmax}_{t_i} P_i(s/t_i)$.[1] Conditions (a), (b) and the fact that $P_i(s/t_i)$ is strictly quasi-concave in t_i ensure that $r_i(s)$ must exist and be unique. We shall say that $r: S \to S$ is a best response function if, for all $s \in S$, $r(s) = (r_1(s), \ldots, r_n(s))$.

Since S_i is compact and convex for all i, it follows that S is compact and convex.

Next, it will be shown that r is continuous. Clearly, it is sufficient to prove that r_i is continuous for all i.

Suppose not. Then there exists $s \in S$ and a sequence $\{s^n\}$ in S such that $s^n \to s$ but $r_i(s^n)$ does not converge to $r_i(s)$. This and the compactness of S implies that there is a subsequence which converges to $t_i \neq r_i(s)$. Without loss of generality, suppose that $\{s^n\}$ itself is such a subsequence. Since $P_i(s^n/r_i(s^n)) \geq P_i(s^n/r_i(s))$, for all n, it follows from the continuity of P_i that

$$P_i(s/t_i) \geq P_i(s/r_i(s))$$

This is a contradiction, since $r_i(s)$ is the unique best response of player i to s.

Since r is continuous and S is compact and convex, we know by Brouwer's fixed point theorem[2] that there exists $s^* \in S$ such that $r(s^*) = s^*$. That is, for all $i \in N$,

$$P_i(s^*) \geqslant P_i(s^*/s_i) \qquad \text{for all } s_i \in S_i$$

In other words, s^* is a Nash equilibrium. ■

What is unfortunate about this theorem is that it is inapplicable to a large class of games, for instance those in which players have finite strategies. That is, for some i, $\# S_i < \infty$. Hence, the Prisoner's Dilemma, the Battle of the Sexes and the game described below are excluded from the purview of the above theorem.

Player 2

		s_2	t_2
s_1		4, 3	3, 4
t_1		3, 4	4, 3

G_2: Player 1

Hence for such games we cannot be sure of the existence of Nash equilibria. Indeed the game G_2 just described does not have an equilibrium.

One way of getting around this problem is to allow players to use "mixed strategies." A player is said to be using a mixed strategy if he decides on a certain probability for playing each of his strategies and then uses a random procedure to pick the *pure strategy* he actually plays. To avoid confusion, what was earlier referred to as a strategy will be called a pure strategy whenever we are allowing for mixed strategies as well.

Let us restrict attention to games in which players have finite (pure) strategies. Consider a game $G = (N, S, P)$. Let $\# S_i = m_i$ for all i. Then a *mixed strategy* for player i is a function $\sigma_i : S_i \to R$ such that, for all $s \in S_i$, $\sigma_i(s) \geqslant 0$ and $\Sigma_{s \in S_i} \sigma_i(s) = 1$.

Given game G, we could define a game $G_M = (N, \bar{M}(S), \bar{P})$ which is a mixed-strategy counterpart of G. $\bar{M}(S)$ is defined as follows: $\bar{M}(S) = M(S_1) \times \ldots \times M(S_n)$, where $M(S_i)$ is the set of all mixed strategies open to player i. It is easy to see that $M(S_i)$ could be thought of as a unit simplex in an m_i-dimensional Euclidean space.

To see this suppose that player i has three pure strategies denoted a, b and c. That is, $S_i = \{a, b, c\}$. In figure 2.3, let the axis marked a represent the probability of playing a, likewise for b and c. The point $(1, 0, 0)$ is the mixed strategy which entails playing a for sure. Similar interpretations can be given to points $(0, 1, 0)$ and $(0, 0, 1)$. It is obvious that any mixed strategy is a convex combination of these three points. Hence the set of all mixed strategies open to player i is nothing but the unit simplex, that is, the triangle ABC.

The pay-off function of player i in G_M is defined as follows: $\bar{P}_i : \bar{M}(S) \to R$ such that, for all $\sigma \in \bar{M}(S)$,

$$\bar{P}_i(\sigma) = \sum_{s \in S} \sigma_1(s_1) \ldots \sigma_n(s_n) P_i(s) \qquad (2.1)$$

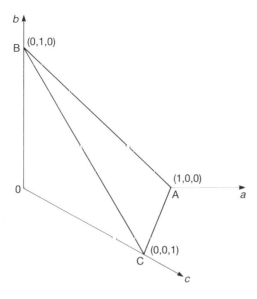

Figure 2.3

It is now easy to show that, even if a game G (with finite strategy sets) does not have an equilibrium, its mixed-strategy counterpart must have an equilibrium. This is usually stated as follows: for every game G with finite strategies there exists at least one Nash equilibrium in mixed strategies.

Theorem 2.2 If $G = (N, S, P)$ is a game with finite strategy sets, then its mixed-strategy counterpart G_M has at least one Nash equilibrium.

PROOF Since $M(S_i)$ is a unit simplex, it follows that for all $i \in N$ the set of strategies open to i in the game G_M is compact and convex. The pay-off function $\bar{P}_i$, being an expected utility function, must be continuous. This is easily checked using (2.1), above. Next, it will be shown that $\bar{P}_i$ is quasi-concave in its ith argument. In other words we have to show that if $\lambda \in (0, 1)$ then $\bar{P}_i(\sigma/(\lambda \sigma_i' + (1 - \lambda)\sigma_i'')) \geqslant \min\{\bar{P}_i(\sigma/\sigma_i'), \bar{P}_i(\sigma/\sigma_i'')\}$. Note that the left-hand expression is equal to

$$\sum_{s \in S} \{\sigma_1(s_1) \ldots \sigma_{i-1}(s_{i-1}) [\lambda \sigma_i'(s_i) + (1 - \lambda)\sigma_i''(s_i)]$$
$$\times \sigma_{i+1}(s_{i+1}) \ldots \sigma_n(s_n)\} P_i(s)$$
$$= \lambda \bar{P}_i(\sigma/\sigma_i') + (1 - \lambda)\bar{P}_i(\sigma/\sigma_i'')$$
$$\geqslant \min\{\bar{P}_i(\sigma/\sigma_i'), \bar{P}_i(\sigma/\sigma_i'')\}$$

Hence G_M satisfies all the properties required in theorem 2.1. It follows that G_M has at least one Nash equilibrium. ∎

Remark 2.1 If G is such that, for all i, S_i is compact and P_i is continuous, even then the existence of a Nash equilibrium in mixed strategies is guaranteed. This is so by the *Glicksberg theorem* (Glicksberg, 1952).

The game G_2 described above can serve as an example. Since in this game each player has only two pure strategies, we can represent player 1's strategy by a single number p, where p is the probability of his playing s_1. Similarly we shall use q to denote the probability of player 2 playing s_2. Distorting our notation a little we could write each player's (expected) pay-off in the mixed strategy game as follows:

$$\bar{P}_1(p, q) = 4pq + 3p(1 - q) + 3(1 - p)q + 4(1 - p)(1 - q)$$
$$\bar{P}_2(p, q) = 3pq + 4p(1 - q) + 4(1 - p)q + 3(1 - p)(1 - q) \tag{2.2}$$

It is easy to check that $p = \frac{1}{2}$, $q = \frac{1}{2}$ is the only mixed-strategy equilibrium. In equilibrium player 1's expected utility is $3\frac{1}{2}$, likewise for player 2. Let us check that no player can benefit through a unilateral deviation. If $q = \frac{1}{2}$, then 1's pay-off, as is easily checked using (2.2), is

$$\bar{P}_1\left(p, \tfrac{1}{2}\right) = 3\tfrac{1}{2}$$

In other words, player 1 cannot do better by deviating. Of course, he cannot do worse either, since p does not figure in the pay-off. In fact this is always the case in equilibria involving mixed strategies. Why? Before you try to answer this let me make the proposition a bit more precise. Let G be a game with n players and $(\sigma_1, \ldots, \sigma_n)$ be a mixed-strategy equilibrium. If σ_i attaches positive probability to all pure strategies in $S_i' \subset S_i$, then, with other players' strategies remaining unchanged, player i must be indifferent between all the pure strategies in S_i'. Proof?

As a final exercise, try and locate the mixed-strategy Nash equilibrium in G_1 described above.

The Nash equilibrium as a solution concept has been subjected to many different kinds of criticism. It can be argued that in too many games there are too many Nash equilibria. It would be useful if we could find a solution concept which is a *refinement* of Nash, that is, for every game it specifies a subset of the Nash equilibria as the set of plausible outcomes. It can also be argued that the Nash equilibrium concept is too "narrow" to be able to predict outcomes accurately and what we need is not a refinement but a *coarsening*. In the two sections that follow I take up both these criticisms in order.

There are several solution concepts which are stronger than Nash but many of these suffer from the problem of nonexistence. Consider, for instance, the idea of a dominant-strategy equilibrium. If for each player i there exists a strictly dominant strategy s_i^*, that is, a strategy which is strictly better than i's other strategies, no matter what the other players do, then $(s_1^*, \ldots, s_n^*)$ is a *dominant-strategy equilibrium*. The most celebrated example of a game with a dominant-strategy equilibrium is the Prisoner's Dilemma. G_3 illustrates such a game.

			Player 2	
			Cooperate	Defect
G_3:	Player 1	Cooperate	5, 5	0, 6
		Defect	6, 0	2, 2

The two strategies open to each player are called Cooperate and Defect. Note that for each player it is better to play Defect rather than Cooperate, no matter what the others do. The interesting feature of the Prisoner's Dilemma, which has caught the imagination of the social sciences, is the fact that the equilibrium, despite involving the use of dominant strategies, is Pareto suboptimal.[3]

The Prisoner's Dilemma game, when played repeatedly, raises some deep issues concerning rationality and can give us insights into collusive behavior among oligopolists. We shall encounter some of this in later chapters. For the present, note that not all games have dominant-strategy equilibria and unlike the Nash equilibrium this fact is not changed by allowing players to use mixed strategies. Another refinement of Nash, which has attractive strategic stability properties, is the *strict* (Nash) *equilibrium*. A strategy n-tuple is a strict equilibrium if any unilateral deviation by a player leaves the player strictly worse off. However, as is easy to check, many games have no strict equilibrium.[4]

While looking for refinements of the Nash concept it would be technically useful if we could isolate something which, apart from having other attractive properties, satisfies the "existence requirement" for a large class of games which arise in popular discourse. Perfect equilibrium is one such solution concept.

2.3   A REFINEMENT OF NASH: PERFECTION

The criterion of perfection plays a very important role in extensive-form games. Hence the discussion of normal-form perfection, which will be undertaken in this section, is best viewed as an introduction to extensive-form perfection which occurs later in the book.

Throughout this section we consider games with a finite number of pure strategies and we allow players to use mixed strategies. If σ is a mixed-strategy Nash equilibrium for game G, there should be no confusion if I refer to it simply as a Nash equilibrium of G.

In normal-form games the idea of a perfect equilibrium is closely related to the occurrence of "mistakes." This is captured in the concept of a "perturbed game."

If $G = (N, S, P)$ is a game and $\eta_i : S_i \to R$ such that

$$\eta_i(s_i) > 0$$

and

$$\sum_{s_i \in S_i} \eta_i(s_i) < 1$$

then we use (G, η), where $\eta = (\eta_1, \ldots, \eta_n)$, to denote the following game. N is the set of players. For all $i \in N$, the strategies open to i are $\{\sigma_i \in M(S_i) \mid \sigma_i(s_i) \geq \eta_i(s_i), \forall s_i \in S_i\}$ and the pay-off function $\bar{P}_i$ is the usual pay-off function of mixed-strategy games based on the pay-offs in G.

For visual clarity it may be useful to illustrate diagrammatically a player's strategy set in a perturbed game. Suppose that $S_i = \{a, b, c\}$. Then following a representation similar to that in figure 2.3 player i's set of strategies in a perturbed game is described by the area enclosed by the broken lines in figure 2.4. (G, η) is referred to as an η-perturbed game of G or simply as a *perturbed game*.

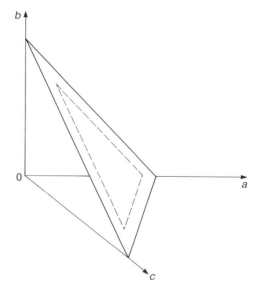

Figure 2.4

Let $G = (N, S, P)$ be a game. Then $\sigma^* \in M(S_1) \times \ldots \times M(S_n)$ is a *perfect equilibrium* of G if there exists a sequence of perturbed games $\{(G, \eta')\}$ such that

(a) $\eta' \to 0$ (as $t \to \infty$) and
(b)   for all t, there exists a Nash equilibrium σ' of (G, η') such that $\sigma' \to \sigma^*$.

Theorem 2.3 A perfect equilibrium of a game is also a Nash equilibrium.

PROOF Let $G = (N, S, P)$ be a game and let σ^* be a perfect equilibrium. Then there exists a sequence of perturbed games $\{(G, \eta')\}$ and a sequence of strategy n-tuples $\{\sigma'\}$ such that σ' is a Nash equilibrium of (G, η'), $\eta' \to 0$ and $\sigma' \to \sigma^*$.

Let $\bar{\sigma}_i \in M(S_i)$, for some $i \in N$. Let $\{\bar{\sigma}_i'\}$ be a sequence in $M(S_i)$ such that $\bar{\sigma}_i' \to \bar{\sigma}_i$ and, for all t, $\bar{\sigma}_i' \in S_i'$, where S_i' is the set of strategies of i in (G, η'). Since σ' is a Nash equilibrium of (G, η'), $\bar{P}_i(\sigma') \geqslant \bar{P}_i(\sigma'/\bar{\sigma}_i')$. Since $\bar{P}_i$ is continuous,

$$\bar{P}_i(\sigma^*) \geqslant \bar{P}_i(\sigma^*/\bar{\sigma}_i) \tag{2.3}$$

Since $\bar{\sigma}_i$ was an arbitrarily chosen element of $M(S_i)$, (2.3) ensures that σ^* is a Nash equilibrium (in mixed strategies) of G.   ∎

Consider the game described below.

$$
G_4: \quad
\begin{array}{c|cc}
 & s_2 & t_2 \\
\hline
s_1 & 5,5 & 0,0 \\
t_1 & 0,0 & 0,0 \\
\end{array}
$$

In G_4, (t_1, t_2) is a Nash equilibrium. A little reflection shows that for every perturbed game player 1's equilibrium strategy is to play s_1 with as large a probability as permitted. Hence (t_1, t_2) is not a perfect equilibrium.

This example coupled with theorem 2.3 establishes that perfect equilibrium is indeed a *refinement* of Nash. What is more, its existence is guaranteed for all games.

Theorem 2.4 If $G = (N, S, P)$ is a game with finite strategy sets, then it has at least one perfect equilibrium.

PROOF Consider $G = (N, S, P)$ and any sequence of perturbed games $\{(G, \eta')\}$ such that $\eta' \to 0$. It is easy to see that by theorem 2.1 every (G, η') must have a Nash equilibrium. Let $\{\sigma'\}$ be a corresponding sequence of Nash equilibria. Since $M(S_1) \times \ldots \times M(S_n)$ is compact, $\{\sigma'\}$ must have a convergent subsequence. Without loss of generality, suppose that $\{\sigma'\}$ is convergent and σ^* is its limit. Then σ^* is a perfect equilibrium of G.   ■

There are several alternative characterizations of perfection available in the literature (see, for example, Selten, 1975; Myerson, 1978; Van Damme, 1987). I shall not go into these here but simply take note of a straightforward but important implication of perfection. This is stated as theorem 2.5 below. The proof is omitted – you could try it as an exercise.

Consider a game $G = (N, S, P)$. A mixed strategy $\sigma_i' \in M(S_i)$ is described as *dominated* if there exists $\sigma_i'' \in M(S_i)$ such that for all $\sigma \in M(S_1) \times \ldots \times M(S_n)$

$$\bar{P}_i(\sigma/\sigma_i'') \geqslant \bar{P}_i(\sigma/\sigma_i')$$

and for some $\sigma \in M(S_1) \times \ldots \times M(S_n)$

$$\bar{P}_i(\sigma/\sigma_i'') > \bar{P}_i(\sigma/\sigma_i')$$

An *undominated* strategy is a strategy which is not dominated.

Theorem 2.5 If $G = (N, S, P)$ is a game and σ^* is a strategy combination in which, for some i, σ_i^* is a dominated strategy, then σ^* is not a perfect equilibrium.

That (t_1, t_2) is not a perfect equilibrium of G_4 is a direct implication of theorem 2.5.

Consider now the converse problem. Suppose that s^* is a Nash equilibrium of a game and does not involve any player using a dominated strategy. Does s^* have to be perfect? The example below, taken from Van Damme (1987), shows that the answer is "no."

G_5:

	s_2	t_2
s_1	1, 1, 1	1, 0, 1
t_1	1, 1, 1	0, 0, 1

s_3

	s_2	t_2
s_1	1, 1, 0	0, 0, 0
t_1	0, 1, 0	1, 0, 0

t_3

G_5 is a three-player game in which 1 chooses rows, 2 columns and 3 matrices. Thus if player 3 moves t_3, the right-hand pay-off matrix becomes the relevant one. In each cell, the first, second and third numbers are the pay-offs of players 1, 2 and 3. In G_5, (t_1, s_2, s_3) is a Nash equilibrium; t_1, s_2 and s_3 are not dominated strategies; but (t_1, s_2, s_3) is not a perfect equilibrium. To see this first note that, no matter what others do, 2 would prefer to play s_2 and 3 would prefer to play s_3. Hence in any perturbed game (G_5, η), 2 and 3 would play s_2 and s_3 with as great a probability as permitted.

Hence, if 1 plays t_1, his expected pay-off is $[1 - \eta_2(t_2)][1 - \eta_3(t_3)] + \eta_2(t_2)\eta_3(t_3) \equiv X$. If 1 plays s_1, the pay-off is $[1 - \eta_2(t_2)][1 - \eta_3(t_3)] + \eta_2(t_2)[1 - \eta_3(t_3)] + [1 - \eta_2(t_2)]\eta_3(t_3) \equiv Y$. It is easy to see that as the ηs become small[5] Y becomes larger than X. Hence, player 1 would never play t_1 in a perfect equilibrium. By the same argument as above, it can be seen that (s_1, s_2, s_3) is a perfect equilibrium.

Remark 2.2 Though in general a Nash equilibrium with undominated strategies need not be perfect, it can be shown that for a restricted class of games this is indeed so. In particular, if s^* is a Nash equilibrium of a two-person game and if, for all i, s_i^* is not dominated, then s^* must be perfect (Van Damme, 1987, theorem 3.2.2).

One must be cautious in interpreting theorem 2.5. It does *not* mean that if in a game there are two Nash equilibria and one Pareto dominates the other then the Pareto-dominated strategy combination cannot be a perfect equilibrium. Consider the game G_6, below.

		s_2	t_2
G_6:	s_1	1, 1	2, 0
	t_1	0, 2	2, 2

This game has two Nash equilibria (s_1, s_2) and (t_1, t_2), and (t_1, t_2) *Pareto dominates* (s_1, s_2). That is, for all i, $P_i(t_1, t_2) \geqslant P_i(s_1, s_2)$ and, for some i, $P_i(t_1, t_2) > P_i(s_1, s_2)$. But far from (s_1, s_2) being ruled out from being perfect, it is in fact the only perfect equilibrium of the game. That (t_1, t_2), despite being Nash, is not perfect is immediately obvious by an application of theorem 2.5. How reasonable this feature of perfection is is indeed open to question.

Another feature which I find troubling is this. Consider game G_7.

		s_2	t_2
G_7:	s_1	1, 1	1, 0
	t_1	0, 1	2, 2

In this game (s_1, s_2) and (t_1, t_2) are both perfect but (t_1, s_2) and (s_1, t_2) are not (indeed, neither are they Nash). In other words, by the criterion of perfection we would predict that (s_1, s_2) might occur or (t_1, t_2) might occur. Nothing else is possible. But this immediately suggests some pre-play communication between the players in order to rule out the following kind of misunderstanding: player 1, thinking that (s_1, s_2) will occur, moves s_1 and player 2, thinking that (t_1, t_2) will occur, moves t_2.

But if players do communicate to rule out such mismatches, it seems reasonable to expect that they will also agree to play a Pareto-dominant strategy combination among the equilibrium combinations. That is, (s_1, s_2) should not at all be treated as a possible outcome.

One implication of this argument is that if a solution concept is such that for some games (with no pre-play communication) it specifies more than one strategy combination as possible outcomes, then it should also treat as possible a strategy combination in which each strategy belongs to a strategy combination which is considered to be a possible outcome. This line of argument takes us very close to the concept of rationalizability, which is the subject matter of the next section.

2.4 A COARSENING OF NASH: RATIONALIZABILITY

One can question whether in single-shot games it is at all meaningful to think of a player deciding to play a particular strategy on the ground that the other player actually plays a specific strategy. If it is truly a single-shot game with no pre-play communication between the players, then such *conditional* strategies are difficult to interpret. Yet the justification for using the Nash equilibrium concept lies precisely on such conditional considerations.

One defense of Nash is that in most real situations players do communicate in advance. If that is so, however, then the interaction is not really a one-shot interaction. We should instead think of an extensive-form structure in which the players "talk" in the first few rounds and then play the game in the final round. We should be able to deduce the Nash outcomes as the equilibria of such a game. This is a task that remains to be performed.

In the meantime what we can do with normal-form games is to make each player go through a process of introspection and decide what his "reasonable" moves are. He bases his decision not on the *actual* move of the other player but on his *conjecture* of what the other player might do. This he achieves by imagining himself to be in the shoes of the other player. But once he does that, he has to get back into his own shoes in order to do the thought experiment for the other player. It should be clear now that there is an infinite regress problem here. Whether this process of decision-making gives us a manageable solution for games or not depends on how well the infinite-regression argument can be formalized into a simple and usable form. Fortunately this has been achieved in two interesting papers by, respectively, Bernheim (1984) and Pearce (1984).[6]

In their formulation players do the introspective reasoning based on a "common knowledge" of their mutual rationality. I should emphasize that the common-knowledge assumption is *not* used formally in these papers but merely for purposes of motivation. The assumption that the players' rationality is *common knowledge* means the following: every player knows that every player is rational; every player knows that every player knows that every player is rational; and so on *ad infinitum*.

Let us see intuitively what we can deduce, armed merely with the common-knowledge assumption. Consider the game G_8.

$$G_8: \quad \begin{array}{c|cc} & s_2 & t_2 \\ \hline s_1 & 1, 2 & 2, 1 \\ t_1 & 2, 2 & 1, 1 \end{array}$$

Would it be rational for player 1 to play s_1? The answer is: it would if 1 believes that 2 may play t_2. That is, it would if 1 believes that it is rational for player 2 to play t_2. But will 1 believe this? The answer is: no, because 1 can see that playing t_2 is not a best response of player 2 for any conjecture 2 may have about 1's play. Hence s_1 is not "rationalizable." It can be checked that t_2 is not rationalizable either.

Is t_1 rationalizable? Let us check. Playing t_1 would be rational for player 1 if he believes that it is rational for 2 to play s_2. But is it rational for 2 to play s_2? The answer is yes, because no matter what 2 believes about 1, it is rational for 2 to play s_2. Hence this chain of reasoning does not bump into irrationality anywhere. So in this game t_1 and s_2 are the only rationalizable strategies. Here rationalizability coincides with Nash. This need not always be so, however.

Refer back to game G_2. Let us check if s_1 is rationalizable. The answer is yes and for the following reason. It is rational for 1 to play s_1 if he believes that it is rational for 2 to play s_2. It is rational for 2 to play s_2 if it is rational for 1 to play t_1. It is rational for 1 to play t_1, if it is rational for 2 to play t_2. It is rational for 2 to play t_2 if it is rational for 1 to play s_1. We have caught up now with the first statement of this chain. So the sequence is unending. It can be checked by a similar reasoning that all moves by all players are rationalizable in this game. Note, however, that this game has no Nash equilibrium (in pure strategies).

Let us now proceed towards a formal definition of rationalizability. We shall for most of this section focus on games with finite (pure) strategies.

Consider the game $G = (N, S, P)$. Let $B_i \subset M(S_i)$, $b \in B_i$ and $m \in M(S_1) \times \ldots \times M(S_n)$. We say that b is a *best response* in B_i to m if

$$\bar{P}_i(m/b) \geqslant \bar{P}_i(m/d) \qquad \text{for all } d \in B_i$$

For each $i \in N$, define a sequence $\{H_i(t)\}_t$ by induction, as follows:

$$H_i(0) = M(S_i)$$

and, for all $t = 1, 2, \ldots,$

$H_i(t) = \{b \in H_i(t-1) \mid$ there exists $m \in M(H_1(t-1)) \times \ldots \times M(H_n(t-1))$ such that b is a best response in $H_i(t-1)$ to $m\}$

Remember that $M(H_i(t-1))$ is the set of mixed strategies which are supported by $H_i(t-1)$. With $H_i(t-1)$ as a subset of a unit simplex, $M(H_i(t-1))$ is simply its convex hull. The set of *rationalizable strategies* of player i is given by

$$R_i = \bigcap_{t=0}^{\infty} H_i(t)$$

We shall say that $m \in M(S_1) \times \ldots \times M(S_n)$ is *rationalizable* if, for all $i \in N$, $m_i \in R_i$.

In the above definition of $H_i(t)$ we require m to belong to $M(H_1(t-1)) \times \ldots \times M(H_n(t-1))$ instead of $H_1(t-1) \times \ldots \times H_n(t-1)$ because we are allowing players to entertain probabilistic conjectures about what others might do. Suppose $H_2(t-1)$ consists of only two strategies, s_2 and t_2. We wish to permit others to hold conjectures as follows: the probability of 2 playing s_2 is p and the probability of 2 playing t_2 is $1-p$. The set of all such conjectures is just $M(H_2(t-1))$.

An obvious but interesting property of rationalizability as a solution concept is worth noting. If $B \subset M(S_1) \times \ldots \times M(S_n)$ is the set of all rationalizable strategies and B_i is the projection of B on $M(S_i)$, that is, $B_i = \{b \in M(S_i) \mid$ there exists $m \in M(S_1) \times \ldots \times M(S_n)$ such that $m/b \in B\}$, then $B = B_1 \times \ldots \times B_n$. If B was the set of Nash equilibria, then this would not, in general, have been true. This is what ensures that whether a particular strategy of a particular player is rationalizable or not does not depend on what strategy others are *actually* using.

Theorem 2.6 For every game $G = (N, S, P)$ and for every $i \in N$, the set of rationalizable strategies R_i is non-empty and $R_i = H_i(k)$ for some k.

Though theorem 2.6 is easy to prove directly, I prove it via two lemmas which are of some interest in themselves. In what follows, if s_i is a pure strategy and $B_i \subset M(S_i)$, I shall use $s_i \in B_i$ to mean that the mixed strategy, which entails playing s_i for sure, belongs to B_i.

Lemma 2.1 For all i and all t, if $\sigma \in H_i(t)$ and $\sigma' \in M(S_i)$ such that the support of σ' is a subset of σ (i.e. the pure strategies which receive a positive probability under σ' receive a positive probability under σ), then $\sigma' \in H_i(t)$.

The proof of lemma 2.1 is obvious and therefore omitted.

Lemma 2.2 For all i, for all t, $H_i(t)$ is non-empty and compact.

PROOF Let us first prove the compactness. Since $H(t)$ is obviously bounded, we simply have to prove that it is closed. Note that $H_i(0)$ is closed. Assume that $H_i(t-1)$ is closed for all i. Now consider a sequence $\{b_i^r\}$ in $H_i(t)$ such that $b_i^r \to b_i$. Since $H_i(t-1)$ is closed, $b_i \in H_i(t-1)$. From the definition of $H_i(t)$, there must exist a sequence $\{m^r\}$ in $M(H_1(t-1)) \times \ldots \times M(H_n(t-1))$ such that b_i^r is a best response to m^r in $H_i(t-1)$. The compactness of $H_i(t-1)$ ensures that $\{m^r\}$ has a convergent subsequence, converging to $m \in M(H_1(t-1)) \times \ldots \times M(H_n(t-1))$. Without loss of generality, suppose that $\{m^r\}$ is such a sequence.

We know that

$$\bar{P}_i(m^r/b_i^r) \geqslant \bar{P}_i(m^r/d_i) \qquad \text{for all } d_i \in H_i(t-1)$$

Hence

$$\bar{P}_i(m/b_i) \geqslant \bar{P}_i(m/d_i) \qquad \text{for all } d_i \in H_i(t-1)$$

Hence $b_i \in H_i(t)$. Therefore, by induction, $H_i(t)$ is compact for all i, for all t.

Next assume that $H_i(t-1)$ is non-empty. Choose any $m \in H_1(t-1) \times \ldots \times H_n(t-1)$. Since $H_i(t-1)$ is compact and $\bar{P}_i$ is continuous, there must exist $b \in H_i(t-1)$ which is a best response in $H_i(t-1)$ to m. Hence $b \in H_i(t)$. Since $H_i(0)$ is non-empty, it follows by induction that $H_i(t)$ is non-empty, for all i, for all t. ∎

PROOF OF THEOREM 2.6 Since $H_i(t)$ is non-empty and compact (lemma 2.2), it follows from a standard theorem in mathematics that $\bigcap_{t=0}^{\infty} H_i(t)$ is non-empty.

Next define $Z = \{D \subset M(S_i) | D = M(X_i)$, where X_i is a non-empty subset of $S_i\}$. Lemma 2.1 implies that, for all k, $H_i(k)$ is a union of the elements of some subset of Z. Since Z has a finite number of elements, it follows that $R_i = H_i(t)$, for some t. ∎

There is an alternative route available which enables us to locate the rationalizable strategies without having to go through this process of recursion. To illustrate this a definition needs to be introduced first.

An n-tuple $(A_1, \ldots, A_n)$, where $A_i \subset M(S_i)$, has the *best response property* if, for all i and all $b \in A_i$, there exists $m \in M(A_1) \times \ldots \times M(A_n)$ such that b is a best response in $M(S_i)$ to m.

Theorem 2.7 For all i, $R_i = \{b \in M(S_i) \mid$ there exists $A_1, \ldots, A_n$ with the best response property and $b \in A_i\}$.

PROOF Define $E_i = \{b \in M(S_i) \mid$ there exists $A_1, \ldots, A_n$ with the best response property and $b \in A_i\}$.

Let $b \in R_i$. From theorem 2.6 we know that there exists k such that $R_i = H_i(k)$, for all i. Clearly, $(H_1(k), \ldots, H_n(k))$ has the best response property. Hence $b \in E_i$.

Now suppose that $x \in E_i$. Hence, there exist $A_1, \ldots, A_n$ which have the best response property and $x \in A_i$. It is obvious that, for all j, $A_j \subset H_j(0)$. If, for all j, $A_j \subset H_j(t)$, it is easy to check that, for all j, $A_j \subset H_j(t+1)$. Hence, by induction, $A_j \subset H_j(t)$, for all t, for all j. It follows that $A_i \subset R_i$ and hence $x \in R_i$. ∎

Theorem 2.8 If $(b_1, \ldots, b_n)$ is a Nash equilibrium, then $(b_1, \ldots, b_n)$ is rationalizable.

PROOF Let $(b_1, \ldots, b_n)$ be a Nash equilibrium. Then $\{b_1\}, \ldots, \{b_n\}$ has the best response property and $b_i \in \{b_i\}$. It follows, by theorem 2.7, that $b_i \in R_i$. ∎

This theorem, coupled with the example concerning game G_2, establishes that the solution concept of rationalizability is indeed a coarsening of Nash equilibrium.

Remark 2.3 Although in this section attention was restricted to games with finite strategy sets, in some of the applications of rationalizability that occur later the underlying games have infinite strategy sets. Fortunately, most of the claims made here remain valid if the strategy sets are compact and the pay-off functions are continuous. Thus, for instance, for every game with compact strategy sets and continuous pay-off functions, the set of rationalizable strategies can be shown to be non-empty and compact.

From the discussion preceding the definition of "rationalizable strategies" a useful, if somewhat blunt, method of locating some rationalizable strategies is suggested for two-player games. Write down the strategies of players 1 and 2 as vertical and horizontal points (figure 2.5); it is assumed that $S_1 = \{s_1, t_1\}$ and $S_2 = \{s_2, t_2\}$. Suppose we want to check whether s_1 is rationalizable. Look for a strategy of player 2 to which s_1 is a best response. Join s_1 to such a strategy with a line and an arrow facing away from s_1. Let us suppose the game under consideration is G_2. Then the line joins s_1 and s_2. Next check which strategy of 1 would make s_2 a best response for 2. Link up s_2 with such a strategy similarly. Continue with the same process.

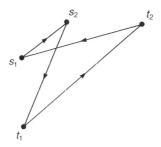

Figure 2.5

Clearly a "path" will be demarcated. Figure 2.5 illustrates the path in the case of G_2. If it so happens that the path thus chalked out returns to the original strategy or to some other strategy which lies on the path, then the original strategy is rationalizable. Hence s_1 is rationalizable.

To take another example, consider game G_9 shown below. In this game, strategy M is rationalizable as is checked by generating the path shown in figure 2.6.

		L	R
	T	1, 1	0, 0
G_9:	M	0, 1	1, 0
	B	0, 0	1, 1

While not a formal algorithm, this is useful for back-of-the-envelope analysis of simple games. Also note that this method does not locate *all* rationalizable strategies. It gives a sufficient condition for a strategy to be rationalizable. One reason for this is that a rationalizable strategy may be a best response not to a pure strategy of the other player but to a mixed

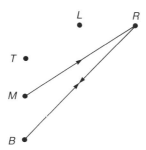

Figure 2.6

strategy. Although the method of figures 2.5 and 2.6 can be adapted to allow for this, as it stands it would miss out on such a strategy.

NOTES

1 Let $f(x_1, \ldots, x_m)$ be a real-valued function on R^m. Then $\mathrm{argmax}_{x_i} f(x_1, \ldots, x_m)$ is the set of values of the ith argument at which $f(\cdot)$ attains its maximum given that $(x_1, \ldots, x_{i-1}, x_{i+1}, \ldots, x_m)$ is fixed. Clearly $\mathrm{argmax}_{t_i} P_i(s/t_i)$ is the same as $\mathrm{argmax}_{s_i} P_i(s)$. If x^* is a *unique* element of $\mathrm{argmax}_{x_i} f(x_1, \ldots, x_m)$ we may write $x^* = \mathrm{argmax}_{x_i} f(x_1, \ldots, x_m)$ instead of using the inclusion symbol.

2 Let $B \subset R^m$ and $f: B \rightarrow B$. Then *Brouwer's fixed-point theorem* asserts that if B is compact and convex and f is continuous then there must exist a *fixed point*, that is, $x^* \in B$ such that $f(x^*) = x^*$.

3 The birth of the Prisoner's Dilemma makes for an interesting digression. In 1950 A. W. Tucker - yes, of Kuhn-Tucker fame - was visiting the mathematics department of Stanford (on leave from Princeton) and because of some space problems was given an office in the psychology department. His neighbors, curious about his research, asked him to give a talk to their department. Tucker, who wanted to demonstrate to the psychologists how a dominant-strategy equilibrium could be suboptimal, invented the Prisoner's Dilemma. (I owe this account to a conversation with Harold Kuhn.)

It has been pointed out that the purely mathematical aspect of the Prisoner's Dilemma was not new even in 1950; that scientists at Rand had worked it out earlier. While this is probably true, it is arguable that for a game like the Prisoner's Dilemma (and in fact most results in economics) the purely mathematical part is the least of the intellectual challenge. What is most demanding is the application of abstract reason to social and economic contexts.

4 One way to remedy this "existence problem" is to look for a set-valued counterpart of the strict equilibrium, that is, for a specification of *sets* of strategies for players such that, if each player believes that others will remain within their sets, then he strictly prefers to remain within his set. A class of solutions of this kind is explored in Basu and Weibull (1991).

5 A sufficient condition is that $\min\{\eta_2(t_2), \eta_3(t_3)\} < \frac{1}{3}$.

6 Related ideas which involve the iterated deletion of strategies which are dominated in some sense are discussed by Luce and Raiffa (1957) and Moulin (1979).

3

The Standard Market Structures

3.1 INTRODUCTION

The purpose of this chapter is a brief review of the standard market structures that dominated courses in industrial economics and microeconomic theory before the rise of the new industrial organization literature. In other words, it is a short account of competition, monopoly, oligopoly and some related market structures. Some deep institutional questions arise even about these standard concepts but we do not go into these here. As we venture into more complicated problems of monopoly or oligopoly in later chapters, I often have to contrast results with what happens in textbook models of monopoly, oligopoly or competition. This chapter provides an encapsulated view of such models.

3.2 MONOPOLY

In some ways monopoly is the simplest market structure, with wide consensus as to what it represents. The consensus has not been easily achieved, however. At the turn of the century, we find Ely (1900, p. 1) writing: "The term monopoly . . . stands in the popular mind not merely for many different ideas, but for a multiplicity of ideas some of which are antagonistic to each other." He later goes on to clarify that this is so not just "in the popular mind" but "even to our experts in economics." While it is true that by 1838 Cournot had worked out a model of monopoly (see his chapter 8) very similar to what we see in our contemporary microeconomics books, Ely was right, because, despite Cournot's work, there was still a great abundance of views about what monopoly meant – rather like what we have today for important concepts like "power" and "coercion." For some authors monopoly was almost any market in which a producer had more influence than a perfectly competitive agent; Edgeworth's (1897) usage on the other hand was much closer to our contemporary one.

Nowadays a monopoly is treated essentially as an industry in which one firm or supplier confronts the entire demand for a product. Suppose that the total consumer demand x for a certain good is a function of the good's price p, and the *demand function* is denoted by

$$x = x(p) \tag{3.1}$$

Let us assume that this is continuous, differentiable, and strictly downward sloping wherever $p > 0$ and $x(p) > 0$. Hence, an inverse of the function $x(\cdot)$ exists; we shall refer to it as the *inverse demand function* and denote it as follows:

$$p = p(x) \tag{3.2}$$

Hence, for all prices p', $p(x(p')) = p'$.

Since we have a monopoly, only one firm exists to serve this industry. Let this firm's (*total*) *cost function* be

$$c = c(x) \tag{3.3}$$

This is also continuous and differentiable and we shall generally assume that the *average cost* $c(x)/x$ as a function of x is U-shaped and that *marginal cost* $c'(x)$ rises with x whenever x is such that $c'(x) > c(x)/x$.

Equations (3.1) and (3.3) describe the *industrial structure*. What we have to describe now is how the firm or monopoly will behave. It will be assumed that the monopolist is a profit-maximizer. The profit-maximization assumption has come under fire in recent times and there is an interesting literature examining the internal structure of firms and their motivation (see, for example, Schmalensee and Willig, 1989, vol. 1, part I, and, in particular, Holmstrom and Tirole, 1989). We shall see some cases of this later, but if we had to attribute one objective function to each firm the profit function is probably still the best choice.

In the *standard* monopoly analysis the monopolist chooses price p in order to maximize profit. Actually whether we have the monopolist choose price or quantity does not matter because selecting one immediately fixes the other by (3.1).[1] Hence, we may write the monopolist's profit function as follows:

$$\pi(x) = xp(x) - c(x) \tag{3.4}$$

At equilibrium this is maximized. Hence, if (p^*, x^*) is an equilibrium price–quantity vector then

$$x^* p'(x^*) + p(x^*) = c'(x^*) \tag{3.5}$$

This is the first-order condition of maximizing $\pi(x)$. When the marginal cost curve is U-shaped and there are two values of x at which (3.5) is satisfied, it is easy to see that profit is maximized where x is larger. Hence x^* is *that* value and $p^* = p(x)$. The equilibrium is illustrated in figure 3.1.

Consider an exercise. Suppose a monopolist's cost of production rises. That is, he has a new cost function $\hat{c}(x)$ such that, for all x, $\hat{c}(x) > c(x)$. Show that the monopolist's profit must fall. Try this yourself before reading on. This problem is very easy to solve using a revealed-preference argument. Instead of plunging into complicated geometry or algebra, it is worth trying this out.

Denote the monopolist's profit function after the cost function changes from $c(\cdot)$ to $\hat{c}(\cdot)$ by $\hat{\pi}(\cdot)$. Let $(\hat{p}, \hat{x})$ be the new equilibrium. Clearly

$$\pi(\hat{x}) > \hat{\pi}(\hat{x})$$

since $\hat{c}(\hat{x}) > c(\hat{x})$. Also,

$$\pi(x^*) \geqslant \pi(\hat{x})$$

by revealed preference since x^* maximizes π. Hence,

$$\pi(x^*) > \hat{\pi}(\hat{x})$$

which completes the proof that, after the cost rises, the new profit must be less.

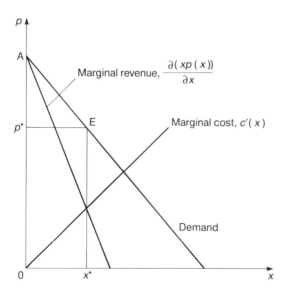

Figure 3.1

In the paragraph introducing equation (3.4) the word "standard" was italicized. This was to stress that the standard analysis is emphatically not the only one. At first sight it appears that there is not much else that a monopolist can do but choose either price or quantity. But notice that the monopolist just described is not a very extortionate person. After buying from the monopolist the consumers earn a net consumers' surplus of $p*AE$.[2] Since the consumers are dealing with a monopolist and therefore have no other producer to turn to, if the monopolist somehow asked them to pay more money, up to $p*AE$, they would agree to pay it. Hence the textbook monopolist extracts less profit than he can extract in principle. This happens because we restrict his strategy to setting p or setting q. If he is allowed to use more complicated strategies or contracts, he will be able to earn more profit. Several monopolistic practices which occur in reality, but look strange to someone only familiar with the textbook story of monopoly, become easy to explain once they are viewed as mechanisms for extracting consumers' surplus. This is an interesting and developing subject and is where some of the main interactions between antitrust legislation and economics occur. Most of chapter 5 is devoted to this topic.

3.3   COMPETITION

As Stigler (1957, p. 1) has observed, the idea of "competition" came into economics from common discourse where it represented rivalry between two or more persons. It is in this sense that Adam Smith (1776) argued that, if the supply of a good exceeded demand, "competition" among producers would lead to a lowering of the price. However, the most striking early analysis of perfect competition occurs in Cournot's chapter entitled "Of unlimited competition." Here Cournot (1838) visualizes a competitive industry as the limit of oligopolies with a larger and larger number of firms. He describes a competitive industry as one where the change in the output of a single firm is negligible from the point of view of the entire industry's output and therefore has no influence on price.

This is clearly very close to the modern view. In contemporary textbooks one finds the description that in a perfectly competitive industry

(a)   there are a large number of firms producing a homogeneous good.

From this it is deduced that

(b)   each individual firm is unable to influence the price (i.e. is a price-taker).

The analysis then proceeds by treating (b) as the basic axiom of perfect competition.

It is interesting to note here that the classical view that (b) follows from (a) is not strictly valid. This is because no matter how large the number of firms, as long as it is finite, if the aggregate demand curve is downward sloping, individual firms cannot be confronting horizontal demand curves.

There are two ways out of this. First, we could assume that the industry has not just a large number of firms but a continuum of them. If (a) is interpreted in this extreme and clearly unrealistic way, then (b) can be compatible with (a) (see Aumann, 1964; Hildenbrand and Kirman, 1976).

The second approach is to use, instead of (b), the following variant, in which

(b′) each individual firm *believes* that it cannot influence the price.

If (b′) is treated as the basic descriptive axiom of perfect competition, then a perfectly competitive equilibrium price $p*$ is one where aggregate demand equals aggregate supply and no individual firm wants to change the amount it supplies, given (b′). The fact that the belief would not hold if it was put to test does not matter.[3]

If we adopt interpretation (b′) and treat it as the basic axiom, the assumption about the large number of firms is no longer germaine to perfect competition. Nor is it important for firms to be identical in the sense of having identical cost functions.

Let me briefly describe a standard model of competitive equilibrium (for more elaborate discussions see, for example, Varian, 1983, or Kreps, 1990). As before the aggregate demand curve faced by the industry is

$$x = x(p)$$

It has the usual properties. There are n firms and firm i's cost function is

$$c_i = c_i(x)$$

As before the average cost curve is U-shaped and the marginal cost is upward sloping wherever marginal cost exceeds average cost. In addition, let me rule out the complications of "variable" and "fixed" costs by assuming $c_i(0) = 0$.

An equilibrium is now easy to define. A price $p*$ is a *perfectly competitive equilibrium price* if there exists $(x_1^*, \ldots, x_n^*)$ such that

(i) $x_i^* = \underset{x}{\operatorname{argmax}} \{p*x - c_i(x)\}$ for all $i = 1, \ldots, n$

and

(ii) $\sum_{i=1}^{n} x_i^* = x(p*)$

The first condition, (i), is where (b') is used. Each firm acts as if it has no power to influence price. Condition (ii) asserts that demand must be equal to supply.

A more graphic description of the above equilibrium which one can find in virtually any textbook of microeconomics is this. In perfect competition each firm's supply curve is its marginal cost curve above the average cost curve (supply being zero for all $p < \min\{c_i(x)/x\}$). The industry's supply curve is a horizontal summation of all individual firm's supply curves. A perfectly competitive equilibrium occurs at a price where aggregate supply ·+|···|· ·+ɡɡ·· ɡ·+|· ·|· ··+·+··|

At times another feature (i.e. apart from axiom (b')) is treated as a basic description of a perfectly competitive industry. This is the assumption of "free entry." Though not essential, it is best understood under the assumptions that all firms are identical (i.e. $c_i(x) = c(x)$ for all x) and that there are an infinite number of firms. Free entry implies that as long as firms in the industry earn positive profit more firms from outside will be attracted into the industry. Equilibrium occurs when profit goes to zero.

Hence, in a *perfectly competitive industry with free entry*, $\hat{p}$ is an *equilibrium price* if

$$\hat{p} = \min\{c(x)/x\}$$

Note that, at $\hat{p}$ profit is zero and firms are indifferent between entering the industry and not entering. Ignoring the integer problem, we could say that the number of firms in the industry in equilibrium will be

$$x(\hat{p}) \Big/ \operatorname*{argmin}_{x}\{c(x)/x\}$$

In the case where firms are nonidentical, there are limits on the profit that the "marginal" firm in the industry (i.e. the first firm that would exit if price fell) can earn. Intramarginal firms, however, can earn large profit (see Friedman, 1976).

Although among competitive models *perfect* competition was the prototype, by the 1930s it was clear that a perfectly competitive economy was based on too many slender assumptions. In order to capture reality it seemed essential to allow for the fact that in most industries, even when competition is rife, the product concerned is seldom perfectly homogeneous: packaging differs, location differs, even when the product is the same. Hence, it is possible that, if a single firm lowers price slightly, (i) its demand increases but not all consumers rush to it and (ii) its demand increases by more than what it would if all firms had lowered their prices. With this if we introduced the assumption of free entry, which would imply zero profit in equilibrium, the model we would have is one of monopolistic competition as developed by Chamberlin (1933).[4] Nowadays, when discussing industries with goods which are close, but not perfect, substitutes it is common to use specific characterizations of quality or brand differentials. We shall encounter several such models in later chapters.

3.4 OLIGOPOLY

So much of the book will deal with the oligopoly question that this introductory section can be brief. Some historical remarks concerning the emergence of oligopoly analysis occurred in chapter 1. Here I confine the discussion to a recapitulation of Cournot oligopoly and introduce terms and definitions which are used later.

As before, let the aggregate demand and inverse demand functions be given by (3.1) and (3.2), above. However, there are n firms in the industry and these are not price-takers. In Cournot's formulation what firm i chooses is the output to be produced by firm i, that is, x_i. Hence, when all firms have taken their decisions, industry's price turns out to be $p(x_1 + \ldots + x_n)$. If firm i's cost function is $c_i(\cdot)$, then firm i's profit π_i is given by

$$\pi_i(x_1, \ldots, x_n) = p(x_1 + \ldots + x_n)x_i - c_i(x_i) \qquad (3.6)$$

If we think of these n firms as n players, x_i as a strategy of firm i and π_i as a pay-off function of i, then the model of a Cournot oligopoly fits into the classical description of a normal-form game as seen in chapter 2.

The definition of a Cournot equilibrium is easy once we exploit this analogy: $(x_1^*, \ldots, x_n^*)$ is a *Cournot equilibrium* if it is a Nash equilibrium of the above game.

If we assume that $p(\cdot)$ and $c_i(\cdot)$ are continuous, $\pi_i(\cdot)$ will be continuous. If $c_i(x_i)$ is always positive we can think of a sufficiently large real number Z such that no firm will ever want to produce more than Z. Hence, we could restrict the output choice of firm i to $[0, Z]$. Hence each firm's strategy set is compact. If, in addition, we assume that $\pi_i(\cdot)$ is quasi-concave in its ith argument (which is indeed so under fairly general restrictions on the demand and cost functions), all the preconditions of theorem 2.1 are satisfied. Hence, under these conditions the existence of a Cournot equilibrium is ensured.

A diagrammatic representation of the Cournot equilibrium in the case of a duopoly, that is, where $n = 2$, is shown in figure 3.2. For this the main ingredient is the *reaction function*. The reaction function of a firm shows the amount that it will produce (in order to maximize its profit) given the other firms' outputs. In a duopoly firm i's reaction function $\phi_i(x_i)$ is defined as follows:

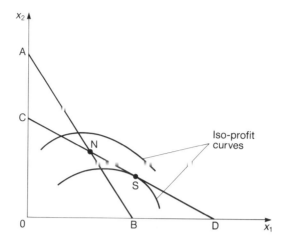

Figure 3.2

$$x_i = \phi_i(x_j) \equiv \operatorname*{argmax}_{x_i} \pi_i(x_1, x_2) \qquad \text{where } i = 1, 2, \quad j \neq i$$

In figure 3.2, AB is firm 1's reaction function and CD is 2's reaction function. A moment's reflection shows that the Cournot equilibrium occurs where the two reaction functions intersect. So N denotes the Cournot equilibrium point.

Another useful character in the geometry of Cournot analysis is the iso-profit curve. The *iso-profit curve* of firm i is a locus of all points (x_1, x_2) such that the profit of firm i remains constant, for instance at k.

$$\pi_i(x_1, x_2) = k \tag{3.7}$$

By varying k we can get a whole family of iso-profit curves. A set of iso-profit curves of firm 1 is shown in figure 3.2. It is easy to see that firm 1's reaction function is a line joining the peaks of firm 1's iso-profit curves as shown.

An influential modification of the Cournot model was provided by Stackelberg (1934). In a Stackelberg equilibrium one firm acts as the "leader" and chooses its output by taking account of the other's reaction function. Thus if 1 is the leader, the output levels $(\hat{x}_1, \hat{x}_2)$ are a *Stackelberg equilibrium* if

$$\hat{x}_1 = \operatorname*{argmax}_{x_1} \pi_1(x_1, \phi_2(x_1))$$

and

$$\hat{x}_2 = \phi_2(\hat{x}_1)$$

Such a Stackelberg equilibrium is depicted by point S in figure 3.2. Once we have studied extensive-form games it will be evident that the Stackelberg equilibrium has a formal game-theoretic interpretation as a subgame perfect outcome of a two-period game.

3.5 DOMINANT FIRMS AND FRINGES

A market structure that cannot be straitjacketed into any of the categories discussed above is one where a small number of large firms play a "dominant" role and there is a "fringe" of small firms which may be competitive in structure. Such a market would combine features of Cournot, Stackelberg, and the competitive model. The dominant-firm-with-fringe has been discussed in the literature but not as much as one would expect given its empirical importance.

One of the earliest models, developed by Stigler (1950), consists of an industry with one dominant firm and a price-taking competitive fringe.[5] The equilibrium in such a market has an interesting characterization.

Let the aggregate demand curve faced by the industry be given by (3.1) above. Let the supply curve of the competitive fringe be

$$s = s(p) \tag{3.8}$$

We shall assume that the competitive fringe consists of n identical price-taking firms, that is, $s(p)/n$ is the supply curve of each firm (which is, of course, the marginal cost curve of each firm).

Suppose now that the dominant firm decides to charge a price p and sell x units of the good. In brief, it chooses (p, x). The fringe, being price-takers, will respond by supplying $s(p)$. If $x + s(p) > x(p)$, then the price will fall. That is, (p, x) is not a feasible plan. Hence, (p, x) is feasible from the dominant firm's point of view only if $x + s(p) \leqslant x(p)$. Therefore, if the dominant firm sets price equal to p, the maximum it can sell is $x(p) - s(p)$. Hence, we could think of the following *residual demand curve* as the demand faced by the dominant firm:

$$x = x(p) - s(p) \tag{3.9}$$

If (3.1) is downward sloping and (3.8) is upward sloping, as usual, then the residual demand curve will be downward sloping. If $c(\cdot)$ is the dominant firm's total cost function, its profit is given by

$$\hat{\pi}(p) = p[x(p) - s(p)] - c(x(p) - s(p))$$

If $p^* = \text{argmax}\{\hat{\pi}(p)\}$, then p^* will be described as the equilibrium price in this industry. In equilibrium, the dominant firm supplies $x(p^*) - s(p^*)$ and the competitive fringe supplies $s(p^*)$.

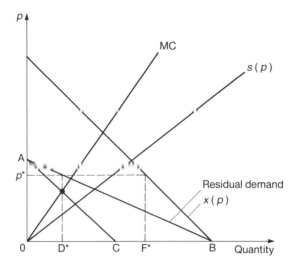

Figure 3.3

The equilibrium just described has a simple diagrammatic representation. Let the aggregate demand curve $x(p)$ and the supply curve of the fringe $s(p)$ be as shown in figure 3.3. The residual demand curve, derived by subtracting $s(p)$ from $x(p)$ at each price p, is as shown. Let the monopolist treat this as the demand curve confronting him and select the profit-maximizing price. If MC is the monopolist's marginal cost curve then p^* is such a price. Hence, in equilibrium, p^* is the price, $0D^*$ is the amount supplied by the dominant firm and D^*F^* is the equilibrium supply of the competitive fringe.

There is no reason, however, why there should be a single dominant firm. The model would be empirically more relevant if we allow for a small group of dominant firms to coexist with a fringe of many small firms. As Dixit and Stern (1982, p. 137) point out, an example of this is "the world petroleum market, where the major companies (and countries) attempt to exercise leadership and the dependents follow."

In the spirit of Stigler's argument we could think of the dominant firms as behaving like Cournot oligopolists among themselves while the fringe reacts by taking price as given and responding with a supply. This has been analyzed by Encaoua and Jacquemin (1980). Let us suppose that there are m identical dominant firms, each having a total cost function $c(\cdot)$, like the dominant monopolist just described.

If these firms produce $(x_1, \ldots, x_m)$, the price that will prevail in the market is defined implicitly by

$$x_1 + \ldots + x_m + s(p) = x(p)$$

which is the same as

$$x_1 + \ldots + x_m = x(p) - s(p) \tag{3.10}$$

One way of explaining why such a price would prevail is through a rational expectations argument. The fringe determines its supply on the basis of a conjectured price. If, given such a supply, the market-clearing price happens to be the conjectured price, that is, (3.10) is valid, then the price satisfies rational expectations.

An inspection of (3.10) makes it clear that if we treat the residual demand curve $x(p) - s(p)$ as the demand curve faced by the m dominant firms and work out the Cournot equilibrium price, that will be the price that will prevail in equilibrium in the market with m dominant firms and a competitive fringe with a supply schedule $s(p)$.

To see this more clearly, let $g(q)$ be the inverse of the function $x(p) - s(p)$, that is, $g(x(p) - s(p)) = p$ for all p. In other words $g(q)$ is the inverse residual demand function. Hence, firm i's profit function is

$$\pi_i(x_1, \ldots, x_m) = g(x_1 + \ldots + x_m)x_i - c(x_i)$$

Following the method of section 3.5, let $(x_1^*, \ldots, x_m^*)$ be the Nash equilibrium of this game. Then in this industry with m dominant firms and a competitive fringe the equilibrium price is $p^* \equiv g(x_1^* + \ldots + x_m^*)$, the quantity produced by the fringe is $s(p^*)$ and the quantities produced by the dominant firms are $x_1^*, \ldots, x_m^*$.

NOTES

1 Another way of doing the same analysis is to suppose that the monopolist chooses *p and x*, in order to maximize profit, subject to (3.1).
2 I am assuming that income effect is zero. If income effect is positive the consumers' surplus will be less than p^*AE (see Hicks, 1956). Most measures of consumers' surplus – for example, Marshall's measure, compensating variation, and equivalent variation – coincide when income effect is zero. Since my occasional venture into welfare matters is not central to this book, I shall use the simplifying assumption of zero income effect wherever the need arises.
3 For a very insightful discussion of the role of *conjectured* demand curves in the analysis of industry see Kaldor (1934).
4 See also Robinson (1933). Joan Robinson's model, however, is not as similar to that of Edward Chamberlin's as is at times presumed. Chamberlin has stressed this in the preface to the sixth edition, 1948, of his book (see also Williams, 1978, chapter 5, for a discussion). For a modern formalization of the Chamberlin model, see Hart (1985).
5 For a survey of dominant-firm behavior and its relation to entry deterrence, see Encaoua et al. (1986).

4

Oligopoly and Some Non-Cournot Equilibria

4.1 INTRODUCTION

Although the Cournot outcome as outlined in chapter 3 is the most standard equilibrium notion that is used in the analysis of oligopoly, it is by no means the "obvious" one or the only reasonable one. With the rise of game theory it has become increasingly transparent that, even with the industrial structure (that is, the specification of aggregate demand and cost functions of the firms in the industry) remaining unchanged, several competing predictions of outcomes are possible. This is because there are several competing equilibrium notions, with attractive formal properties and intuitive appeal, that can be used.

Some economists have viewed this as a weakness of modern industrial organization theory. But if the modern theory is convincing as to why no unique or "narrow" prediction of outcome is the only reasonable one, then clearly that is not a weakness of the theory. To castigate the theory on such a ground is like throwing out the messenger who brings unwanted news. Ultimately theories have to be accepted or rejected on grounds of empirical relevance. The purpose of theory is to lay out a menu with *a priori* analytical appeal.

By combining the game theory of chapter 2 and the industrial models of chapter 3 we can gain considerable insight into the possibility of different kinds of equilibrium analysis. Note that in Cournot's analysis (i) firms' strategies consist of choosing quantities to be sold and (ii) the equilibrium notion used is that of Nash. Hence, two (among other possible) routes for doing non-Cournot analysis are to retain (i) and use an alternative equilibrium concept such as rationalizability or to retain Nash and change the strategic variable from quantity to price. The purpose of the next two sections is to explore these two models. This is done through illustrations. I consider some special cases of the general industrial structure described in chapter 2; in particular, I consider cases with linear demand and cost functions. In the process of discussing these models I also introduce some topics of historical interest, such as the works of Bertrand and Edgeworth.

4.2 RATIONALIZABILITY AND OLIGOPOLY

In a standard model of oligopoly, what output configurations would we predict using the rationalizability criterion?

Suppose there are n identical firms confronting the following aggregate inverse demand function:

$$p = a - bx$$

where p is price, x is quantity and a and b are both positive.

Let each firm i's total cost function be linear and with marginal cost equal to c. Hence,

$$c(x_i) = cx_i$$

where x_i is the output produced by firm i. We shall assume $c < a$. Otherwise the industry is not viable.

It is easy to check that firm i's reaction function will be as follows:

$$x_i = \frac{a - c}{2b} - \frac{1}{2} (x_1 + \ldots + x_{i-1} + x_{i+1} + \ldots + x_n) \qquad (4.1)$$

The Cournot equilibrium is the solution of the n equations (one for each firm) of the above kind that we have. Thanks to our strong assumption, namely that of linearity, a Cournot equilibrium will always exist. Let us denote a vector of Cournot equilibrium outputs by $(x_1^C, \ldots, x_n^C)$.

What are the rationalizable outcomes in such an oligopoly? Curiously, it depends critically on whether $n = 2$ or $n > 2$.

The rationalizability discussion in chapter 2 needs to be technically adjusted slightly for application here. This is because each agent has a continuum of strategies open to him, and also because I shall assume that each agent makes pointwise conjectures about what others may play. That is, the conjectures always take the form that another firm will make such a move with probability 1.

If $n = 2$, there is only one rationalizable outcome and it coincides with Cournot. This is very easy to check and there is no need for any formalism. The reaction functions of the two firms are illustrated in figure 4.1.

To keep the strategy sets compact, let us suppose that each player can choose any output from the interval $[0, Z]$, where Z is such a large number that it will never pay to choose an output above Z. For instance, we could

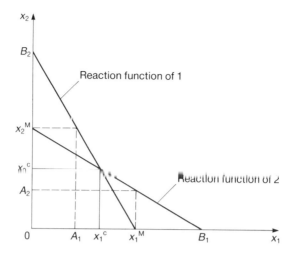

Figure 4.1

have $Z = a/b$, where a and b are the coefficients in the demand curve.

Following the notation of chapter 2, we have $H_1(0) = H_2(0) = [0, Z]$. Figure 4.1 makes it clear that

$$H_1(1) = [0, x_1^M]$$

and

$$H_2(1) = [0, x_2^M]$$

Recall the definition of $H_1(1)$:

$$H_1(1) = \{x \in H_1(0) \mid \text{ there exists } y \in H_2(0) \text{ such that } x \text{ is the best response to } y\} \tag{4.2}$$

Note that since we are using pointwise conjectures we are justified in using $H_2(0)$ instead of the set of all probability measures on $H_2(0)$. From (4.2) it is easy to see that $H_1(1)$ must be $[0, x_1^M]$.

By a similar argument, we get

$$H_1(2) = [A_1, x_1^M]$$
$$H_2(2) = [A_2, x_2^M]$$

It is easy to satisfy oneself that x_1^C is the only element that belongs to all $H_1(t)$. That is,

$$\{x_1^C\} = R_1$$

and similarly

$$\{x_2^C\} = R_2$$

To describe the collection of rationalizable outcomes when $n > 2$ we need another notation. Let x^M be the monopoly output of firm i. Since all firms are identical, there is no need to have an i subscript. Formally,

$$x^M = \operatorname*{argmax}_x \{ (a - bx)x - cx \} = \frac{a - c}{2b} \tag{4.3}$$

If $n > 2$, then for each firm i to produce any output in the interval $[0, x^M]$ is rationalizable.[1] That is, $R_i = [0, x^M]$.

To prove this, note that R_i must be a subset of $[0, x^M]$ because it is never worthwhile for a firm to produce more than x^M no matter what he expects the other firms to do. Hence the proof is completed by showing that $[0, x^M] \subset R_i$. This may be proved by induction. Certainly, $[0, x^M] \subset H_i(0)$ for all i. Assume $[0, x^M] \subset H_i(t - 1)$ for all i. Consider now $x \in [0, x^M]$. If every other firm produces $[2/(n - 1)](x^M - x)$, it follows from the reaction function of firm i that i's best response is indeed x. This is obvious from

$$x_i = x^M - \frac{1}{2} (x_1 + \ldots + x_{i-1} + x_{i+1} + \ldots + x_n) \tag{4.4}$$

which is derived by substituting (4.3) into (4.1). It is easy to check that

$$\frac{2}{n - 1} (x^M - x) \in [0, x^M]$$

Recalling that $n > 2$ and $x \in [0, x^M]$, note that the largest that $[2/(n - 1)] \times (x^M - x)$ can be is x^M. Hence there exists a conjecture of other players' moves which lie in $H_1(1 - t) \times \ldots \times H_n(t - 1)$ and for which x is a best response from i's point of view. Hence $x \in H_i(t)$. Since x was an arbitrary point in $[0, x^M]$, it follows that $[0, x^M] \subset H_i(t)$. Hence $[0, x^M] \subset R_i$.

By adapting theorem 2.7 to the case where strategy sets are infinite but compact, as in this chapter, a shorter, though less transparent, proof of the fact that $[0, x^M] = R_i$ is possible. Try it.

What the above argument shows is that if we have an oligopoly with more than three firms, many more things can happen by the criterion of rationalizability than what the traditional Nash–Cournot analysis leads us to believe.

It is worth discussing to what extent the above "claims" transcend the linear case. Suppose that we simply know that the industrial structure is such that there is a unique Nash equilibrium (which is "stable" in the sense that the reaction functions intersect in the "right" direction). Conditions which guarantee this are fairly general (see, for example, Friedman, 1977). If there are only two firms, it is easy to extend the above argument and show that the rationalizable solution continues to coincide with the Nash solution. For

$n > 3$, however, it is no longer guaranteed that the entire interval $[0, x^M]$ will be rationalizable.

4.3   BERTRAND EQUILIBRIUM AND THE EDGEWORTH INDETERMINACY

In the discussion on oligopoly thus far it was assumed that firms decide on their respective output with prices being determined by the market. This was the assumption of Cournot and it is fair to describe it as the dominant tradition even today. However, there is also a large and growing literature which uses Nash equilibrium as the appropriate equilibrium notion but, unlike Cournot, treats prices as the instruments controlled by the firms. In other words, the firm's set of strategies is simply the set of all possible prices. The foundations of this approach, as noted in chapter 1, owe much to a brief review article of Bertrand published in 1883, and also to some remarks by Marshall in one of the earlier editions of his *Principles*. Life was injected into the subject by Edgeworth's brilliant essay on duopoly entitled "The pure theory of monopoly"! The English version of this is printed in Edgeworth (1925) but it is a translation of an article written as early as 1897 in Italian. Actually, the Italian one is in turn a translation of an original English piece which has been lost.

Edgeworth's paper deals with several issues of taxation and monopoly but, and this is what is relevant to us here, it also devotes a section to what we now call "Bertrand equilibrium." Edgeworth shows that if capacity constraints exist then a Bertrand equilibrium might not exist.

Let me begin by describing a Bertrand oligopoly formally. Suppose the aggregate demand function is, as before,

$$x = A - Bp$$

There are two firms that can produce this good at the constant marginal cost c. There are no fixed costs. Each firm treats price as its strategic variable. That is, firms 1 and 2 announce the prices. We shall assume that if $p_i < p_j$ then everyone buys from firm i, and if $p_i = p_j$ each firm gets to serve half the market. Hence the profit function of firm 1 may be defined as

$$\pi_1(p_1, p_2) = \begin{cases} \frac{1}{2}(A - Bp_1)(p_1 - c) & \text{if} \quad p_1 = p_2 \\ (A - Bp_1)(p_1 - c) & \text{if} \quad p_1 < p_2 \\ 0 & \text{if} \quad p_1 > p_2 \end{cases}$$

$\pi_2(p_1, p_2)$ is defined symmetrically.

We say that (p_1^*, p_2^*) is a *Bertrand equilibrium* if (p_1^*, p_2^*) is a Nash equilibrium. Hence the only difference between Bertrand and Cournot is in the specification of the strategy sets.

It is simple to check that there is a unique Bertrand equilibrium for the duopoly just described: at equilibrium $p_1^* = p_2^* = c$; firms earn zero profit and total output equals $A - Bc$. The equilibrium is depicted in figure 4.2.

As a digression, observe that the Bertrand equilibrium is a Nash equilibrium involving the use of dominated strategies. This is because if firm i sets price equal to c it will earn zero profit no matter what the other firm does. On the other hand, if price is set above c (and below A/B) profit is zero if the other firm's price is less than p_i and positive otherwise. One can apply the criterion of perfection discussed in chapter 2 here by making a small modification. Suppose the firm's price cannot take any positive value but only certain values on a grid. We could for instance assume that price must never be in fractions of cents. Let us also assume that p_i cannot exceed A/B. Thus if P is the set of nonnegative integers below A/B, price (in cents) must be an element of P. That is, $p_i \in P$ for all i. For simplicity, suppose $c \in P$. By the same kind of reasoning as used above, $p_1^* = p_2^* = c$ is a Bertrand equilibrium of this duopoly. But is it perfect? By a direct application of theorem 2.5, we know that $p_1^* = p_2^* = c$ is not a perfect equilibrium. By theorem 2.4 we know that there must exist another Nash equilibrium in prices (which may, however, involve mixed strategies). It is therefore easy to see that in a "perfect Bertrand equilibrium," firms earn positive profit.

Let us return to the original Bertrand framework, that is, the one discussed before the previous digression. The Edgeworth problem arises if each firm has a capacity constraint which is between its Cournot output and E in figure 4.2. Let us, in particular, suppose that the maximum that a firm can produce lies between F and E, that is, in the interval $((A - Bc)/2, A - Bc)$. Let L

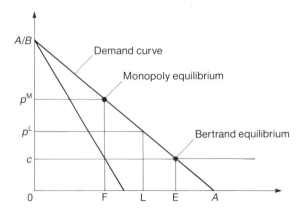

Figure 4.2

(figure 4.2) be such an amount. It will be shown that the model has no Bertrand equilibrium.

Consider first the case where $p_1 = p_2$. If $p_1 = p_2 > c$, then there must exist at least one firm which could supply more. Such a firm would do better by undercutting a little.[2] If $p_1 = p_2 = c$, both firms are earning zero profit. If one firm raises price slightly, all consumers will flock to the other firm, true, but the other firm will fail to satisfy all customers because of its capacity constraint. So some customers will come to this firm. Since its price is above c now, it will earn positive profit, that is, better than zero; therefore $p_1 = p_2 = c$ cannot be a Bertrand equilibrium. That $p_1 \neq p_2$ cannot be a Bertrand equilibrium is left as an exercise.

Edgeworth, it should be emphasized, did not describe this as a case of *nonexistence* of equilibrium but of "indeterminate" equilibrium with prices cycling within a certain range.[3]

The source of the problem is not difficult to see. It lies in the discontinuous relation between a firm's price and profit. One way of eliminating this discontinuity is to assume that the duopolists do not produce identical goods but close substitutes. In such a case one firm charging a slightly lower price would not attract all the consumers, because consumer preferences are usually heterogeneous. Hence the Bertrand analysis may be particularly well suited to industrial setups that produce substitutes. It is interesting to note that for the purpose of economics substitutes can be defined in two ways: (i) the usual way, for example, Coke and Pepsi, or (ii) Coke sold at location A and Coke sold at location B. The latter is clear if we think of people living around A. To them "Coke sold at A" is not exactly the same thing as "Coke sold at B," and, in fact, even if "Coke sold at B" were slightly cheaper they may continue to buy "Coke sold at A." This should make it clear that there is a close connection between models of location, product differentiation and brand competition. It is therefore possible to study these together as we shall do later.

Throughout this chapter, we talked in terms of prices *or* quantities being the strategic variable. In reality, strategies may be more complicated. Firms may first produce quantities and then compete over prices (Kreps and Scheinkman, 1983; Osborne and Pitchik, 1986). Firms may look at one another's production plans and alter their own plans before finally taking their outputs to the market (Saloner, 1987; Basu, 1990b). But such models involve extensive-form interactions and their discussion will therefore be postponed to a later chapter.

NOTES

1 This result, proved in Bernheim (1984), is true only for the linear case. If demand and cost curves are nonlinear but the Cournot equilibrium is "stable," what can be

shown is this. If $n = 2$, the only rationalizable outcome is the Cournot equilibrium. But as n becomes larger, the set of rationalizable outcomes of a firm converges to the interval from zero output to the monopoly output (Basu, 1991a).

2 Strictly speaking, we should first write the profit function $\pi_i(\cdot)$ of each firm as a function of p_1 and p_2 taking the capacity constraints into account. Then we could go through this kind of argument formally. However, since my analysis would be valid under most reasonable specifications of the profit function – for instance, the one used by Benoit and Krishna (1987) – greater formalism seems unnecessary.

3 For a formal analysis of the Edgeworth problem, see Levitan and Shubik (1972) and Shubik (1980); see also Maskin and Tirole (1988).

5

Nonlinear Pricing

5.1 INTRODUCTION

The textbook monopolist is a wasteful agent. As we have already seen in chapter 3, he lets the consumer get away with more surplus than he needs to. Consider the standard monopoly equilibrium depicted in figure 5.1 below. Let us assume that the demand curve is that of a single *price-taking* consumer.

The monopoly equilibrium, according to tradition, occurs at B, a point vertically above where marginal cost intersects marginal revenue. To avoid the problem of which measure of consumers' surplus to use, I shall, as before, assume that the income effect is zero for the good illustrated in figure 5.1. As demonstrated in chapter 3, the textbook monopolist, by letting the consumer pay $0\bar{p}B\bar{x}$, is losing out on some money, namely $AB\bar{p}$, unnecessarily.

Hence, if the monopolist is really a profit-maximizer, it is not clear why he should sell at a price $\bar{p}$ as he is expected to do. Indeed, if he did extract the full available surplus from the consumer, B would no longer be the equilibrium. It will be clear as we go along that equilibrium will occur at D. It may be countered that to extract all the consumers' surplus the monopolist needs to know the exact shape of the demand curve and in reality he would not know this. This may be true and would explain why a monopolist would not succeed in extracting the full surplus, but it does not explain why the traditional equilibrium will be an equilibrium. To show that, we have to produce a good argument as to why under incomplete information it may be best to behave like the traditional monopolist. If this can be done, it will be a nice justification for the textbook model. But right now we must regard this as an open problem.

The monopolists in the real world are much more ingenious than their textbook counterparts, however. They have devised several mechanisms

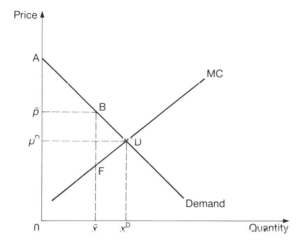

Figure 5.1

for extracting more consumers' surplus. Many pricing and marketing institutions that we encounter in industries and that, on the face of it, look innocuous are actually devices for earning a larger profit. It is possible, for instance, to show (Braverman et al., 1983) that a monopolist may prefer to produce a good with a higher probability of its being defective than he is technically capable of and offer consumers a repair service because that allows him to extract a larger payment from the consumers. That is, it allows him to collect a part of $AB\bar{p}$ in figure 5.1.

Interlinkage, tie-ins, full-line forcing, cluster markets and two-part tariffs, or more generally nonlinear pricing, may all be viewed as devices for extracting the full amount that the consumer is willing to pay under all-or-nothing offers. I shall first take up the simple yet instructive case of two-part tariffs.

5.2 TWO-PART TARIFFS

Suppose that the sole owner of a giant-wheel is considering what pricing strategy to follow. Being a monopolist, he could set the price of each ride on the wheel very high – certainly above marginal cost. Alternatively, he could charge an "entry fee" for entering the park where the giant-wheel is located and then give away the joy rides at a low price, equal to the marginal cost. Oi (1971) posed this problem and analyzed it with great lucidity; he showed that it is better to charge a two-part tariff, that is, an entry fee plus a low price for each ride. I shall here demonstrate this and some other features of two-part tariffs with the help of a simple diagrammatic technique, used in Basu (1987b).

Two-part tariffs are charged in many markets. Transport companies often offer monthly passes, which amount to paying an entry fee and then taking as many rides as one wants at a low price or even for free.

The particular good being discussed does not matter. So consider any good, say hats, being sold by a monopolist to a single, price-taking consumer. Let the monopolist charge a two-part tariff (T, p), where T is the entry charge and p the per-unit price of hats. In other words, any consumer who wants to buy hats must first pay a fee of T to the monopolist. Then he can buy as many hats as he wants at a price of p per hat.

It should immediately be clear that, for goods which are easily sold from one consumer to another, the above scheme might not work too well because one consumer could buy for himself and n other consumers and save paying n entry fees. Since I cannot buy bus rides for my friends, neither take joy-rides for them, nor watch films for them, these are goods where two-part tariffs can be effective. "Hats" are not a good example but it is a small word and you could think of "hats" as slang for "joy-rides on a giant-wheel."

So, to return to the example, let x be the number of hats bought by the consumer and y the consumer's income. This is a two-good economy and the other good has a price of 1. If $x > 0$, the consumer has to pay $T + px$ to the monopolist. If $x = 0$, he pays nothing to the monopolist. Hence, in figure 5.2, his budget set consists of the line segment yA and all points in 0AB.

The indifference curve that passes through y plays a very important role.

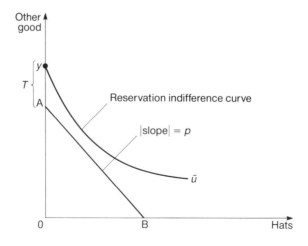

Figure 5.2

I shall refer to it as the "reservation indifference curve." If $\tilde{u}$ is the utility level depicted by it, then $\tilde{u}$ is the "reservation utility" of the consumer. In other words, the monopolist can never get the consumer to accept an offer which lands him with a utility below $\tilde{u}$, since the consumer can always refuse to buy anything from the monopolist and thereby ensure himself a utility level of $\tilde{u}$. In the case illustrated in figure 5.2, the consumer will in fact do without hats.

To see how well a monopolist charging two-part tariffs can do, suppose that he plans to sell some arbitrary number x_0 of hats. The maximum he can get from the consumer for this is given by GJ in figure 5.3. This he does by setting p equal to the marginal rate of substitution at J and T equal to yA'. Then the consumer faces the budget set yA' and $A'B'0$ and his optimum is to buy x_0 units and pay GJ = yD of which yA' is the entry fee and $A'D$ equals x_0 multiplied by p. It follows that if we draw a horizontal line through y and turn the diagram upside down, we could think of $\tilde{u}$ as the total revenue (TR) curve faced by the monopolist charging a two-part tariff. We could call such a monopolist a two-part tariff monopolist or, following Oi's example, a Disneyland monopolist.

Let yE be the *offer curve*, that is, the locus of equilibrium points on all budget constraints that can be drawn through y. You should check that for the traditional monopolist (who charges only a per-unit price) yE is the TR curve (with the diagram turned upside down). Since the offer curve through y must be above the indifference curve through y (strictly so, if preferences are strictly convex), the Disneyland monopolist necessarily earns a larger profit than the traditional monopolist. Of course, that the Disneyland monopolist must be able to earn at least as much as the traditional monopolist is

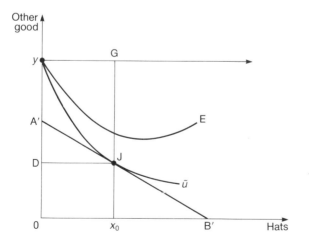

Figure 5.3

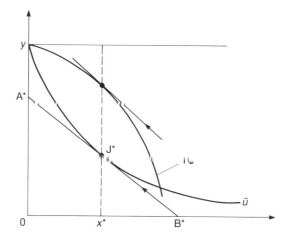

Figure 5.4

obvious because he always has the option of setting the entry fee equal to zero.

   To find out how much these two types of monopolists will produce, we simply have to draw the total cost (TC) curve upside down with y in figure 5.3 as the origin. Each type of monopolist will produce that output which maximizes the vertical distance between the relevant TR curve and the TC curve. Figure 5.4 depicts the equilibrium for a Disneyland monopolist. TC is the total cost curve. In equilibrium, the entry fee is yA*, per-unit price is given by the slope of the line A*B* and the amount sold is x*. Some properties of the Disneyland monopolist's equilibrium are easily deduced from such a geometry. First, output will be such that marginal cost equals the per-unit price p. In other words, in terms of figure 5.1, the equilibrium output occurs at x^D. Second, since in equilibrium the consumer gets his reservation utility $\tilde{u}$, he must be paying sufficiently to the monopolist to have no consumers' surplus left. In terms of figure 5.1, he pays $0ADx^D$ to buy x^D units of the good. Of this total payment, ADp^D is the entry fee.

5.3   MONOPOLY AND EFFICIENCY

The relation between a monopoly equilibrium and Pareto efficiency is at the same time simple and widely misunderstood. Indeed, a considerable amount of policymaking and the drafting and implementation of antitrust legislation has been marred by such misunderstandings.

   Most countries have enacted antitrust laws in some form or other. With its Sherman Act 1890, Clayton Act 1914, Robinson–Patman Act 1936 and many more, the United States has some of the most sophisticated legislation for deterring monopoly and encouraging competition. In Britain the first legislation against monopolistic industrial practices was enacted by the Labour government in 1948 when it passed the Monopolies and Restrictive Practices (Inquiry and Control) Act. The Monopolies and Restrictive Practices Commission was established under this Act. Its powers are more limited than the US Federal Trade Commission because it has no power to *initiate* an inquiry (for discussion see, for example, Guenault and Jackson, 1960; Rowley, 1966). In India the Monopolies and Restrictive Trade Practices Act 1969 is the main legislation for the control of monopolistic practices, although its efficacy has often been questioned (see, for example, Chandra, 1977; Paranjape, 1986). Nevertheless, the *motivation* behind the British and the Indian Acts is very similar to that of the antitrust laws of the United States. In the case of Japan the Antimonopoly Law 1947 was modelled after the US laws and imposed on the country by the Allied Forces (Caves and Uekusa, 1976), but it has undergone substantial changes subsequently (Hiroshi, 1986). The motivation behind all this legislation comes from a belief that monopoly is generally inefficient. This belief was there even before the analysis of monopoly was available in any reasonable form. The Sherman Act was passed a good 10 years before Ely's book, quoted in chapter 3, was published and, as the discussion in chapter 3 shows, the very *concept* of monopoly was still controversial, let alone the *consequences* of monopoly.

It will be argued here that, though some forms of monopoly are inefficient (in the sense of leading to Pareto-suboptimal equilibria), the most extortionate forms of monopoly are not inefficient. This seems paradoxical at first sight; and it is not surprising that lawyers have not appreciated it – or, to use more legally precise language, have not shown evidence of appreciating it.

Since antitrust laws try to prevent some of the most extortionate practices associated with monopolies, the above claim shows that such laws cannot be justified on grounds of efficiency. The justification would have to lie in equity and fairness.

Let me begin by demonstrating why the standard textbook monopolist is indeed inefficient. To do this formally we need to use a general equilibrium model. The simplest model for such an analysis is a 2×2 pure-exchange economy in which the entire initial endowment of good X is owned by agent 1 and the entire endowment of Y belongs to 2. Agent 2 is a monopolist, so he sets price. Agent 1 is a competitor (we could also think of agent 1 being actually a group of a large number of identical consumers), which, recalling the discussion in chapter 3, essentially means that he is a price-taker.

Much of this information is depicted in the Edgeworth box shown in figure 5.5. The endowment point is e and agent 1's offer curve is eE. So eE has the

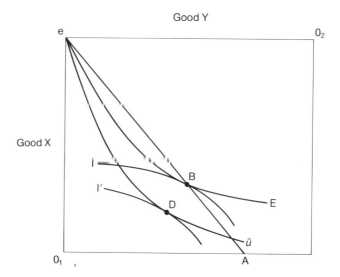

Figure 5.5

same character as yE in figure 5.3. A traditional monopolist will clearly set price so that the budget constraint of agent 1 is eA. Hence, equilibrium occurs at B, where agent 2's indifference curve I is tangential to the offer curve. B is clearly a Pareto suboptimal point.[1] Hence a traditional monopoly indeed leads to inefficiency. This explains the basis of the resentment against monopoly.

However, as we have already seen, the traditional textbook monopolist is a fairly philanthropic character in relation to what is possible. So let us check the welfare properties of a Disneyland monopolist. Let me here interpret a Disneyland monopolist not simply as someone charging a two-part tariff but, more generally, as a monopolist who extorts all the consumer's surplus from agent 1 – perhaps by making a take-it-or-leave-it offer. In other words, the Disneyland monopolist never makes an offer better than the minimum acceptable to agent 1. Hence he chooses a point on e$\bar{u}$, which is 1's indifference curve going through point e. From 2's point of view the best point on e$\bar{u}$ is D, where 2's indifference curve I′ is tangential to e$\bar{u}$. Agent 2 can attain this equilibrium through several mechanisms, such as the two-part tariff discussed in the previous section or take-it-or-leave-it offers which entail 2 offering a deal such as "give me so many units of good A and I will give you so many units of B and if you do not accept this deal then we do not trade."

Quite obviously D lies on the contract curve (not shown) in the Edgeworth box and is a Pareto-optimal point. So if a monopolist becomes more extortionate, the equilibrium changes from being suboptimal to optimal (i.e.

point B to point D)! Hence extortionate monopolistic practices should not be ruled out by law on grounds of their creating inefficiencies – or at least such an argument would require a much more sophisticated route. The justification for antitrust policies has to be based on grounds of equity. This is not impossible to construct because in the efficient monopoly equilibrium, that is, at D, the competitive buyers are exactly as well off as at e. Trade with the monopolist confers no benefit on them. Pareto optimality is achieved by the monopolist by appropriating the entire benefit from trade. One must keep in mind, however, that the fairness argument is complicated by the fact that the monopoly may have many shareholders. If the number of shareholders is very large, greater efficiency need not necessarily mean greater inequity.

5.4 NONLINEAR PRICING

In the last two sections I was assuming that all consumers are identical. The analysis becomes complicated if consumers are heterogeneous as they must be in reality. Barring some special cases, a monopolist cannot extract all the surplus from all consumers (or, equivalently, hold all consumers down on their respective reservation indifference curves) through any single two-part tariff. It would be a good exercise to take a two-consumer example and check that the above claim is true. The reader should also try to construct some exceptional examples where, despite heterogeneity of consumer preferences, a single two-part tariff is adequate to extract all surplus.

With heterogeneous consumers, one way of extracting all surplus is to charge each consumer a different price or two-part tariff. But this is unlikely to be possible for two reasons. First, such a policy may be construed as discriminatory and such discrimination may not be possible because it is illegal or because it causes too much illwill among consumers. Second, its feasibility hinges on the monopolist possessing a lot of information; in particular, he must know which consumer has which kind of preference.

So what can the monopolist do? If he has one kind of information, namely, *he knows what kinds of preferences the consumers have without knowing who has which preference*, the monopolist can do quite well for himself even if he cannot extract all the surplus.

A whole range of "asymmetric information" models in economics have been based on the information assumption stated in italics above. It is probably true that this is not the most common form in which incomplete information manifests itself in reality, but it is better than the full-information assumption, and it has also allowed us to construct realistic models in many areas such as optimal income taxation[2] and interlinkage of factor markets. It is with this information base that I shall now demonstrate how a monopolist firm can effectively use nonlinear pricing schemes.

It is useful to begin by noting that the two-part tariff discussed above is a special kind of nonlinear pricing. To understand this let us check what we mean when we say that the traditional monopolist uses linear pricing.

Let us, in an imaginary figure, represent the amount purchased by a consumer on the x axis and the amount paid by him on the y axis. If a monopolist charges a per-unit price only, then the options open to the consumer are represented by a straight line through the origin. It is in this sense that a traditional monopolist is supposed to use linear pricing. When a monopolist charges a two-part tariff we no longer have a linear function in this space but, in fact, a discontinuous one with the discontinuity occurring at the origin. More generally we could suppose that a monopolist is free to draw any graph in this space and let each consumer choose one point. Such a monopolist is said to be using a nonlinear pricing scheme.

We shall now consider a monopolist who uses such a pricing scheme. But to keep the algebra manageable it is useful to place some restrictions on the types of consumers who wish to buy from this monopolist.

Let us suppose that there are m consumers and they can be partitioned into n "types." Let t_i be the number of consumers of type i. Hence $m = t_1 + \ldots + t_n$. If a consumer of type i consumes x units of the good being supplied by the monopolist and z units of the other good – let us call it "money" – then his utility is given by

$$U^i = U^i(x, z)$$

It is assumed that U^i is increasing in x and z, is differentiable and is strictly concave. It should now be clear that by a consumer of type i we simply mean a consumer whose utility function is $U^i(x, z)$.

The important restriction on inter-consumer preferences which is used in this literature (see Spence, 1977, 1980; Phlips, 1983) is that, between any two consumer types, one can be described as wanting the monopolist's good more intensely. This is known as the *agent monotonicity axiom* and can be stated formally as follows.

Axiom M For all x, z and for all $i \in \{1, \ldots, n-1\}$,

$$\frac{U_1^i(x, z)}{U_2^i(x, z)} < \frac{U_1^{i+1}(x, z)}{U_2^{i+1}(x, z)}$$

U_1^i is used to denote the partial derivative with respect to the monopolist's good and U_2^i is the same with respect to the other good. Axiom M will be assumed to be true throughout section 5.3.

Spence (1977, 1980) and Phlips (1983) assume also that, for all x, y, z, w, for all i and for all real numbers r,

$$[U^i(x,y) = U^i(z,w)] \leftrightarrow [U^i(x,y+r) = U^i(z,w+r)]$$

I shall not use this restriction. This will of course mean that some of the results will be less sharp but, on the plus side, the results will be more generally applicable. I shall, however, assume that all consumers have the same income y. This is a simplifying assumption and, as will be shown later, the results do not depend on it.

As already stated in words, the monopolist's offer to the consumers could be thought of as a real-valued function $r(\cdot)$ which is interpreted as follows. If a consumer buys x units of goods, he has to pay $r(x)$ amount of money to the monopolist. However, it is easy to see that with n types of consumers the monopolist has nothing to gain by making a continuum of offers. He could do as well by offering n pairs of the following kind:

$$((x_1, r_1), \ldots, (x_n, r_n))$$

which I shall denote briefly by $\{x, r\}$. If a consumer chooses to buy x_i units of the good, he has to pay r_i units of money.

There is no discrimination between consumers in the sense that each consumer is free to choose any pair from the n-tuple of pairs offered in $\{x, r\}$. It is purely a matter of labeling and I shall assume that (x_i, r_i) is the one that is chosen by consumers of type i. That is, for all i and all j,

$$U^i(x_i, y - r_i) \geqslant U^i(x_j, y - r_j) \tag{5.1}$$

and

$$U^i(x_i, y - r_i) \geqslant U^i(0, y) \tag{5.2}$$

Condition (5.2) implies that a consumer is free not to buy anything from the monopolist. It will be assumed here that if a type-i consumer is indifferent between (x_i, r_i) and (x_j, r_j) he will choose (x_i, r_i).

Let Z be a collection of n-tuples of ordered pairs defined as follows:

$$Z = \{\{x, r\} \mid (5.1) \text{ and } (5.2) \text{ are satisfied}\}$$

We shall now assume that the monopolist maximizes his profit by offering to the consumers an $\{x, r\}$ from the set Z. It should be clarified that the monopolist's profit-maximization is not constrained by this domain restriction assumption since elements outside Z can be suitably relabeled to bring them into Z. One may get a false impression that the restriction of domain to Z forces the monopolist to transact with all consumers. The impression is false because the monopolist can always set $x_i = r_i = 0$. Of course, this will also mean that consumers of type less than i will not buy goods from the monopolist. But a monopolist who does not want to transact with a consumer of type i will not anyway want to transact with those of types less than i.

Let $c(\cdot)$ be the total cost function of the monopolist. We assume $c' > 0$, $c'' > 0$. If he offers $\{x, r\} \in Z$, his total profit will be

$$\pi(\{x, r\}) = \sum_{i=1}^{n} t_i r_i - c \sum_{i=1}^{n} t_i x_i \qquad (5.3)$$

The monopolist's problem is to maximize this by selecting an $\{x, r\}$ from Z. And as far as we are concerned, the characteristics of a market with nonlinear pricing are those that emerge from the solution of the above maximization problem. It will be assumed that a solution exists and it will be denoted by

$$\{\hat{x}, \hat{r}\} = ((\hat{x}_1, \hat{r}_1), \ldots, (\hat{x}_n, \hat{r}_n))$$

Theorem 5.1 $\{\hat{x}, \hat{r}\}$ satisfies the following: for all i, j,

$$\hat{x}_j \leqslant \hat{x}_i \leftrightarrow \hat{r}_j \leqslant \hat{r}_i \qquad (5.4)$$

$$U^1(\hat{x}_1, y - \hat{r}_1) = U^1(0, y) \qquad (5.5)$$

For all $i > 1$,

$$U^i(\hat{x}_i, y - \hat{r}_i) = U^i(\hat{x}_{i-1}, y - \hat{r}_{i-1}) \qquad (5.6)$$

$$\hat{x}_1 \leqslant \hat{x}_2 \leqslant \ldots \leqslant \hat{x}_n \qquad (5.7)$$

PROOF Relation (5.4) is obvious.

Note that $U^i(\hat{x}_i, y - \hat{r}_i) < U^i(\hat{x}_{i-1}, y - \hat{r}_{i-1})$ cannot be true because i would then prefer $(\hat{x}'_{i-1}, \hat{r}_{i-1})$ to $(\hat{x}_i, \hat{r}_i)$. Now suppose that $U^i(\hat{x}_i, y - \hat{r}_i) > U^i(\hat{x}_{i-1}, y - \hat{r}_{i-1})$. Then the monopolist can raise $\hat{r}_i$ a little and suitably adjust $\hat{r}_{i+1}, \ldots, \hat{r}_n$ upwards and earn more profits. This is a contradiction. Hence (5.6) must be true. (In case it is not clear what "suitably adjust" means, a similar adjustment will be defined rigorously in proving theorem 5.2, below.)

Equation (5.5) is established by a similar argument.

Suppose for some i, $\hat{x}_i < \hat{x}_{i-1}$. Then axiom M and (5.6) imply $U^{i-1}(\hat{x}_i, y - \hat{r}_i) > U^{i-1}(\hat{x}_{i-1}, y - \hat{r}_{i-1})$, which is a contradiction since it violates (5.1). Hence (5.7) must be true.   ∎

If a consumer of type i buys x_i units of the good at a cost of r_i, the marginal rate of substitution (MRS) is defined as

$$\text{MRS}_i(x_i, r_i) = \frac{U_1^i(x_i, y - r_i)}{U_2^i(x_i, y - r_i)}$$

For person i, buying x_i at a cost of r_i, $\text{MRS}_i(x_i, r_i)$ may be thought of as the (implicit) price faced by him.

Theorem 5.2 For all $i < n$,

$$\text{MRS}_i(\hat{x}_i, \hat{r}_i) > c'\left(\sum_{i=1}^{n} t_i \hat{x}_i\right)$$

and

$$\text{MRS}_n(\hat{x}_n, \hat{r}_n) = c'\left(\sum_{i=1}^{n} t_i \hat{x}_i\right)$$

PROOF Throughout the proof we shall use c' to denote $c'(\sum_{i=1}^{n} t_i \hat{x}_i)$.

Suppose there exists $i < n$ such that $\text{MRS}_i(\hat{x}_i, \hat{r}_i) \leqslant c'$. Let j be the smallest integer for which this is true. Assume $\hat{x}_{j-1} = \hat{x}_j$. Then, by (5.4) of theorem 5.1, $\hat{r}_{j-1} = \hat{r}_j$. Hence, by axiom M,

$$\text{MRS}_{j-1}(\hat{x}_{j-1}, \hat{r}_{j-1}) < \text{MRS}_j(\hat{x}_j, \hat{r}_j)$$

But this contradicts the fact that j is the smallest integer for which $\text{MRS}_j(\hat{x}_j, \hat{r}_j) \leqslant c'$. This contradiction and (5.7) of theorem 5.1 imply $\hat{x}_{j-1} < \hat{x}_j$. Hence, (5.6) and axiom M imply

$$U^{j-1}(\hat{x}_{j-1}, y - \hat{r}_{j-1}) < U^{j-1}(\hat{x}_j, \hat{y} - \hat{r}_j) \tag{5.8}$$

(If the j defined above is 1, then we can reach (5.8) by treating $\hat{x}_{j-1} = \hat{r}_{j-1} = 0$ and using a similar argument to that above.)

The situation depicted thus far is illustrated in figure 5.6 to aid intuition. Let us now define a function $r_j(x_j)$ implicitly by

$$U^j(\hat{x}_j, y - \hat{r}_j) = U^j(x_j, y - r_j(x_j))$$

For all $i \geqslant 1$ define $r_{j+i}(x_j)$ recursively as follows: $r_{j+i}(x_j)$ is defined implicitly by

$$U^{j+1}(\hat{x}_j, y - r_j(x_j)) = U^{j+1}(\hat{x}_{j+1}, y - r_{j+1}(x_j))$$

For $i \geqslant 2$ (and, of course, less than or equal to $n - j$), $r_{j+i}(x_j)$ is defined implicitly by

$$U^{j+i}(\hat{x}_{j+i-1}, y - r_{j+i-1}(x_j)) = U^{j+i}(\hat{x}_{j+i}, y - r_{j+i}(x_j))$$

Let the monopolist's profit as a function of x_j be denoted by $\phi(x_j)$, which is defined as follows:

$$\phi(x_j) = \pi((\hat{x}_1, \hat{r}_1), \ldots, (\hat{x}_{j-1}, \hat{r}_{j-1}), (x_j, r_j(x_j)), (\hat{x}_{j+1}, r_{j+1}(x_j)),$$
$$\ldots, (\hat{x}_n, r_n(x_j)))$$

$$= \sum_{i=1}^{j-1} t_i \hat{r}_i \sum_{i=j}^{n} t_i r_i(x_j) - c \left(\sum_{i \neq j} t_i \hat{x}_i + t_j x_j \right)$$

Hence,

$$\frac{\partial \phi(\hat{x}_j)}{\partial r_j} = \sum_{i-j}^{n} t_i \frac{\partial r_i(\hat{x}_j)}{\partial r_j} - t_j c'$$

Note that

$$\frac{\partial r_i(\hat{x}_i)}{\partial x_j} \equiv MRS_j(\ell_j, \ell_j)$$

Hence, from the definition of j,

$$t_j \frac{\partial r_j(\hat{x}_j)}{\partial x_j} - t_j c' \leq 0$$

From the definition of $r_{j+i}(x_j)$, it follows that, for all $i \geq 1$,

$$\frac{\partial r_{j+i}(\hat{x}_j)}{\partial x_j} < 0$$

(Figure 5.6 will help you to see this.) Therefore,

$$\frac{\partial \phi(\hat{x}_j)}{\partial x_j} < 0$$

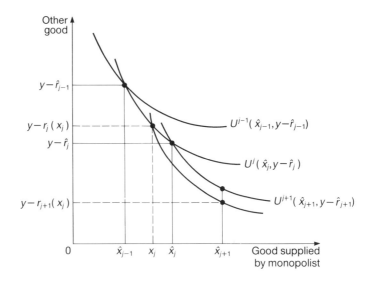

Figure 5.6

Hence if x_j is lowered from $\hat{x}_j$, and r_j, ..., r_n are adjusted suitably, the monopolist's profit rises. It is easy to see that as long as x_j is greater than x_{j-1} this adjustment leaves the monopolist's offer within Z. This contradicts the contention that $(\{\hat{x}, \hat{r}\})$ is the monopolist's optimum and thereby establishes that, for all $i < n$, $MRS_i(\hat{x}_i, \hat{r}_i) > c'$.

The proposition just established and axiom M imply $MRS_n(\hat{x}_{n-1}, \hat{r}_{n-1}) > c'$. From this and (5.6) it is easy to see that if $MRS_n(\hat{x}_n, \hat{r}_n) \neq c'$ the monopolist could increase his profit by changing $(\hat{x}_n, \hat{r}_n)$. ■

Before proving the above theorems, it was asserted that the assumption that all consumers have the same income was not germane to my analysis. To show this I shall now allow different consumer types to have different incomes. With this, if we make an accompanying alteration in axiom M, then exactly the same result as specified in the theorem above goes through. The idea is very simple, and I present it only informally. Suppose persons of type i have an income of y_i each. Figure 5.7 shows the indifference curves of persons of types 1 and 2, which pass through points $(0, y_1)$ and $(0, y_2)$ respectively. Since both these indifference curves are drawn from the same origin, we label the origin $0_1, 0_2$. Now in figure 5.8 we draw the two indifference curves with respect to different origins. In particular we shift 0_2 until y_1 and y_2 meet on the y axis. We label this point y. Some readers may find it easier to understand the above operation with the help of transparencies. Suppose the indifference curve of consumer 1 through y_1 and the indifference curve of 2 through y_2 are drawn on separate transparencies and then the two transparencies are placed on top of each other so that the origins coincide. Figure 5.7 is the projection of this on the wall. Now pick up the

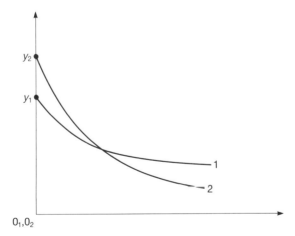

Figure 5.7

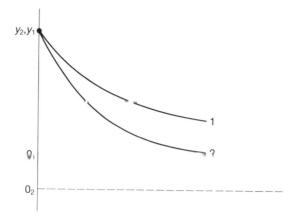

Figure 5.8

transparency of consumer 2 and shift it so that y_1 and y_2 coincide. Figure 5.8 is a projection of this. Similarly by shifting $0_3, 0_4, \ldots, 0_n$ we could ensure that $y_3, y_4, \ldots, y_n$ all start from y. This new set of indifference curves will be referred to as the *origin-adjusted indifference curves*. What we have to do is to impose a condition similar to axiom M on the origin-adjusted indifference curves. That is, we have to assume that, at any point, the origin-adjusted indifference curve of a person of type $i + 1$ is steeper (in terms of magnitude) than that of i. And the stage is set for an analogous proof of the above theorem.

The above restriction may appear mechanical but fortunately it is possible to derive it from economically more meaningful axioms. For instance, we could simply assume that $y_{i+1} \geqslant y_i$ for all i, the good is not inferior and axiom M (without origin adjustment) is true.

Having characterized the monopoly outcome, it is interesting to compare it with the "optimum." If, for instance, the same good were being distributed by a public utility interested in maximizing social welfare, what would the outcome be? The answer depends on what is meant by social welfare. Let us, for simplicity (and certainly without endorsing it), equate social welfare with aggregate money value to the consumers minus aggregate cost.

Define $\psi_i(x_i)$ as the maximum amount a consumer of type i is willing to pay for x_i when faced with an all-or-nothing offer. Thus $\psi_i(x_i)$ is defined implicitly by

$$U^i(x_i, y - \psi_i(x_i)) = U^i(0, y) \tag{5.9}$$

Hence, social welfare W is given by

$$W(x_1, \ldots, x_n) = \sum t_i \psi_i(x_i) - c\left(\sum t_i x_i\right) \tag{5.10}$$

Notice that the amount that consumers have to pay does not enter (5.10) because (5.10) merely determines how the total value generated is shared between the consumers and the government. Since social welfare is treated as simply equal to the total value generated, its distribution is unimportant to us. It should also be mentioned that the consumer's surplus measure implicit in (5.10) is the Marshallian one (see Marshall, 1920; Hicks, 1956).

The first-order condition for maximizing W is given by

$$\psi_i'(x_i^*) = c'\left(\sum_i t_i x_i^*\right) \qquad i = 1, \ldots, n$$

where $(x_1^*, \ldots, x_n^*)$ are the optimum values. From (5.9) we get

$$\frac{U_1^i(x_i^*, y - \psi_i(x_i^*))}{U_2^i(x_i^*, y - \psi_i(x_i^*))} = \psi_i'(x_i^*)$$

Hence,

$$\mathrm{MRS}_i(x_i^*, \psi_i(x_i^*)) = c'\left(\sum_i t_i x_i^*\right) \qquad i = 1, \ldots, n \qquad (5.11)$$

which is the age-old condition that MRS is the same as the marginal cost.

It is therefore clear that the profit-maximizing solution will not be efficient if consumers are heterogeneous since, from theorem 5.2, we know that for all $i < n$ MRS exceeds marginal cost. If consumers are homogeneous, however, and the monopolist is allowed to use nonlinear pricing the outcome will be efficient, but the efficiency will be accompanied by inequity in the sense that all the benefits of the market will be collected by the monopolist. The consumers will be left at a level of welfare where they would be if they had not bought anything from the monopolist.

If we had used the assumption that the indifference curves of each individual are parallel in a vertical direction (see the remarks following axiom M for a formal statement), which implies that the income effect for the monopolist's good is zero, then we would have the result that the monopolist always produces less than the optimum. A formal statement of this follows. Recall that a circumflex denotes monopoly equilibrium values and an asterisk denotes the optimum.

Theorem 5.3 If the income effect is zero for the good in question, then $\Sigma t_i \hat{x}_i < \Sigma t_i x_i^*$.

PROOF Suppose the income effect is zero and

$$\sum_i t_i \hat{x}_i > \sum_i t_i x_i^*$$

Hence $c'(\Sigma t_i \hat{x}_i) > c'(\Sigma t_i x_i^*)$, since $c'' > 0$. This, theorem 5.2 and equation (5.11) imply that, for all i,

$$\mathrm{MRS}_i(\hat{x}_i, \hat{r}_i) > \mathrm{MRS}_i(x_i^*, \psi_i(x_i^*))$$

Since income effect is zero, it follows that

$$\mathrm{MRS}_i(\hat{x}_i, \hat{r}_i) > \mathrm{MRS}_i(x_i^*, r_i) \qquad \text{for all } r_i$$

Since indifference curves are convex, this implies

$$\hat{x}_i < x_i^* \qquad \text{for all } i$$

Hence, $\Sigma t_i x_i < \Sigma t_i x_i^*$, which is a contradiction.   ■

5.5   TIE-INS, CLUSTERS AND INTERLINKAGE

In the previous section, one person having a greater demand for a good than another person implied that the former would buy a larger amount of the good than the latter if both faced the same price and had the same income. This is a direct consequence of the agent-monotonicity axiom. If, however, the product happens to be a durable good, then a "greater demand" can be interpreted in a very different way. Consider, for instance, typewriters. To say that a person has a greater demand for a typewriter does not necessarily mean that he will buy several typewriters. It could simply mean that, once he acquires one, he will use it more intensively than others. If human beings differ in this sense, then it may be in the interest of the typewriter company to "tie-in" typewriter sales with the sales of some other complementary good, like ribbons or cartridges. By this the monopolist may be able to extract more surplus than by the textbook method of simply fixing the typewriter price to his greatest advantage. Such tie-ins have been the source of some very interesting antitrust cases. But before going into that let us clarify what a "tie-in" means.

Broadly speaking, a *tie-in* or a *tying agreement* is said to occur when the sale or lease of one commodity is made conditional on the sale or lease of another (Bowman, 1957; Burstein, 1960).[3] The courts in the United States have generally viewed tie-ins as illegal because it has been supposed that a tie-in amounts to the creation of a second monopoly – though the economics of such a claim is not obvious.

Tie-ins can occur for several reasons. If the price of a monopolist's product is fixed by law, the monopolist could try to circumvent the law by insisting that whoever buys his product also buys some other good from him even though he charges a higher-than-market price for the latter. Thus Bowman (1957) discusses an antitrust case of 1920, where the respondent sold steel ties used for wrapping cotton bales but insisted that the buyers also buy the jute bagging from him. The tie-in apparently was a mode of circumventing the wartime policy of low steel prices.

A different and very simple explanation of tie-in sales, based on the possibility that reservation prices across consumers are heterogeneous, was provided by Stigler (1963) (see also Schmalensee, 1982). Suppose there are two individuals, 1 and 2, and two goods X and Y. Assume that the decision for each consumer is to choose between buying nothing, buying 1 unit of X, buying 1 unit of Y, and buying a unit each of X and Y. Next suppose that the reservation prices of the buyers are as follows:

1 would pay up to 8 dollars for X and 2 dollars for Y
2 would pay up to 7 dollars for X and 3 dollars for Y

If a monopolist (for both goods) tried to sell X and Y separately, he would earn at most 18 dollars (by charging 7 dollars per unit of X and 2 dollars per unit of Y). If, however, he insisted that X and Y be bought as *one* bundle,[4] he could earn 20 dollars by charging 10 dollars for each bundle.

Yet another reason – the one mentioned at the start of this section – for the existence of tie-ins is as a mode of price discrimination between heterogeneous buyers of a durable good. An interesting case of this kind which occurred at the turn of the century is the case between the Heaton–Peninsular Button-Fastener Co. and Eureka Speciality Co. The case involved a newly invented machine for stapling buttons to "high-button shoes" (Bowman, 1957). Let me try to tell the same story with a more contemporary, albeit imaginary, account.

Suppose a company has invented and patented a machine called a photocopier. What people really demand is not the machine but the services that flow out of it. We could measure this in, for instance, pages, that is, the number of pages photocopied. Let us assume that photocopying requires nothing else but the machine and paper. We shall also assume that paper is available competitively at a price equal to the marginal cost of production, c, which is assumed to be constant.

At what price should the company sell the photocopier machines? The answer is very simple using the method of section 5.2, if all consumers are identical. Since people are not interested in the machine *per se* but in the number of pages photocopied, draw a diagram where the horizontal axis represents the number of pages photocopied and the vertical axis the only other good called money.

Let us suppose that the company could tie in the sale of paper with the machines. That is, it insists that whoever buys its machine must also buy all the paper needed for photocopying from it. In that case the company chooses a price pair (T, p) where T is the price of the machine and p the price of paper (which is the same thing as the price of each unit of service from the machine).

Do not forget that, in this model, the photocopier machine is sold by a monopolist and one has to buy the machine to get photocopies.

The rental market is yet to emerge.

Since the machine itself is of no inherent value to the consumer, what we have is a situation identical to the two-part tariff model. If a person does not want to do any photocopying, he can spend his entire income y on the other good. But if he wants to do x pages of photocopying, he can spend only $y - T - px$ on the other good.

We already know (from section 5.2) how the monopolist will set prices. He will set $p = c$ and make T large enough to extract all the consumers' surplus. Note that with p equal to c he makes no profit on the paper sales, so he will be indifferent as to whether the paper is bought from him or from the competitive market at price c. In other words, there will be no tie-ins in this case.

But now suppose that the consumers have differing needs. Some want to use the machine intensively and some occasionally. To rule out the use of nonlinear pricing on paper (which is anyway quite unrealistic) let me assume that the monopolist has to set a fixed price T for the machine and a fixed price p per unit of paper. What should he do? He would ideally like to charge a higher T for those who are the intensive users. But he is not allowed to do this and, even if he were, he would not know who the heavy users were. He will have to devise a method whereby the heavy users will "self-select" themselves and contribute more to his coffers. One way of doing this is to keep T low but set p above c. Then each time a person buys paper from him he will make a small profit of $p - c$. Since the heavy users will buy more often, they will end up making a bigger contribution to the monopolist's profit.[5] This is exactly what was done by the inventor of machines for stapling buttons to high-button shoes (if you do not know what these are you may derive consolation from the fact that neither does the author). He insisted that the buttons also be bought from him. And this is what ran him into the charge of violating antitrust laws.

Of course there are subtle ways of effecting this tie-in without announcing that those who buy photocopier machines must also buy their paper from the same shop. Thus the company could make the machine in a way which requires special paper which only this company manufactures.

The typewriter company that requires the use of special cartridges on its machines, the camera which requires special films, the shampoo that can cause hair loss if it is not followed by the use of conditioner manufactured by the same company could also be instances of tying arrangements.

The view that these amount to violations of antitrust law because they lead to the *creation* of new monopolies – a practice often described as *leverage* – is not transparent. What is more likely is that these tie-ins are often mechanisms for price discrimination where, for some reason, this cannot be practised openly.[6]

Nevertheless, the legal issues raised here are very interesting and some effort has been made in recent times to isolate conditions under which the 'leverage' argument makes economic sense (e.g. Asch, 1983; Carbajo et al., 1990; Whinston, 1990). To see this, note that, while the basic antitrust objection to price discrimination and tie-ins is that they create new monopolies, this can be interpreted in very different ways. I consider two of these. First, suppose that a monopoly firm A offers a nonlinear price schedule such that the larger buyers get a lower price. If the good in question happens to be an input for another industry, then A's pricing policy becomes a cause of increasing returns in the downstream industry that uses the input. This would discourage competition in the downstream industry and may even create a monopoly. The argument has *a priori* appeal and it is interesting to note that one of the sections of the Robinson–Patman Act 1936 in the United States prohibits price discrimination which tends to have this effect. While it would be interesting to construct a theoretical model of the above argument, I shall, instead, illustrate it with a real-life example.

Asch (1983) discusses the Morton Salt Case of 1948 in which the Morton Salt Company was offering a nonlinear price schedule:

Less-than-carload purchases:	$1.60 per case
Carload purchases:	$1.50 per case
5,000-case purchase in 12 months:	$1.40 per case
50,000-case purchase in 12 months:	$1.35 per case

The charge against the company, upheld by the Supreme Court, was that it violated section 2(a) of the Robinson–Patman Act because Morton's price schedule discouraged competition not in the "horizontal sense" involving Morton's competitors but among grocery stores which purchased salt from Morton. Only the larger grocery stores would be able to get salt cheap. Indeed, only five major retail food chains had ever made it to the $1.35 mark.

What is theoretically interesting is to analyze the problem from Morton Salt Company's point of view. If its pricing structure influences the market structure of the downstream industry that buys its product, then what will be the nature of the price schedule in equilibrium? Can it ever be the case that this company actually creates a downstream monopoly?

Leaving these as open issues, I move to the second sense in which a monopoly or monopolistic tendencies can be said to be "created." This may happen in the case of tie-ins. Suppose good x is sold by a monopolist. If the sale of x is tied to the sale of some other good y, the legal view was that this may lead to leverage by making the market for y less competitive. While economists have generally been dismissive of this viewpoint, Whinston (1950) and Carbajo et al. (1990) try to show that under certain situations leverage can be formally explained. One possible line – pursued by Carbajo et al. (1990) – is to consider a firm (call it firm 1) producing two goods A and B. For A it has a monopoly. For B it competes with another firm (call it 2) by setting prices. That is, the B industry is a Bertrand duopoly. Firm 2 produces only good B. Further, good B can be produced by both firms at a constant marginal cost c.

If firm 1 does not bundle goods A and B, that is, consumers buy A and B separately (and the demands for the two goods are unrelated) then in equilibrium the price of good B will settle down to the competitive level, namely c (as we have seen in chapter 4), and the price of A will be the monopoly price. Now suppose firm 1 ceases to sell the two goods separately and instead makes bundles consisting of 1 unit of good A and 1 unit of good B, and sells these bundles. Let us call the bundle good "C." The Bertrand outcome, with its concomitant zero profit, can now no longer obtain because firm 1's good (i.e. C) is a substitute for 2's good (i.e. B) but not a perfect substitute. There are parametric situations, as Carbajo et al. show, and they are easy to construct, such that for firm 1 it is better to bundle the goods. In a sense, therefore, what the bundling is doing is destroying the competitive price (which is also the Bertrand price) which would have prevailed in the market for B otherwise. It is in this sense that we could think of bundling or tie-ins as extending monopoly power from one market to another.

A concept related to tie-ins which has generated some recent controversies in the courts is a "cluster market." In the words of Ayres (1985, p. 109) " 'Tied products' are those sellers *require* to be purchased together. In *cluster cases*, defendant firms offer to sell a number of 'untied products,' but do not require that they be purchased together" (my italics). Thus in United States v. Philadelphia National Bank, 1963, the Supreme Court in the United States described the range of products and services provided by a bank, e.g. "various kinds of credit," "checking accounts and trust administration," as a cluster. In deciding whether some antitrust law was being violated or not one would have to look at a bank's operation over the whole cluster instead of doing an item-by-item analysis.

Ayres points to some of the deficiencies of the courts' definitions and develops the interesting concept of "transactional complementarity." Goods are *transactional complements* if buying them from a single firm significantly reduces consumers' transactions costs. This is one definition, but depending on the context there may be scope for using several definitions. There is room for formal analysis here.

Another related concept on which, unlike in "clusters," much theoretical research has occurred is "interlinkage" in factor markets in backward agrarian economies. It has been widely noted (for two surveys from different perspectives see Bardhan, 1980; Bell, 1988)[7] that in such economies transaction on one market is conditional upon transaction on another market.

A landlord will often give credit only to a person who supplies labor to the landlord. A person will at times rent out his land to another person if that person agrees to do some part-time work for him. Bardhan (1984) had suggested that interlinkage in backward agriculture and tie-ins in modern industry may have some fundamental commonness. I have tried to analyze formally the extent of this commonness in Basu (1987b). It indeed seems possible to argue that interlinkage is a mechanism for extracting a larger surplus than would be possible under the textbook framework of single-market single-price interactions.

NOTES

1 This was once fairly standard analysis; see Schydlowsky and Siamwalla (1966).
2 The seminal work using this method is the paper by Mirrlees (1971).
3 Closely related concepts have been analyzed by many other economists under different labels: e.g. "commodity bundling" (Adams and Yellen, 1976); "full-line forcing" (Burstein, 1960); "block booking" (Stigler, 1963). For a lucid survey of price discrimination and bundling, see Varian (1989).
4 Such offers are usually described by sellers as: "Buy one unit of x and get one unit of y free."
5 It is generally believed that in a case like this, whenever paper is sold as a *tied* product, it will be sold above the competitive price. This is not necessarily so. The reader should try to construct a case with heterogeneous consumers where the monopolist's best strategy is to sell paper at a price below its marginal cost.
6 In the United States, for instance, certain forms of price discrimination are prohibited under the Clayton and Robinson–Patman Acts. In Britain also the Monopolies Commission has generally been hostile towards price discrimination and nonlinear pricing (see Rowley, 1966, chapter 14). A firm's apprehension that nonlinear prices may be treated by the courts as violation of one of these Acts may lead it to seek camouflage.
7 See also Braverman and Srinivasan, 1981; Braverman and Stiglitz, 1982; Basu, 1990c.

6

Quality

6.1 INTRODUCTION

Though we often speak in our models of several firms producing the same homogeneous product, this is an abstraction seldom encountered in reality. Although we speak of the "footwear" industry or the "automobile" industry, there is no homogeneous and well-defined object called "footwear" or "automobiles." There are different kinds of footwear and motor cars. If we want to retain the concept of an "industry" as a useful one we need to consider groups of firms which produce the same *kinds* of goods instead of the same good. This compels us to confront the idea of quality differentials or brands within the same product group.

As Eaton and Lipsey (1989) point out, there is no unique way of defining the concept of product quality differentials. Until such a definition is found we shall have to be content with several views of product differentiation (see Waterson, 1984, chapter 6). The present chapter and the next two chapters investigate a class of models which explore related themes, like brand proliferation, location choice, and product durability. The purpose of the present chapter is to introduce some ideas concerning product quality. It may therefore be viewed as a precursor to more specific formulations where quality takes particular forms such as durability and locational advantage – two topics which occur in succession in the next two chapters.

Gabszewicz and Thisse (1979) have developed a characterization of quality variation where the focus of consumer decision is shifted away from the conventional to a polar extreme. The decision problem then is not "how many to buy" but "which brand to buy." This is a useful change of focus since when a consumer thinks of buying a piano, a computer, or a carpet, the central problem is not how many to buy but which of the several competing brands to buy. Their characterization of quality differentiation also has the advantage – or disadvantage, as the case may be – that implicit in it is a *hierarchy* of quality such that a higher income person would tend to go for a higher quality good. This is distinct from the location models, discussed in chapter 8. The next section provides a brief introduction to the Gabszewicz–Thisse formulation.

Another formulation for describing oligopoly in a differentiated product market is to use a specific linear demand system. This method also allows us to speak of a market where the goods involved are complements instead of substitutes. Section 6.3 describes such models. At times, we find that we do not have to be very precise about the meaning of product quality in order to be able to deduce interesting conclusions. Section 6.4 illustrates such a case by considering a model which explains why doctors have patients waiting and, in general, why markets do not always clear.

6.2 QUALITY HIERARCHIES

To make fleeting acquaintance with the Gabszewicz–Thisse model consider an industry (the automobile industry for instance) in which there are n different kinds (e.g. Honda, Chrysler, Ford) of goods produced in n different firms, each firm producing one brand. A typical consumer's problem is first to decide whether to buy the good or not and then to decide which brand to buy. He can, it is assumed, buy one unit at most. If the consumer buys a product of firm k (or, which is the same thing, brand k) and his residual income – that is, money left over for the purchase of other goods – is R, then his utility, denoted by $U(k, R)$, is given by

$$U(k, R) \equiv u(k) R \qquad (6.1)$$

where, for all j, $u(j)$ is a nonnegative number such that $j > i$ implies

$$u(j) > u(i) \qquad (6.2)$$

We shall follow the convention of putting $k = 0$ if the consumer decides not to buy any brand. Hence, the consumer's decision problem is simply to choose $k \in \{0, 1, \ldots, n\}$.

From (6.1) and (6.2) it follows that if a consumer's income is equal to W and if the prices of the n kinds of goods are $p_1, \ldots, p_n$, then if he buys brand k his utility is given by $u(k)(W - p_k)$. If he does not buy this product at all, his utility is $u(0) W$. It follows that a consumer with income W will prefer k to j if

$$u(k)(W - p_k) > u(j)(W - p_j) \qquad (6.3)$$

It is interesting to note that, by this characterization, products of different firms are not just different but have a definite hierarchy in that as a person's income rises he prefers products of a firm denoted by a higher integer. That is, if a consumer with income W rejects goods of brand below k, then the consumer with income above W will certainly reject brands below k. To see this, rewrite (6.3) as follows:

$$[u(k) - u(j)] W > u(k)p_k - u(j)p_j \tag{6.4}$$

Clearly, if $u(j) < u(k)$, then, as W rises, condition (6.4) will continue to hold. It is for this reason that, if $j < k$, it is said that k is a *better quality* good than j. Observe also that, if $j < k$, p_j will be less than p_k because otherwise no person, irrespective of income levels, would ever buy from firm j.

Hence, if we think of consumers as having different levels of incomes, we shall find that purchases of brands occur in a stratified fashion, with the poorest people buying nothing, the richest buying the most expensive brands, the middle income group buying the middle brands, etc. Hence firms could be thought of as having market shares with different firms selling to different income groups. The sizes of the groups will, of course, depend on the prices of the goods. And it is possible to characterize a Bertrand equilibrium for such an industry.

To take a step towards this, suppose that there are only two firms and consumers have income levels between $\underline{W}$ and $\overline{W}$ and are uniformly distributed on this interval. I shall refer to a consumer by his income level. Let $v_i(W)$ be consumer W's reservation price for brand i. That is, if the price of i is $v_i(W)$ consumer W will be indifferent between buying brand i and not buying anything. Hence,

$$v_i(W) = \frac{W[u(i) - u(0)]}{u(i)}$$

In figure 6.1 $v_1(W)$ and $v_2(W)u(2)/u(1)$ are plotted as functions of W. With p_i denoting firm i's price, the same figure shows the heights p_1 and $p_2u(2)/u(1)$. The market shares of the two firms are now easy to represent on the diagram. Let W_* be such that $v_1(W_*) = p_1$ and W^* be such that $AB = CD$. It is easy to see that consumers in the interval $[\underline{W}, W_*]$ will not buy any brand, those in $[W_*, W^*]$ will buy brand 1, and those in $[W^*, \overline{W}]$ will buy brand 2.

Obviously W_* and W^* are functions of p_1 and p_2. Hence the market shares of the two firms, and therefore the profits, will depend on p_1 and p_2. Unlike in the Bertrand model with homogeneous goods, in this model a Nash equilibrium always exists and the firms may earn positive profits. Equilibria can be of different types depending on the values of $u(2)$ and $u(1)$. In particular, it is possible that only one firm will exist in equilibrium. This model can be used for a variety of analyses as shown by Gabszewicz and Thisse (1979, 1980) and Shaked and Sutton (1983).

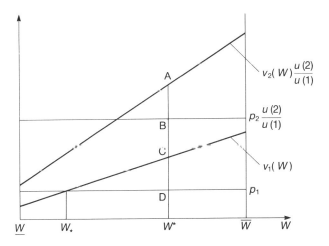

Figure 6.1

6.3 STRATEGIC SUBSTITUTES AND COMPLEMENTS

The broadest notion of two goods being of the same kind is captured by the concept of "substitutes." And one of the simplest ways of formalizing the concept of substitutes (and complements) in industrial organization theory is to consider a class of utility functions which yields linear demand systems. The form used by Dixit (1979) has turned out to be particularly influential. This is the quadratic utility function

$$u = m + a_1 x_1 + a_2 x_2 - \tfrac{1}{2}(b_1 x_1^2 + 2d x_1 x_2 + b_2 x_2^2)$$

where x_i is the amount of good i consumed and m is the money left over after buying x_1 and x_2. It is assumed throughout this section that the utility function is strictly concave. In particular,

$$b_1 > 0 \qquad b_2 > 0 \qquad d^2 - b_1 b_2 < 0$$

The utility function yields the following inverse demand functions:

$$p_1 = a_1 - b_1 x_1 - dx_2 \tag{6.5}$$

$$p_2 = a_2 - b_2 x_2 - dx_1 \tag{6.6}$$

What is convenient about this system is that the sign of the coefficient d captures fully the idea of substitutability between goods.

By solving (6.5) and (6.6) for x_1 and x_2, it is easy to see that if $d > 0$ then a rise in p_i causes x_{3-i} to rise. Hence goods 1 and 2 are *substitutes*. If $d < 0$ the goods are *complements*.

This definition is pivotal because, as noted by Singh and Vives (1984), many properties of the Nash equilibrium of a differentiated-products duopoly depend critically on whether d is positive or negative. Thus, for instance, profits are larger in Cournot than in Bertrand competition if and only if the goods are substitutes, that is, $d > 0$.

Subsequent work, notably by Bulow et al. (1985), show that in general what matters critically in a differentiated-goods duopoly is whether the goods are "strategic" substitutes or not. To define these important terms formally suppose that the profit functions of the two firms are given by $\Pi^1(\Delta_1, \Delta_2)$ and $\Pi^2(\Delta_1, \Delta_2)$, where firm i's "action" Δ_i is any real number. At this point it is not necessary to be more precise about what a firm's action or strategy consists of. It could be price, quantity, location, or something else. It will be assumed that Π^i is strictly concave in Δ_i.

The actions of firms 1 and 2 are defined to be *strategic substitutes* (*strategic complements*) if the reaction functions in the (Δ_1, Δ_2) space are downward (upward) sloping. Note that if $\phi_i(\Delta_j)$ is i's reaction function, then

$$\Pi^1_1[\phi_1(\Delta_2), \Delta_2] \equiv 0$$

and

$$\Pi^2_2[\Delta_1, \phi_2(\Delta_1)] \equiv 0$$

where Π^i_j is the derivative of Π^i with respect to Δ_j.

By differentiating the first equation with respect to Δ_2, we obtain

$$\Pi^1_{11} \phi'_1(\Delta_2) + \Pi^1_{12} = 0$$

Hence

$$\phi'_1(\Delta_2) = -\frac{\Pi^1_{12}}{\Pi^1_{11}}$$

Since $\Pi^1_{11} < 0$, the reaction function is negative (i.e. $\phi'_1(\Delta_2) < 0$) if and only if $\Pi^1_{12} < 0$. Hence the two actions are *strategic substitutes*[1] if $\Pi^i_{12} < 0$, $i = 1, 2$. They are *strategic complements* if $\Pi^i_{12} > 0$, $i = 1, 2$.

Note that in Dixit (1979), if the two firms choose quantities and the cost of production is zero, then

$$\Pi^1(x_1, x_2) = (a_1 - b_1 x_1 - d x_2) x_1$$

Check that $\Pi^1_{12} = -d$. Similarly $\Pi^2_{12} = -d$.

Hence, if $d > 0$, the two goods are not just substitutes, as described by Dixit (1979) and Singh and Vives (1984), but they are *strategic* substitutes; and it is the latter which is, in general, the critical property for predicting the outcomes of oligopolies. We shall see some illustrations of this later when discussing switching costs and lock-ins.

To complete the taxonomy it is worth mentioning that Bulow et al. (1985) describe the actions Δ_1 and Δ_2 as *conventional complements* if $\Pi_2^1(\Delta_1, \Delta_2) > 0$ and $\Pi_1^2(\Delta_1, \Delta_2) > 0$. Conventional substitutes are defined likewise. It is easy to check that while *strategic* complementarity implies an upward-sloping reaction function, *conventional* complementarity implies that the iso-profit curves of firm 1 in the (Δ_1, Δ_2) space are U-shaped. Conventional substitutability implies that the iso-profit curves are inverted U-shaped. Since the pay-off functions are concave, it follows that if the iso-profit curves are U-shaped (inverted U-shaped), then the higher (lower) curves give higher profit.

6.4 QUALITY, STATUS AND MARKET DISEQUILIBRIA

Interesting issues arise even when a product's quality is not directly observable or is not an innate characteristic of a good. Indeed quality may not even be definable in a precise way as in section 6.2. At times the value of a good to a person may depend on who its other consumers are. Fashion products and status goods fall in this category. In such cases some interesting real-life questions can be answered even without formally characterizing quality. I do this in the present section by considering a single good where, as in the Gabszewicz–Thisse model, the decision problem of the consumer is not how much to buy but whether to buy or not. The model is based on Basu (1987a); for a more recent model expressing the same idea, see Becker (1991). Unlike in section 6.3, the present model is concerned with a monopoly market.

To buy certain products where quality is important, for example, Jaguar cars, the newly released shares of a company, meals at a popular Chinese restaurant, or consultation with a "good" doctor, one has often to join a waiting list. In other words, these "firms" price their products so as to maintain an excess demand. At first sight this is paradoxical. Why does the doctor not raise his fees and eliminate or shorten the waiting list of patients? While this may be attributed to the benevolent spirit of the medical profession, the present section provides an explanation of such behavior in terms of selfishness and, in particular, profit maximization. It presents a theory of why and under what circumstances it pays a firm to follow a strategy of maintaining excess demand.

There is a long tradition in economics – dating back to at least Scitovsky's paper of 1944 – of modeling markets where consumers judge quality by price. In a situation of price rigidities, a natural analog of this is that consumers will judge quality by also observing the aggregate excess demand for the good. At first sight, this seems to provide an explanation of why a firm may wish to maintain a price at which there is an excess demand: because by this it manages to increase the desirability of its product to individual consumers. Indeed, in India, Bajaj scooters not only *has* an excess demand but it takes out large newspaper advertisements publicizing the fact that one has to wait to get a Bajaj scooter.[2]

This argument, however, turns out to be inadequate if demand functions are continuous. Consider a monopoly. In the presence of excess demand its sales need not be affected by small changes in price. In other words, it is possible for the firm to raise price a little without having to sell less, thereby increasing its profit. Hence, an excess-demand situation cannot be a profit-maximizing one.

Note that the above reasoning makes use of the continuity of demand. Hence, if it were the case that people judge quality by excess demand and the demand function is discontinuous, only then may it be possible to explain excess demand in equilibrium. What is interesting, and this is the central point of this section, is that if the people actually judge quality by excess demand, then the demand function automatically turns out to be discontinuous and under certain conditions this discontinuity is precisely of the kind that results in price rigidities and excess demand. It is important to emphasize that the discontinuity of demand which plays a crucial role in the model is not an assumption but arises naturally in this framework. It arises even though the utility function or the *n*-function (defined below), that is, all the basic ingredients of the model, are continuous.

The model about to be developed has several applications. First, it can be applied to the supply side. For instance, by thinking of jobs as work environments or certificates of prestige which people buy, my argument can be inverted to explain wage rigidities in the face of excess supply of labour (see Basu, 1989a). Second, it could apply to markets where the quality of the product is not in question but where people buy a good or service to establish their own social status or worth. The membership of a club could be a symbol of status. Calcutta's old colonial Calcutta Club provides an example of this. One reason why an individual covets membership of this club is because there are others who covet the same but nevertheless fail to become members. Aggregate excess demand for membership enhances an individual's value of the membership.

Let $H = \{1, \ldots, h\}$ be the (finite) set of consumers. It will be assumed that there is only one producer of a certain good, for example cars. Each person i in H can buy at most one car, and the maximum amount of money, v_i, that he is willing to pay for the car depends on the excess demand z (i.e. the difference between aggregate demand and aggregate supply) that exists. Hence, for all i in H,

$$v_i = v_i(z) \qquad v_i' \geqslant 0 \tag{6.7}$$

If p is the price of a car and z is the excess demand for it, a person i will want to buy the car if and only if $v_i(z) \geqslant p$, and the total demand n for cars (which is equal to the total number of people who want to buy) is given by[3]

$$n = n(z,p) = \#\{i \in H | v_i(z) \geqslant p\} \tag{6.8}$$

Given (6.7), it follows that, as z increases or p falls, n will not fall. Since each individual can buy at most one car, n can take values between 0 and h. Finally, the finiteness of H ensures that, for a sufficiently large value of p, n is zero. Within these restrictions, the function $n(z,p)$ can take any form. Hence, we may treat the function $n(z,p)$ as a "primitive" as long as we keep the above restrictions in mind. In this chapter we do precisely that and, in addition (this is a harmless and mathematically convenient assumption), we ignore the fact that n and z can take only integer values.

Hence, from now on we shall treat n as a mapping (R being used to denote the set of all real numbers and R_+ the set of all non-negative real numbers),

$$n: R \times R_+ \to [0, h]$$

which is continuous, monotonically non-decreasing in the first variable and non-increasing in the second variable. Also, for a sufficiently large value of the second variable n takes the value zero, and for a sufficiently small value of the second variable n equals h. I shall refer to this as an n-function.

Given a price $\hat{p}$ and a supply $\hat{x}$, what are the equilibrium amounts that may be demanded? Before giving a formal answer, it is useful to have a diagrammatic representation.

Figure 6.2 shows the function $n(z,\hat{p})$ for different values of z. The amount supplied is measured from the origin in the left-ward direction and excess demand is measured in the right-ward direction. In this case, the amount supplied is marked by $\hat{x}$. Given any level of demand d, to find out the amount of excess demand, we simply have to mark a distance d from $\hat{x}$ (to the right of $\hat{x}$). Thus, if d_2 is demanded, the excess demand is equal to 0A.

Now draw a 45° line through $\hat{x}$, as shown. Let us check whether a particular level of demand is compatible with $\hat{x}$ being supplied at price $\hat{p}$. Consider the demand given by the distance $\hat{x}$B in the diagram. This implies an excess demand of 0B, which in turn implies that aggregate demand will be BD. But BD is greater than BE, which equals $\hat{x}$B. Hence, demand equilibria are given by the points of intersection between the n-function and the 45° line. Therefore demand levels of d_1, d_2 and d_3 are the only demands compatible with $(\hat{x}, \hat{p})$. This is an essential part of a rational expectations equilibrium. According to this an individual's valuation of the goods depends not on excess demand, as in (6.7), but on his expectation of excess demand. An equilibrium occurs when the expected value matches the actual value.

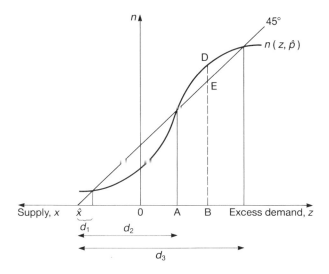

Figure 6.2

Now for the formal derivation. The set of demands compatible with
(x, p) – in the sense of expectations being rational – is denoted by $D(x, p)$
and defined as follows:

$$D(x, p) = \{r \in R_+ \mid n(r - x, p) = r\} \tag{6.9}$$

Let us define $d(x, p)$ as the largest element in the set $D(x, p)$.

It is assumed that, given (x, p), the producer knows that only the demand
levels in the set $D(x, p)$ can persist and he can choose any of these. As will
be obvious as we go along, from his point of view it is always best to set the
demand at $d(x, p)$. What we have to determine next is which (x, p) is the
best from the monopolist's point of view.

Let $c(x)$ be the cost function, which is continuous and monotonically
increasing in x. Hence the producer's profit function is given by

$$\pi(x, p) = p \min\{x, d(x, p)\} - c(x) \tag{6.10}$$

It is assumed that the producer maximizes π by choosing (x, p). Throughout
the remaining pages I use (x^*, p^*) to denote an output level and a price
which maximizes profit.[4] Thus

$$(x^*, p^*) = \text{argmax } \pi(x, p) \tag{6.11}$$

(x^*, p^*) is referred to as the *equilibrium*. The trivial case of zero production
is ruled out by assuming throughout that $x^* > 0$.

To aid intuition, let us draw a picture of $D(x, p)$ for a fixed value of
x, say $\hat{x}$. This is done in figure 6.3. As p is raised, the n-function shifts

down. By plotting the points of intersection between the 45° line and each n-function corresponding to a price in the lower diagram, we get a picture of the correspondence $D(\hat{x}, p)$ for different values of p. Thus, for example, $D(\hat{x}, p') = \{d_1', d_2', d_3'\}$. It is easy to see that $d(\hat{x}, p)$ plotted against p is the thick discontinuous line abce, which at p'' takes the value d_2'' instead of d_1''.

The discontinuity is now clear. If, starting from a price p'', the producer increases price a little, the maximum sustainable demand for his product drops from d_2'' to below d_1''. If, holding p'' constant, he raises supply to slightly above $\hat{x}$ (which will shift the 45° line up) a similar sharp decline in demand occurs. It is this kind of discontinuity which can explain why it may be profit maximizing for a producer to maintain an excess demand for his product.

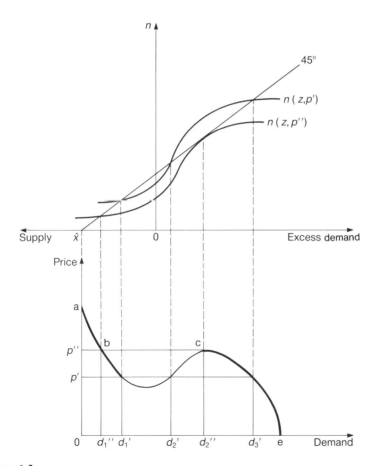

Figure 6.3

There are many parametric situations in which an excess-demand equilibrium occurs. I shall here identify a fairly transparent condition which is sufficient for excess demand to prevail in equilibrium.

Let $p(x)$ be the value of p defined implicitly by the condition $n(0, p) = x$. For all x, the existence of such a p is guaranteed because of the assumptions on the n-function. If, now, the n-function has the property that, for all $x > 0$, there exists $z > 0$, such that $n(z, p(x)) > x + z$, then we shall say that *individual valuation is strongly responsive to excess demand*. My choice of terminology is clear once it is appreciated that this property requires that for a "large" number of people v_i rises sharply in response to an increase in excess demand.

Theorem 6.1 If individual valuation is strongly responsive to excess demand, then all equilibria exhibit demand, that is, $d(x^*, p^*) > x^*$.

PROOF Assume individual valuation is strongly responsive to excess demand and $d(x^*, p^*) \leqslant x^*$.

Step 1 Let us first suppose $d(x^*, p^*) < x^*$. There are two possibilities: (i) $n(0, p^*) \geqslant x^*$ or (ii) $n(0, p^*) < x^*$. If (i), then since n can take a maximum value of $\#H$, and the n-function is continuous, there must exist $\hat{z} \geqslant 0$ such that $n(\hat{z}, p^*) = \hat{z} + x^*$. Hence, $\hat{z} + x^* \in D(x^*, p^*)$. Since $\hat{z} + x^* > d(x^*, p^*)$, this is a contradiction. Now suppose (ii) is true. Define $\hat{x} = n(0, p^*)$. It follows from definition (6.9) that $\hat{x} \in D(\hat{x}, p^*)$. Hence,

$$d(\hat{x}, p^*) \geqslant \hat{x} \tag{6.12}$$

Since n is nondecreasing in z, we have $n(0, p^*) \geqslant n(d(x^*, p^*) - x^*, p^*)$. Hence,

$$\hat{x} \geqslant d(x^*, p^*) \tag{6.13}$$

and

$$\begin{aligned}
\pi(\hat{x}, p^*) &= p^*\hat{x} - c(\hat{x}) && \text{by (6.12)} \\
&\geqslant p^*d(x^*, p^*) - c(\hat{x}) && \text{by (6.13)} \\
&> p^*d(x^*, p^*) - c(x^*) && \text{since } \hat{x} < x^* \\
&= \pi(x^*, p^*) && \text{since } d(x^*, p^*) < x^*
\end{aligned}$$

This contradicts the fact that (x^*, p^*) maximizes profit, and thereby establishes that $d(x^*, p^*)$ cannot be less than x^*.

Step 2 Suppose that $d(x^*, p^*) = x^*$. Hence $p(x^*) = p^*$. Since individual valuation is strongly responsive to excess demand, there exists $z' > 0$ such that $n(z', p^*) > x^* + z'$. Hence, $x^* + z' \in D(x^*, p^*)$, which is a contradiction.

Together with step 1, this establishes a contradiction of the initial assumption that $d(x^*, p^*) \leqslant x^*$. ∎

In theorem 6.1, if it was the case that, although $d(x^*, p^*) > x^*$, $x^* \in D(x^*, p^*)$, then the theorem would be uninteresting. After all the producer, having picked (x^*, p^*), could set demand at x^* instead of $d(x^*, p^*)$ since x^* has the "rational expectations" property and he loses nothing by this. It is easy to show, however, that if individual valuation is strongly responsive, not only is $d(x^*, p^*) > x^*$, but also $x^* \in D(x^*, p^*)$. This is because if $x^* \in D(x^*, p^*)$ then the strong responsiveness of individual valuation implies that there exists $z' > 0$ such that $n(z', p^*) > x^* + z'$. Hence, there exists $p' > p^*$ such that $n(z', p') = x^* + z'$. Therefore

$$d(x^*, p') \geqslant x^* + z'$$

Now,

$$\pi(x^*, p') = p' x^* - c(x^*) \qquad \text{since } z' > 0$$
$$> p^* x^* - c(x^*)$$
$$\geqslant \pi(x^*, p^*) \qquad \text{since } x^* \leqslant d(x^*, p^*)$$

Hence, if $x^* \in (x^*, p^*)$, (x^*, p^*) cannot be the monopolist's optimum.

In the above model, I did not begin from utility maximization on the part of the consumers. Indeed no utility function was defined. We began with each person i's v_i function (6.7), which was then aggregated to (6.8). Can these be derived from standard utility maximization? The answer is yes, and one simple way of doing this is to use the model described in section 6.1. Suppose that there is a continuum of consumers on the interval $[0, h]$. Each consumer $t \in [0, h]$ has an income of $W(t) = W_1 + W_2 t$, where W_1 and W_2 $(\geqslant 0)$ are exogenously given parameters. The utility that consumer t gets by consuming a unit of the good, characterized by price p and excess demand z, is $u(z)[W(t) - p]$, where $u(z)$ is a nondecreasing function of z. The utility that he gets if he does not consume the good is given by $W(t)u_0$. It is easy to check that the number of people demanding the good characterized by (p, z) is[5]

$$n(z, p) = h - \frac{u(z)p}{u(z) - u_0} + \frac{W_1}{W_2}$$

So what was earlier treated as a primitive, to wit, the n-function, is now derived from a standard utility function.[6] Of course, the important question as to how the function $u(z)$ is, in turn, derived is not answered here.

To end with some open motivational issues, note that this model began with equation (6.7) as a primitive. An interesting direction to pursue is to explain this basic equation from more fundamental assumptions of consumer theory. Without going into a formal analysis of this here, I want to comment on two alternative and reasonable motivations that can be used.

There is a large body of literature which argues that individual welfare depends, among other things, on what an individual consumes relative to others (see, for example, Frank, 1985). One interpretation of this is that, if a certain product or service is desired by many, but not everybody who desires it gets it, then this is an additional reason for individuals to covet it. In other words, human beings seek exclusiveness. Leibenstein's (1950) analysis of a "snob" effect was based on a similar argument. This provides an immediate and direct justification for the basic equation. What is interesting but was overlooked by the earlier writers in this field is the fact that the basic equation can explain price rigidities and excess demand equilibria.

The other approach to the basic equation is to claim that human beings are really interested in product quality. But since this cannot be directly observed, they treat excess demand as a signal for quality, in the same way that education is a signal for productivity in Spence's (1974) model. This approach, however, leads to an open question which deserves further research: under what circumstances is there reason for consumers to treat excess demand as an index of quality?

Finally, a comment on labour markets. There has been a large recent literature on "efficiency" wages (e.g. Shapiro and Stiglitz, 1984), which explains downward wage rigidity in terms of the employer's preference for not lowering wages. The model of their paper can be used to construct a new efficiency wage argument (see Basu, 1989a).

Consider a person seeking a job and evaluating alternative possibilities. There is a lot of sociological evidence (Jencks et al., 1988) that a person will be concerned about, among other things, the social status of a potential job. And one way of judging the status associated with a firm is by the excess supply of employees faced by it. Admittedly this argument would be more applicable to salaried and higher paid jobs, in contrast with several existing theories which apply mainly to the low wage sector (e.g. Mirrlees, 1975). But this complementarity may well be its advantage.

NOTES

1 In Bulow et al.'s terminology, if $\pi^{i}_{12} < 0$, then i regards Δ_i to be a strategic substitute for Δ_j. Thus, in my usage, actions Δ_1 and Δ_2 are strategic substitutes if 1 *and* 2 regard Δ_1 and Δ_2 to be strategic substitutes for Δ_2 and Δ_1 respectively.
2 See, for example, *The Times of India*, New Delhi, November 24, 1987, page 11. And going by Liv Ullman's account in *Changing* (Alfred Knopf, New York, 1977, page 21) Hollywood does not run on very different lines either: "Quite a few people have gathered for lunch. New film projects are discussed. Success is measured by

the number of offers one receives. The more money you are offered, the more producers ring your agent and offer yet more.

"This is Hollywood's way of talking about the weather."

3 It is worth noting that a more sophisticated theory would require v_i to be a function of z and p, that is, $v_i(z, p)$, instead of (6.7). But this complication is not essential, given the problem addressed in this chapter. It will be clear as we go along that as long as aggregate excess demand figures in the individual demand function – no matter in what form – the model developed in this chapter will be relevant. Hence there is no harm in using the simple idea captured in (6.7).

4 The existence of a maximum is guaranteed by the following argument. Let P be a price such that for all prices above this π is nonpositive. The existence of such a P follows from the properties of the n-function. Clearly there is no advantage in raising x to above h. Hence x may be taken as varying between 0 and h. Hence the domain of the function $\pi(\cdot)$ is $[0, h] \times [0, p]$, which is compact. It is easy to check that $\pi(\cdot)$ is upper semi-continuous, thereby ensuring that it achieves a maximum somewhere in the domain (Berge, 1963, p. 74). A function $f: R^n \to R$ is described as *upper semi-continuous* (u.s.c.) if, for all $x_0 \in R^n$, for all $\varepsilon > 0$, there exists a neighborhood $U(x_0)$ such that $x \in U(x_0)$ implies that $f(x) < f(x_0) + \varepsilon$. An equivalent definition of u.s.c. is a function $f: R^m \to R$ such that, for all λ, $\{x \mid f(x) \geq \lambda\}$ is closed. Consider the partly specified function $f: [0, 1] \to [0, 1]$ described in the figure, in which a discontinuity occurs at x_0. If $f(x_0) = B$, then f is not u.s.c. If $f(x_0) = A$, then f is u.s.c. This figure also gives a hint as to why the existence of a maximum is not hurt by a discontinuity as long as the function continues to be u.s.c.

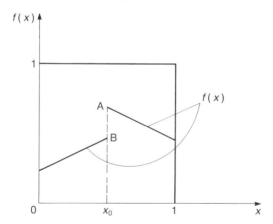

5 Given that the number of people demanding the goods cannot be less than zero or more than h, a more fastidious specification of the n-function is as follows:

$$n(z, p) = \text{mid}\left\{0, h - \frac{u(z)p}{u(z) - u_0} + \frac{W_1}{W_2}, h\right\}$$

where $\text{mid}\{a, b, c\}$ is a number which is the second largest (ties being broken arbitrarily) of a, b and c.

6 Further, $n(z, p)$ is concave if $u(\cdot)$ is concave.

7

Durability

7.1 INTRODUCTION

Product quality can be factorized into many different things and, of these, one of the most important is durability. Thus, for instance, a product may be considered better than another on the grounds of being more durable. The subject of durability also happens to be of interest in itself. One of the challenges of durability is that it is possible to construct models where the extent of durability of a product is a "choice" variable. Note that in chapter 6 the quality of a product was taken as given. Thus firm A may be producing a high quality product and B a low quality product; or consumers may be uncertain about the quality of products and treat other indicators, such as excess demand, as signals of quality; but no firm had actually to take the decision of whether to improve a good's quality or not.[1] Interesting problems arise if quality is a variable (see, for instance, Sheshinski, 1976; Mussa and Rosen, 1978). In the section that follows we do exactly this. With the extent of durability being treated as a variable which the producer has to choose, we address questions such as: which market structure is most conducive to manufacturing more-durable products?

As mentioned above, the subject of durability is of interest in itself and one of the reasons for this is the so-called "Coase conjecture" (Coase, 1972), which speculates that, with durable goods, even in a monopoly, prices will get driven down to the competitive level. Interest in this area has been revived with the work of Stokey (1981) and Bulow (1982) and this has sparked off an interesting debate concerning the pricing of durable goods. Section 6.3 is a discussion of this problem.

7.2 DURABILITY UNDER MONOPOLY AND COMPETITION

For the present I shall be concerned with durable consumer goods which depreciate over time, such as clothes, footwear, carpets, wallpaper, and scissors. With any of these goods the consumer has to decide, at some point, whether to continue to use them or to discard them and buy afresh. This, in turn, presents the producer with a problem: how durable should he make his product? The relation between market structure and durability has been the subject of considerable debate.[2]

At first glance, it seems that increasing durability would reduce profit by reducing the frequency of purchase. This was Chamberlin's (1957) view; but it is flawed because, as the producer raises durability, he can raise price to compensate for the reduction in sales (see for example Barro, 1972). It therefore seems (and this belief is widely shared in the literature) that a profit-maximizing monopolist would raise durability as much as possible, if production costs were independent of durability and the capital market were perfect. I shall in this section first show how the problem of durability as a variable can be modeled. Then it is shown that, if the standard models are generalized to allow for heterogeneous consumers, then the position that monopolists always make goods of optimal durability ceases to be tenable. The intuitive argument is interesting and involves price discrimination of the kind seen in chapter 5 but implemented through a more subtle mechanism.

This idea is formalized here by assuming that there are two types of consumers: the "lavish," who are fastidious about quality and would buy a new unit as soon as the old one was slightly worn, and the "thrifty," who are carefree and would prefer to use goods up to a point of greater depreciation. Now, even if a monopolist has to charge the same price to each consumer, he can discriminate between the two groups by choosing a suitable amount of durability. For instance, if he makes the good less durable, the lavish consumers make more frequent purchases per unit of time. Hence, although both consumer types pay the same price per unit of commodity, the lavish ones pay more per unit of time. That is, they pay a higher effective price. Hence, by making the product less durable, the monopolist manages to price-discriminate between consumers. I am concerned with a consumer good that depreciates over time. It is not a good that remains new for n days and then disintegrates but, more realistically, one that loses its newness with time before finally disintegrating.[3] The simplest way to capture this idea is to assume that the good lasts one period (and then completely disintegrates) but, within this period, during the first q units of time the good is new and has a quality level of N units, and during the remaining $1 - q$ units of time it is depreciated and has a quality level of D units. Of course, $N > D$. The quality profile of one unit of such a good is illustrated in figure 7.1.

The extent of durability of the good is captured by the parameter q. If q becomes larger, I shall say that the good is now "more durable" or that it "depreciates more slowly." If $q = 1$, the good is described as "fully durable." If $q = 0$, then this good is never new. I am here interested in goods that are new for some time, however little. Hence it is assumed that there exists a very

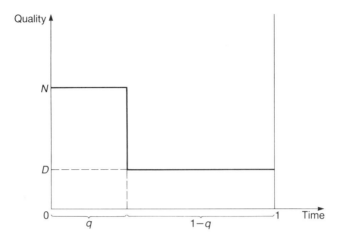

Figure 7.1

small real number $e > 0$ such that q must be greater than or equal to e. Throughout, it is assumed that q is a variable which the producer has to select from the interval $[e, 1]$. But before we go on to the question of the producer's decision, we need to model the consumer.

For simplicity, I shall suppose that we are talking of a good which, by its very nature, is such that the consumer would want to possess at most one unit at each point of time. Toothbrushes, pianos, dining tables, and wallpaper are examples of such goods. Hence, the consumer's main problem is whether to buy the good and, if "yes," how often to replace it (i.e. discard it and buy a new one). Hence the good in question is the kind we have encountered in chapter 6 but with the additional feature here that it decays over time. So it is like Gabszewicz and Thisse's (1979) piano but it is a piano which may have to be replaced after a certain length of time.

Since at any point of time a consumer can have at most one unit of the good, the quality level that he gets at any point of time is N, D, or zero. It is being supposed that not to possess the good is to get zero "qualits," which is our word for the unit by which quality is measured.

Assume that there are n consumers, indexed by i. Let f^i be a function which shows the value (in money terms) to consumer i of consuming different levels of quality at each point of time. Operationally this means that if within one period consumer i consumes N qualits for fraction n of the period, D qualits for fraction d and zero qualits for fraction $1 - n - d$, and the consumer's income is M_i and he spends X_i on the good in question, then his utility over the period is given by

$$U^i = nf^i(N) + df^i(D) + (1 - n - d)f^i(0) + M_i - X_i$$

Since the origin of the utility function does not matter and I shall not consider changes in income, it is harmless to suppress the term M_i. In addition I shall make an innocuous normalization by assuming that, for all $i, f^i(0) = 0$. Hence, from now on the utility function of i is

$$U^i = nf^i(N) + df^i(D) - X_i \qquad (7.1)$$

Since each period looks the same, U^i may be interpreted as the average utility over a steady state.

Let us compute the utilities associated with three specific options. First, if the consumer does not buy this good at all, the number of qualits he gets at each point of time is zero (it is being assumed that quality is something that only this good provides) and $X_i = 0$. Hence, from the above equation we get

$$U^{iO} = 0$$

where U^{iO} is the utility that person i gets by not buying the good.

Second, let U^{iL} be the utility that he gets if he decides to buy afresh as soon as the old good depreciates in quality. Then, if the price of the good is p and its durability parameter (explained above) is q, it is obvious[4] that

$$U^{iL}(p, q) = f^i(N) - p/q \qquad (7.2)$$

If a person buys afresh as soon as the good depreciates we shall say that he acts *lavishly*.

Third, let U^{iT} be the utility he gets if he chooses to buy one unit at the beginning of the period and not buy again in this period, that is, he acts *thriftily*. Clearly,

$$U^{iT}(p, q) = f^i(N)q + f^i(D)(1 - q) - p \qquad (7.3)$$

We have so far considered three options: acting lavishly, acting thriftily, and not buying. There are other options, such as buying one unit, after it depreciates continuing with it for some time, and then buying a new one again. It is easy to check that such options can be ignored because the consumer's best strategy always includes one of not buying, being thrifty, and being lavish. To see this, suppose a consumer chooses to have high quality for a period $n \in [q, 1]$ and depreciated quality for the remainder. If the good is characterized by (p, q), then the consumer's utility is given by

$$W(n) = nf^i(N) + (1 - n)f^i(D) - np/q$$

Note that if $f^i(N) - f^i(D) - p/q \geqslant 0$, then $W(1) \geqslant W(n)$. If $f^i(N) - f^i(D) - p/q \leqslant 0$, then $W(q) \geqslant W(n)$. But $W(1) = U^{iL}(p, q)$ and $W(q) = U^{iT}(p, q)$. Hence, $W(n) \leqslant \max\{U^{iO}, U^{iL}(p, q), U^{iT}(p, q)\}$.

In the light of the above claim, the following tie-breaking assumption is fairly innocuous and is maintained throughout this section. Faced with a (p, q), if a consumer is indifferent between buying and not buying a good, he buys it; and, having decided to buy, if he is indifferent between acting thriftily and lavishly, he acts lavishly.

Let us first analyze the case of a monopoly producer. Suppose there is one producer and he offers the price–durability pair (p, q). Let c be the cost of producing each unit of good. It is assumed for simplicity that the cost does not depend on the product's durability.[5] Note that this is the most adverse assumption for what I am trying to establish.

If $n^L(p, q)$ and $n^T(p, q)$ are the numbers of consumers who act lavishly and thriftily, then the monopolist's profit R is given by

$$\pi(p, q) = (p - c) \left[\frac{n^L(p, q)}{q} + n^T(p, q) \right] \tag{7.4}$$

Definition 7.1 (p^*, q^*) is a *monopoly equilibrium* if and only if

$$\pi(p^*, q^*) \geqslant \pi(p, q), \text{ for all } p \in [0, \infty) \text{ and } q \in [e, 1]$$

It will be assumed throughout that there exists some (p, q) that gives the monopolist a positive profit.

It will now be shown that, although it does not cost the monopolist anything to make the product more durable, he may nevertheless prefer to make it less durable (i.e. to set $q < 1$). For this result and other discussions in this section, I make use of the fact that a monopoly equilibrium always exists. Hence, we first need to establish existence.

Let P be a price at which consumer demand is zero. Define a set K as follows:

$$K = \{ (p, q) \mid p \in [c, P], q \in [e, 1] \}$$

Consider the real-valued function π on K. It may be checked that π is an upper semi-continuous function. This follows from our tie-breaking assumption made above which says that, whenever a consumer is indifferent between any two of the options in the set { not buy, act lavishly, act thriftily }, he will choose the one that gives the producer a larger profit. Since K is compact, it follows that π attains a maximum in K (see chapter 6, note 4). Since, for all (p, q) not belonging to K, $\pi(p, q) \leqslant 0$ and we have assumed that, for some (p, q), $\pi(p, q)$ must be positive, it follows that the maximum value attained by π in K is greater than zero. Hence, that is also the maximum value that π attains on an unrestricted domain of price–durability pairs, that is, with $p \in [0, \infty)$ and $q \in [e, 1]$. The existence of monopoly equilibrium being assured, we may now examine the relation between monopoly and durability.

Theorem 7.1 There exist equilibria where monopolists sell goods of limited durability (i.e. $q < 1$). A necessary condition for this to happen is that consumers have heterogeneous preferences.

PROOF The following example establishes the first part of the theorem. Assume there are only two consumers, with the following characteristics:

$$f^1(N) = 4 \qquad f^1(D) = 0$$
$$f^2(N) = 2 \qquad f^2(D) = 1$$

In addition, assume $c = 0$ and $e \leqslant 1/4$. Using equations (7.2) and (7.3), we obtain

$$U^{1L}(p, q) = 4 - p/q \qquad U^{1T}(p, q) = 4q - p$$
$$U^{2L}(p, q) = 2 - p/q \qquad U^{2T}(p, q) = q + 1 - p \tag{7.5}$$

Let us check the maximum profit that the monopolist can earn, given that q is fixed at 1 (i.e. we want the value of max $\pi(p, 1)$). Inserting $q = 1$ in (7.5), it is clear that as long as $p \leqslant 2$ he can sell two units (one each to consumers 1 and 2), and if p is in $[2, 4]$ he can sell one unit (to consumer 1). Hence, max $\pi(p, 1) = \pi(4, 1) = \pi(2, 1) = 4$. To prove the theorem, we merely have to show that there exists q in the interval $[e, 1]$ such that, for some p in $[0, \infty)$, $\pi(p, q) > 4$. Consider $q = 1/4$ and $p = 1$. Inserting these in (7.5) we get

$$U^{1L} = 0 \qquad U^{1T} = 0$$
$$U^{2L} = -2 \qquad U^{2T} = 1/4$$

Hence, 1 will act lavishly and 2 thriftily. That is, 1 will buy four $(= 1/q)$ units and 2 will buy one unit. Hence $\pi(1, 1/4) = 5$. Since we know that a monopoly equilibrium always exists, the equilibrium value of q must be less than 1.

In order to prove the second part, suppose $f^1 = \ldots = f^n$, (p^*, q^*) is a monopoly equilibrium and $q^* < 1$. Since consumers are identical, either (i) everybody acts lavishly or (ii) everybody acts thriftily. Suppose (i). Then

$$\pi(p^*, q^*) = (p^* - c)\frac{n}{q^*} \tag{7.6}$$

and from (7.2) and (7.3) it follows that (since $U^{iL} \geqslant U^{iT}$)

$$f^i(N) - f^i(D) \geqslant p^*/q^* \qquad \text{for all } i \tag{7.7}$$

If the monopolist raises p and q proportionately (i.e. ensuring that $p/q = p^*/q^*$), then (7.7) implies that everybody remains lavish and (7.6) implies an increase in profit.

Suppose (ii). Then choose $p > p^*$ and $q > q^*$ so that

$$U^{iT}(p, q) = U^{iT}(p^*, q^*)$$

Two things can happen in this case: (a) people remain thrifty, or (b) people become lavish. If (a), then

$$\pi(p, q) = (p - c)n > (p^* - c)n = \pi(p^*, q^*)$$

If (b), then

$$\pi(p, q) = (p - c)\frac{n}{q} > (p^* - c)n = \pi(p^*, q^*)$$

This contradiction establishes that the original situation could not have been an equilibrium.　　■

There are several models (e.g. Parks, 1974) in which monopolists offer many price–durability (or price–quality) pairs and practice price discrimination. In such models it is expected that monopolists would be able to screen consumers because the problem is analogous to the screening in standard nonlinear pricing and optimal income tax theory.[6] What is interesting in the present model is that, even by offering a unique price–durability pair, the monopolist manages to price-discriminate. He does this by inducing different consumers to respond differently and thereby to pay different effective prices for the good.

Finally, note that, while the question of durability is obviously related to that of quality, my central theorem exploits the natural relation between durability and the frequency of purchase. Hence, this problem is distinct from the problem of quality choice as discussed in, for instance, Sheshinski (1976) and Mussa and Rosen (1978).

Now consider the case where the durable goods industry is *competitive with free entry*. Suppose, as before, that there are n consumers and a (countably) infinite number of identical producers. They are identical in the sense that for each firm the cost of producing each unit of the good is c. It will be obvious later that we do not really need the assumption of an infinite number of firms. It is enough if the number of firms is large and, in particular, exceeds n/e.

Each producer i posts outside his shop his product's price–durability information, that is (p_i, q_i). Let us use the notation

$$((p_1, q_1), (p_2, q_2), \ldots) \equiv \{p, q\}$$

I shall assume that each consumer chooses one shop and then makes all purchases from there. (Actually, this is not an assumption. It can be shown that buying from several shops cannot in this model enhance a consumer's utility.) If a consumer is indifferent between several shops, we can use an arbitrary tie-breaking rule. I shall assume that the consumer goes to the shop with the lowest index.

Let $n^{iT}(\{p,q\})$ and $n^{iL}(\{p,q\})$ be the number of consumers who go to firm i and act thriftily and the number who go to i and act lavishly. Clearly, each firm i's profit depends on every firm's announcement. Hence,

$$\pi^i(\{p,q\}) = (p_i - c)\left[\frac{n^{iL}(\{p,q\})}{q_i} + n^{iT}(\{p,q\})\right]$$

Each firm's strategy consists of choosing $(p_i, q_i) \in [0, \infty) \times [e, 1]$. Hence we have a normal-form game where the firms are the players.

Definition 7.2 $\{p^*, q^*\}$ is a *competitive equilibrium* if it is a Nash equilibrium of the above game.

Let $\{p^*, q^*\}$ be a competitive equilibrium. Every firm i for which $n^{iT}(\{p^*, q^*\}) + n^{iL}(\{p^*, q^*\}) = 0$ will be described as being "out" of the industry. All other firms are "in." It will now be obvious that if the number of firms exceeds n/e then some firms must be out of the industry in equilibrium, and that is all we need for the next theorem.

Theorem 7.2 In a competitive equilibrium, every firm i that is "in" the industry (i.e. its sales are positive) sets $q_i^* = 1$.

PROOF Let $\{p^*, q^*\}$ be a competitive equilibrium. Obviously some firms must be "out" of the industry. These firms earn zero profit. Suppose i (which is "in" the industry) earns positive profit. It follows that $p_i^* > c$. If a firm j which is outside the industry changes its price p_j^* to p_j such that $c < p_j < p_i^*$ and changes q_j to q_i^* then he will get all of i's customers and earn a positive profit. It follows that in a competitive equilibrium all firms must earn zero profit.

Next suppose that for some i that is "in," $q_i^* < 0$. From the above paragraph we know $p_i^* = c$. Now let i raise q_i a little and p_i a little so that at least one of the earlier buyer's utility is unchanged. Hence i now earns a positive profit. Since this has happened through a unilateral deviation, it is a contradiction. ∎

The above model of competition is interesting because its difference with oligopoly turns out to be simply a matter of industry size. Suppose the industry has m firms and they announce the following strategies: (p_1, q_1), ..., (p_m, q_m). Then firm i's profit, $\pi_i((p_1, q_1), \ldots, (p_m, q_m))$, is defined in the same way as profit in the competitive model. $((p_1^*, q_1^*), \ldots, (p_m^*, q_m^*))$ is an *oligopoly equilibrium* if it is a Nash equilibrium.

Although by this formulation the oligopoly equilibrium looks very similar to the competitive equilibrium, its properties are likely to be very different. Note that if m is sufficiently small each firm's profit does not have to be zero. Since, the competitive equilibrium was characterized essentially by exploiting this zero-profit property (see the proof of theorem 7.2), an oligopoly equilibrium with small m has to be analyzed by a different method. Such an analysis could be of interest and remains to be done.

Another feature worth introducing in the above model is a used-goods market. This may have interesting implications in the model of this section, because such a market allows for mutually profitable transactions between the "lavish" customers and others. I leave this as an open problem and turn instead to examine the subtle role of the used-goods market in the Coase model of durable goods.

7.3 DURABLE GOODS: RENTING AND SELLING

Let us here stay away from the subject of durability of durable goods. Suppose there is a good that lasts forever and does not depreciate. Some interesting problems arise when such a product is sold by a monopolist, because sales in different periods compete with each other because of the unchanging quality of the goods. In such a case it is possible for the monopolist to compete against himself and drive the price of the good to the competitive level. This is the conjecture outlined by Coase (1972) in a seminal paper and it has been the subject of considerable recent research.[7]

To see the problem let us, following Coase, suppose that all land is owned by one person, the monopolist, and the demand for land is given by AB in figure 7.2. The cost of supplying land is zero. The total availability is given by S. If marginal revenue is given by AM, it appears at first sight that the monopolist will sell M units of land at price p. Suppose the monopolist does so. Clearly in the next period he could sell more land (half of MB if the demand curve is a straight line), and charge a price below p. And he can continue doing so until price drops to the competitive level, in this case zero, and total sales equal B. If the time periods are made arbitrarily small, then the entire process would occur in the "twinkling of an eye." Moreover, it is arguable that consumers will realize this and so no one will buy any land at a positive price. It is possible to formalize this argument by developing a rigorous model of the interaction. But I shall here confine attention to a two-period model and, following Bulow (1982) and Tirole (1988, pp. 81–2), demonstrate the "Coase problem" in such a limited context and illustrate the problem of selling versus renting.

Note that in the above model when the monopolist decides on a second round of sales, at a price below p, this lowers the value of land held by the

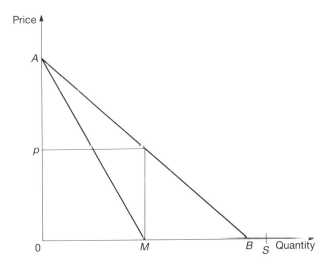

Price

A

p

0   *M*   *B*   *S*   Quantity

Figure 7.2

people who bought it in the first round. Since this negative externality of second-round sales does not affect the monopolist, the sales are worthwhile from his point of view. One way in which a monopolist can alter this and thereby halt this inexorable process towards the competitive price is by *renting out* the good in the first period. Then, at the beginning of the second period, all goods are back to the monopolist, and all the externalities of second-period behavior are now internalized. It seems likely that it is better, from the monopolist's point of view, to rent out a product instead of selling it. This is indeed true as may be illustrated with an example.

Let a consumer's utility depend on the number of units of the durable good he has during periods 1 and 2, and the amount of money he has. Denoting these by, respectively, x_1, x_2, and m, I shall specifically assume that

$$u(x_1, x_2, m) = m + x_1 - \frac{x_1^2}{2} + \delta\left(x_2 - \frac{x_2^2}{2}\right)$$

where $\delta \in (0, 1)$. It will be assumed that x_i is always less than or equal to 1. Hence u_1 and u_2 are positive.

Suppose that the consumer's (present value of) total income is fixed at y. If p_i is the price of possessing the good for period i, the interest rate is r, and, the capital market being perfect, $1/(1 + r) = \delta$, then the consumer's budget constraint is

$$m + p_1 x_1 + \delta p_2 x_2 \leq y$$

Maximizing $u(x_1, x_2, m)$ subject to this budget constraint gives us the first-order conditions

$$1 - x_1 = p_1 \tag{7.8}$$

$$1 - x_2 = p_2 \tag{7.9}$$

These are the demand functions that Tirole (1988) uses, and so we can follow him and consider a monopolist who *rents* (or leases) the good to the consumer. Confronted with demand curves (7.8) and (7.9), and assuming that the cost of production is zero, the monopolist will clearly lease out 1/2 unit in each period and charge a price of 1/2. That is, in equilibrium,

$$r_1 = r_2 = 1/2 \text{ and } p_1 = p_2 = 1/2$$

Hence, profit earned by *renting out* the product, π^R, is given by

$$\pi^R = (1 + \delta)/4$$

Now suppose that the monopolist can only *sell* the product. Let x_i be the number of units sold in period i. Note that since this is a durable good with no depreciation, if x_1 and x_2 units are *sold* in the two periods, the number of units possessed by the consumer in periods 1 and 2 are x_1 and $x_1 + x_2$.

When we study extensive-form models formally we shall see that these problems are usually solved backwards (in time). Following this cue, assume x_1 units of goods have been sold in period 1. Now consider the problem in period 2. From (7.9) it is obvious that, if x_2 units are sold in period 2, the price of each unit in period 2 will be

$$p_2 = 1 - x_1 - x_2$$

Hence, in the second period the monopolist's problem is to maximize $(1 - x_1 - x_2)x_2$ by choosing x_2. Since the choice is a function of x_1, we write

$$x_2(x_1) = (1 - x_1)/2 \tag{7.10}$$

Hence, profit earned in period 2 is $(1 - x_1)^2/4$.

Let P_i be the price of *selling* a unit of the good in period i. This is distinct from p_i which is the price for being able to possess and use the machine for period i (i.e. it is a rental charge). If the monopolist sells x_1 units in period 1, he can set price equal to

$$\begin{aligned} P_1 &= (1 - x_1) + \delta[1 - x_1 - x_2(x_1)] \\ &= (1 - x_1) + \delta(1 - x_1)/2 \end{aligned} \tag{7.11}$$

This makes use of the fact that consumers know that if he sells x_1 in period 1 he will sell $x_2(x_1)$ in period 2.

Hence, if the monopolist sells x_1 units in period 1, his total profit is

$$\pi(x_1) = (1 - x_1)x_1 + \frac{\delta(1 - x_1)x_1}{2} + \frac{\delta(1 - x_1)^2}{4} \qquad (7.12)$$

Maximization of this gives us the first-order condition

$$x_1 = 2/(4 + \delta)$$

Hence, by inserting this in (7.12) we get the profit π^s earned by the monopolist by *selling* the product:

$$\pi^s = \frac{(2 + \delta)^2}{4(4 + \delta)}$$

Check that

$$\pi^s < \pi^R$$

Hence, a monopolist is better off renting his product.

It is easy to see that $\pi^s < \pi^R$ essentially because a monopolist who sells the product cannot precommit his behavior in the next period. If he could, then he would announce in period 1 that his sales in the two periods will be x_1 and x_2. If he could commit himself to this and the consumer believed him, his profit would be

$$\hat{\pi}(x_1, x_2) = (1 - x_1)x_1 + \delta(1 - x_1 - x_2)x_1 + \delta(1 - x_1 - x_2)x_2$$

It may be checked that max $\hat{\pi}(x_1, x_2) = \pi^R$. Hence, renting turns out to be advantageous only when it is impossible to precommit credibly. We are using here reasoning which will be more systematically undertaken after chapter 9.

An implication of this model is that a durable-good monopolist who sells his good may have a strategic interest in raising the marginal cost of production. Suppose the firm faces a choice between installing a technology with a higher marginal cost and installing another with a lower marginal cost. It is possible to show that in some situations it may prefer the higher cost even when the savings in fixed costs are not enough to compensate for this. The reason is straightforward. If marginal cost is high, it is in the firm's interest to sell less. Hence, raising marginal cost is a way of precommitting credibly to producing less.

Despite the advantages of renting described above, it may not always be possible or desirable to rent out goods. First, there is the problem of moral hazard whereby a consumer may misuse a rented good in a way that he would not if he had bought it. Moreover, as Bulow (1982, p. 315) has argued, for certain goods it is in the buyers' interest to *buy* the product or get it on such a long lease that it is almost equivalent to buying it. Thus, when replacing iron railroad tracks with steel ones, it is impractical to rent the steel because the disruption costs would be enormous if the next round of renting negotiations failed. In principle, it should be possible to construct a generalized model which takes such matters into consideration. Whether selling or renting occurs will then depend on the trade-offs between these competing advantages.

NOTES

1 It is possible to interpret the previous section's model such that quality is an endogenous variable. This would be so if we thought excess demand was not an *indicator* of quality but was an inherent feature of quality. Thus, if people buy Bajaj scooters not because they treat the excess demand as an indicator of quality but because they attach extra value to a good for which demand exceeds supply, then indeed "quality" was an endogenous variable in section 6.2. In this section, however, quality will be a control variable in a more direct sense.

2 See, for example, Levhari and Srinivasan (1969), Sieper and Swan (1973), Kamien and Schwartz (1974), and Leibowitz (1982). The analysis that follows is taken from Basu (1988).

3 This kind of assumption is used by, among others, Leibowitz (1982) and Bond and Samuelson (1984). Stokey's (1981) and Bulow's (1982) durable goods, on the other hand, never lose their newness.

4 We ignore the problem that p/q might not be an integer.

5 Several authors in this area make this same assumption: see, for example, Barro (1972).

6 It is easy to demonstrate that in some situations a monopolist, given a choice, will prefer to offer more than one (p, q) pair and to offer at least one less durable product. Consider the example where $f^1(N) = 5$, $f^1(D) = 0$, $f^2(N) = 2$, $F^2(D) = 1$, $e = 1/8$, and $c = 1$. If the monopolist has to offer one (p, q) pair, he would choose $(5, 1)$ and his profit would be 4. It is easy to see that, if he were allowed to offer more than one type of good, he could earn a larger profit by offering, for example, the following (p, q) pairs: $(5, 1)$ and $(1, 1/6)$. Person 1 would choose the former and 2 the latter, and profit would be equal to 4 plus 1/6.

7 See, for example, Stokey (1981), Bulow (1982), and Gul et al. (1986).

8

Location, Brands and Advertising

8.1 INTRODUCTION

As has already been remarked, there is a certain analogy between the economics of location and the economics of product brands. This was evident to Hotelling (1929) who observed that the problem of two firms selling a homogeneous good at two different locations on a line could, alternatively, be thought of as two firms choosing to sell cider of two different degrees of sourness from within a continuum of possibilities. This analogy has been used very effectively in the existing literature (see Salop, 1979).

The purpose of this chapter is to introduce some issues in location economics based on the classic framework of Hotelling. While there is a large literature on this (see Gabszewicz et al., 1986, for a survey), my aim here is much more limited. It is to introduce the problem with a view to taking the reader on to the analysis of brand proliferation and in particular the work of Schmalensee (1978). In the last section of this chapter we discuss the economics of advertising in this context and otherwise.

8.2 LOCATION

Suppose there are two firms 1 and 2 selling a homogeneous good. They can situate themselves anywhere on a line of length k kilometers. Consumers live all along this line; in fact, they are uniformly distributed on this line. The total number of consumers is k. There is no loss of generality in both the length and the population size being k, since this is simply a matter of choice of units. For a consumer to have to travel 1 kilometer and back costs c in money terms. Hence, if a consumer has to go t miles to buy a product of price p_i, the cost or *effective price* to the consumer is $p_i + ct$. It will be assumed that each consumer buys exactly one unit and he buys this from wherever the

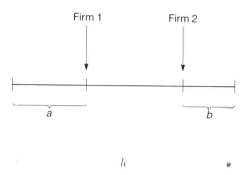

Figure 8.1

effective price is lower. If both firms charge the same price and have the same location, they will, it is being assumed, share the market equally.

To focus attention exclusively on spatial competition, assume that the price charged by both firms is fixed exogenously. In particular, $p_1 = p_2 = p$. The only decision problem of the firms is to choose their location. I shall here define firm 1's location in terms of distance a from the left-hand corner and firm 2's location in terms of distance b from the right-hand corner. All this is illustrated in figure 8.1.

It is very easy to see that the Nash equilibrium of this model is one where both firms locate themselves in the centre. That is, $a = b = k/2$. To see this assume, without loss of generality, that 2 is located to the right of the midpoint. There are two possibilities for 1. It may be located at the same place as 2 or at some other place. If the latter is true, then the locations cannot be a Nash equilibrium because whichever firm is on the left side can increase its profit by shifting right without crossing over the other firm. On the other hand, if both are at the same point, each firm could do better by moving slightly to the left. Hence, both firms being located in the centre is a Nash equilibrium. This has come to be known as Hotelling's *principle of minimum differentiation*.

This principle is not as robust as appears at first sight, however. If, for instance, there are three, instead of two, firms, the Nash equilibrium ceases to exist. If there are two firms but the costs of transportation are strictly convex, instead of being linear, then again the principle might fail. Indeed if the cost of transportation is quadratic the firms would try to move away from each other. That is, we get a principle of maximum differentiation (see D'Aspremont et al., 1979). What is even more troublesome is that if we allow each firm to choose not only location but location *and* the price of the product then no Nash equilibrium exists.

To prove this, let us retain all the assumptions of the model just described except price rigidity. So now firm 1 chooses (a, p_1) and 2 chooses (b, p_2) simultaneously. It can be proved that this game does not possess any Nash equilibrium. Before demonstrating this formally, it is useful to introduce some notation. Let $\pi_2(a, b, p_1, p_2)$ be the profit function of firm i when firm 1 chooses (a, p_1) and 2 chooses (b, p_2). From the description above the following is easy to see.

$$
\pi_1(a, b, p_1, p_2) = \begin{cases} 0 & \text{if } c(k - a - b) + p_2 < p_1 \\ kp_1 & \text{if } c(k - a - b) + p_1 < p_2 \\ \dfrac{1}{2}(k + a - b)p_1 + \dfrac{1}{2c}p_1 p_2 - \dfrac{1}{2c}p_1^2 \\ & \text{if } |p_1 - p_2| \leqslant c(k - a - b) \end{cases}
$$

$\pi_2(\cdot)$ is defined analogously.

To see this, note that, if $c(k - a - b) + p_2 < p_1$, then for a person living exactly where firm 1 is it is better to buy the product from firm 2. Clearly then everybody would prefer to buy from firm 2 and 1's profit is zero. The second line of the above profit function is derived by a symmetrically opposite argument. If $|p_1 - p_2| \leqslant c(k - a - b)$, clearly there exists a critical point d somewhere between 1's location and 2's location such that people at d are indifferent between the two firms. I shall measure d from the left end of the line. We could think of d as a function of (a, b, p_1, p_2). It is easy to check that $d(a, b, p_1, p_2)$ is implicitly defined by

$$c(d - a) + p_1 = c(k - b - d) + p_2$$

The last line of the profit function is simply $p_1 d(a, b, p_1, p_2)$.

It can now be shown that there is no Nash equilibrium in the above game where firm 1 chooses (a, p_1) and 2 chooses (a, p_2). To prove this by negation suppose that (a^*, p_1^*), (b^*, p_2^*) is a Nash equilibrium.

Consider first the case $a^* + b^* = k$. It is obvious that $p_1^* \neq p_2^*$ cannot be a Nash equilibrium; neither can $p_1^* = p_2^* > 0$. So suppose $p_1^* = p_2^* = 0$. If firm 1 relocates itself somewhere else and sets a price slightly above zero, it can earn positive profit. So this cannot be a Nash equilibrium either.

Suppose now $a^* + b^* < k$. Without loss of generality suppose $\pi_2(a^*, b^*, p_1^*, p_2^*) \equiv \pi_2^* \geqslant \pi_1(a^*, b^*, p_1^*, p_2^*)$. Then neither firm earns zero profit in equilibrium. Denote $d(a^*, b^*, p_1^*, p_2^*)$ by d^*. Note that $\pi_2^* = (k - d^*)p_2^*$. Clearly

$$\pi_1(k - b^*, b^*, p_2^* - e, p_2^*) = k(p_2^* - e)$$

Hence, for a sufficiently small e,

$$\pi_1(k - b^*, b^*, p_2^* - e, p_2^*) > \pi_2^*$$

Since $\pi_2^* \geqslant \pi_1(a^*, b^*, p_1^*, p_2^*)$, it follows that (a^*, p_1^*), (b^*, p_2^*) is not a Nash equilibrium.

What happens if the firms do not choose both location and price? For instance, if a and b are exogenously given and firm i chooses p_i, what will the equilibrium look like? Such questions are now easy to answer (see also D'Aspremont et al., 1979) and will not be pursued here. Instead we proceed to apply the algebra of location to problems of brand selection and proliferation.

8.3 BRAND PROLIFERATION

In both the United States and the United Kingdom the breakfast cereal industry has faced charges of violating antitrust legislation by practising entry deterrence. While entry deterrence as a full-fledged issue will be studied later and in the extensive form, what is of interest here is the possibility of brand proliferation being used by the incumbent firms to deter potential entrants. This is exactly the charge that was brought by the US Federal Trade Commission in 1972 against four manufacturers of breakfast cereal – Kellogg, General Mills, General Foods, and Quaker Oats. It was alleged that through multiplying their brands and differentiating products they were erecting barriers to entry.

Schmalensee (1978) constructed a model to capture this allegation. He shows that (i) brand proliferation can be used to deter entry and at the same time yield "supernormal" profits to the incumbents and (ii) a collusive industry may prefer to deter entry by multiplying brands instead of lowering prices (i.e. instead of using limit pricing). While the model is based on very strong assumptions, it demonstrates well how a location model can be used to analyze practical industrial problems relating to product differentiation.

Let us think of n brands of a certain good as n retail outlets of the same good on a circle of unit circumference. This will imply "localized rivalry" where each brand competes directly only with its (two) neighboring brands. If the brands are equally spaced, then the distance between any two adjacent brands, for example h and $h + 1$, is $1/n$.

If x units of a certain brand are produced, the cost C of producing these is given by

$$C = F + vx \tag{8.1}$$

where $F, v > 0$. The establishment of a new brand entails considerable initial cost, for instance in promotion activities. This is captured by F. This also suggests that the shifting of an existing brand (i.e. changing the location of, for instance, h) is very expensive. It is cheaper in such a case to close down the brand and start a new one.

If n brands are equally spaced on the circle and p is the price of the

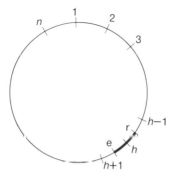

Figure 8.2

good no matter which brand, then I shall assume, following Hotelling, that consumers from an interval of length $1/n$ will demand each brand (i.e. consumers living on the segment er in figure 8.2 would be buying brand h). Unlike in the model of section 8.2, it will be assumed that each consumer's intensity of demand depends on p. This is captured by the term $a(p)$, where $a'(p) < 0$. Hence if there are n equally spaced brands charging price p, the demand x for each brand is

$$x(p, n) = a(p)/n \qquad (8.2)$$

Let I be the set of positive integers. It will be assumed throughout that $n \in I$.

Note that (8.2) is, in a sense, only a partially specified demand function. If brand prices vary or the brands are not equally spaced, (8.2) will not be able to tell us the demand for different brands. Given the limited nature of our exercise, it is enough to have this partial specification.

If there are n equally spaced brands with price of all brands set at p, the profit π earned by each brand is

$$\pi(p, n) = (p - v)x(p, n) - F \qquad (8.3)$$

Define $\hat{n}(p)$ to be the value of n such that $\pi(p, \hat{n}(p)) = 0$. Hence

$$\hat{n}(p) = (p - v)a(p)/F$$

Following Schmalensee let us assume that a potential entrant can only make a price-matching entry. This could be justified by presupposing that, when all incumbents charge the same price, if a new firm sets price above the incumbents' price no consumer buys from the new firm, and if it sets price below the incumbents' price no additional consumer is attracted to the new firm because of its lower price.

It is easy to see that if there are n equally spaced brands charging p, a potential entrant's expected profit is given by $\pi(p, 2n)$. There are several ways of seeing this. One instructive route is to suppose that the entrant locates himself midway between two incumbent brands. Then in the locality of the entrant it is *as if* there are $2n$ equally spaced firms on the circle. Since there is localized rivalry between brands, all that matters for a brand's profit is the characteristics in its neighborhood. Hence, his profit is $\pi(p, 2n)$.

It follows that a potential entrant expects to earn a nonpositive profit on entry if $2n \geqslant \hat{n}$ or $n \geqslant \hat{n}/2$. Incumbents earn a positive profit if $n < \hat{n}$. Hence claim (i) discussed at the start of this section is established: it is possible to have an equilibrium where all incumbents earn a positive profit and yet an entrant expects a zero or a negative profit on entry. This happens if $n \in [\hat{n}/2, n]$.

Let us now consider a group of incumbent firms which decide to block entry collusively. To keep the analysis simple it will be assumed that the incumbent firms have to confine their strategy to choosing the number n of equally spaced brands they wish to produce and the price p per unit of the good. The total profit of all incumbent firms selling n brands at price p is given by

$$V(p, n) = n\pi(p, n)$$

Hence

$$V(p, n) = a(p)(p - v) - nF$$

Let $(p^m, n^m) \equiv \text{argmax } V(p, n)$. Hence (p^m, n^m) is the strategy chosen when there is no threat of entry. Since n has to be chosen from the set I, it is obvious that $n^m = 1$. From the first-order condition we know that p^m is given implicitly by

$$(p^m - v)a'(p^m) + a(p^m) = 0$$

To see what strategies will be used to deter entry, let us now consider the problem of collusive profit maximization subject to entry deterrence.

$$\max V(p, n)$$
$$\text{subject to } \pi(p, 2n) \leqslant 0$$

The same problem may be written more elaborately as follows:

$$\max\{a(p)(p - v) - nF\}$$
$$\text{subject to } 2nF \geqslant (p - v)a(p)$$

Let the solution of this be denoted by (p^d, n^d).

It will now be shown that $p^d = p^m$ and $n^d \geqslant n^m$. Since (p^d, n^d) is the deterrent strategy, this means that price is not used as an instrument of deterrence. Deterrence is achieved through the multiplication of brands. To prove this, suppose $p^d \neq p^m$. Define $\Delta \equiv (p^m - v)a(p^m) - (p^d - v)a(p^d)$, and let $\bar{n}$ be such that $2\bar{n}F - 2n^dF \equiv \Delta$. Note that $\Delta > 0$ because p^m is the unconstrained best and $p^d \neq p^m$. It is now easy to check that $V(p^m, \bar{n})$ $> V(p^d, n^d)$. Since $2n^d F \geqslant (p^d - v)a(p^d)$, it follows that $2\bar{n}F \geqslant (p^m - v)a(p^m)$. Hence if the incumbents alter (p^d, n^d) to $(p^m, \bar{n})$ they will earn a larger profit and continue to deter entry. This is a contradiction. Hence $p^d = p^m$. If $2n^m F \geqslant (p^m - v)a(p^m)$, then entry is automatically blocked and $n^d = n^m = 1$. If, however, entry is not automatically blocked then $n^d > n^m = 1$. That is, brand proliferation is the deterrent strategy.

This model is based on several very strong assumptions and its ultimate appeal depends on how much these can be relaxed. In future, the assumption that an entrant has to make a price-matching entry should either be relaxed or deduced from more basic and self-evident axioms. Another strong assumption is that incumbents choose their strategies and these are then fixed once and for all. In reality, if entry does occur, it may be worthwhile for incumbents to make adjustments. But such an analysis calls for extensive-form modeling. Though I shall not return to brand proliferation issues, such strategic post-entry interaction will be discussed in a later chapter and the reader is encouraged to return to the subject matter of this section after reading that chapter.

8.4 ADVERTISING

The oligopolistic market with competing brands and marginally differentiated products is ideal ground for the use of "advertising" by firms. Advertising is in general defined as any promotional activity undertaken by a firm (or a group of firms) in order to shift the demand curve confronting the firm to the right.

In the context of product differentiation Schmalensee (1978) has discussed the role of "introductory advertising." He does this by modifying the above model so that the fixed cost F is treated as a choice variable of the firm and represents the amount of introductory advertising. As F is raised, the demand for the brand in question rises. It is possible to show that entry deterrence entails excessive advertising.

Although in the above discussion advertising is used to enhance the demand for a product which is differentiated from others, advertisements can often be used to make a product *appear* differentiated from other identical goods. Some of the early work on advertising, including Dorfman and Steiner's (1954) seminal paper, could be viewed as belonging to this genre.

In Dorfman and Steiner's model, advertising is any expenditure which is a fixed cost – as indeed in Schmalensee (1978) – and which influences the shape and position of the demand curve. In particular, if A is the amount spent on advertising and p is the price, then the demand x for the good is given by

$$x = x(p, A) \qquad x_p < 0, \ x_A > 0 \tag{8.4}$$

The profit earned by a firm is

$$\pi(p, A) = px(p, A) - c(x(p, A)) - A$$

where $c(x)$ is the cost of producing x units of the good.

The first-order condition for profit maximization is given by

$$\frac{\partial \pi}{\partial p} = x + px_p - c'x_p = 0 \tag{8.5}$$

$$\frac{\partial \pi}{\partial A} = px_A - c'x_A - 1 = 0 \tag{8.6}$$

Equation (8.5) implies

$$\frac{p - c'}{p} = \frac{1}{e} \tag{8.7}$$

where $e = -px_p/x$ is the price elasticity of demand. Equation (8.6) implies

$$\frac{p - c'}{p} = \frac{1}{px_A} \tag{8.8}$$

Equations (8.7) and (8.8) give us

$$e = px_A$$

which is the celebrated *Dorfman–Steiner condition*. It asserts that, in equilibrium, price and the extent of advertising will be such that the additional revenue earned by one more unit of money spent on advertising is equal to the elasticity of demand.

The most contentious issue concerning advertising is its goodness or badness. Does it enhance welfare or efficiency? If so, what is the optimal amount of advertising? Does the market result in over-optimal or sub-optimal advertising? All these issues have been debated at great length. Some have argued that advertising is an unmitigated evil causing resources to be wasted and encouraging consumerism. Some have felt that advertising is very useful because it helps disseminate information. Then there are others who feel that the worth of advertising can never be objectively valued because advertisements alter preferences and hence its evaluation has all the problems of interpersonal comparisons.

I do not plan to enter into this labyrinthine literature here (for a discussion see Schmalensee, 1986). But, to give a glimpse of the problem, I shall briefly discuss Dixit and Norman's (1978) ingenious suggestion for evaluating the role of advertising in the Dorfman–Steiner type of model just discussed.

Consider a demand function such as (8.4). Suppose that initially the level of advertising was A^0 and the monopolist was charging p^0 and selling x^0. Later the level of advertising rose to A^1 and the output–price configuration changed to (x^1, p^1). This is illustrated in figure 8.3. D^i is the demand curve when the advertising level is A^i.

One way of viewing the problem is to suppose that the initial demand curve or the final demand curve represents the *true* preference of the consumers. Since *a priori* it is not known which one it is, it is not clear how we should value the change from E^0 to E^1. The way out that Dixit and Norman suggest is to evaluate the welfare change under both D^0 and D^1. If on both criteria there is agreement on something, then that is taken to be true. Otherwise not. What is surprising is that agreement is possible on several matters of importance. In particular, it can be shown that if (i) an increase in advertising always causes both price and quantity to rise (i.e. E^1 is to the northeast of E^0) and (ii) the income effect is zero then

(A) a little advertising is desirable but

(B) the free market results is a level of advertising which is greater than the optimum.

This is true for monopolies and oligopolies.

The intuition behind (A) is easy to see. Since under monopoly or oligopoly

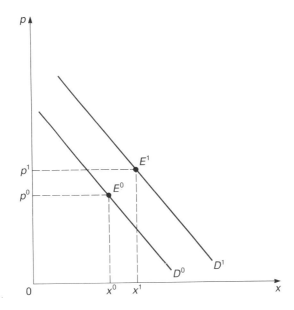

Figure 8.3

the equilibrium production is *below* the optimal one, a little advertising, by increasing sales, shifts the equilibrium towards the optimum. Since this is true with evaluation under the demand curve with zero advertising, it must be true when evaluated under a demand curve with positive advertising.

Proposition (B), which is also the more interesting claim, is more difficult to prove. For a formal proof, begin by supposing that the consumer's utility function is

$$u(x, A, m) = f(x, A) + m \qquad (8.9)$$

where x is the amount of the relevant good consumed, m is the amount of money spent on other goods and A is the amount of advertising (i.e. money spent to promote the good). Let the cost of producing this good be zero. Assume that the utility function that occurs with A fixed at $\bar{A}$ is the utility function of the consumer, which expresses his "true" satisfaction.

It is obvious from (8.9) that the consumer's inverse demand function is

$$p = f_x(x, A) \qquad f_{xx} < 0, \quad f_{xA} > 0 \qquad (8.10)$$

where $f_x(x, A)$ is the derivative with respect to x. Hence if the consumer has x units of the good and A is the amount spent on advertising (and therefore the resource cost of advertising is A) then the total social welfare W is given by

$$W(x, A, \bar{A}) = f(x, \bar{A}) + y - f_x(x, A)x - A \qquad (8.11)$$

where y is the consumer's income. Note that $\bar{A}$ figures in the function as the standard of judgment.

The monopolist's profit is given by

$$\pi(x, A) = f_x(x, A)x - A$$

The amount of the good the monopolist will sell, *if* he spends A on advertising, is given by the following first-order condition:

$$f_{xx}(x, A)x + f_x(x, A) = 0 \qquad (8.12)$$

Let the function $x = g(A)$ be implicitly defined by (8.12). Hence (8.10) implies

$$p = f_x(g(A), A) \qquad (8.13)$$

Now I can formally state the assumption that, as A increases, equilibrium price and quantity increase. Given (8.13) this implies that

$$f_{xx}(g(A), A)g'(A) + f_{xA}(g(A), A) > 0 \qquad (8.14)$$

and

$$g'(A) > 0 \tag{8.15}$$

Writing (8.11) as $W(g(A), A, \bar{A})$, we get

$$\frac{\partial W(g(A), A, \bar{A})}{\partial A} = g'(A)[f_x(g(A), \bar{A}) - f_x(g(A), A)] - 1$$

$$- x[f_{xx}(g(A), A)g'(A) + f_{xA}(g(A), A)] \tag{8.16}$$

Let the monopolist's equilibrium level of advertising be A^m. That is,

$$A^m = \operatorname*{argmax}_A \pi(g(A), A)$$

Then, by (8.14) and (8.16) we get

$$\frac{\partial W(g(A^m), A^m, A^m)}{\partial A} < 0 \tag{8.17}$$

Since $g'(A) > 0$ and $f_{xA} > 0$ (see (8.10)), it follows that

$$g'(A^m)[f_x(g(A^m), 0) - f_x(g(A^m), A^m)] < 0$$

Hence,

$$\frac{\partial W(g(A^m), A^m, 0)}{\partial A} < 0 \tag{8.18}$$

Since in (8.17) $\bar{A} = A^m$ and in (8.18) $\bar{A} = 0$, (8.17) and (8.18) imply the $\partial W / \partial A < 0$ at the monopolist's equilibrium, no matter whether the evaluation is done by using the utility function with zero advertising or the equilibrium amount of advertising. Hence, welfare is enhanced by cutting down the level of advertising. This establishes (B).

Several criticisms of Dixit and Norman's criterion are possible (see Schmalensee, 1986, for some discussion). It will suffice here to note that, in evaluating the welfare change accompanying a change in the level of advertising from A^0 to A^1, the evaluation is done by first assuming that A^0 gives the true utility function and by then assuming that A^1 gives the true function. What is not allowed is to treat A^0 as true when A^0 is the level of advertising and A^1 as true when A^1 is the level of advertising. To state this more precisely, consider (8.11) with $g(A)$ substituted for x. By the Dixit–Norman rule A^1 is socially better than A^0 if an only if

$$W(g(A^1), A^1, A^1) > W(g(A^0), A^0, A^1)$$

and

$$W(g(A^1), A^1, A^0) > W(g(A^0), A^0, A^0)$$

What they do not compare is $W(g(A^1), A^1, A^1)$ with $W(g(A^0), A^0, A^0)$.

This is probably an unduly harsh criticism, though, because in the language of interpersonal comparisons what they are suggesting is this. Suppose we have to compare (i, x) (i.e. person i having consumption vector x) with (j, y). Their criterion amounts to saying that (i, x) is "better off" than (j, y) if, by both i's and j's utility functions, x is preferred to y. What they are not asserting is x valued by i's utility function is greater than y valued by j's utility function. Since, from the literature on interpersonal comparisons, we know that this last comparison is virtually impossible to make on purely objective grounds, the weakness pointed out in the above paragraph should be noted but, at the same time, be treated as virtually inevitable.

A more "manageable" critique is based on questioning why the two levels of advertising used as standards of evaluation are the only relevant standard. If a very high level of advertising is treated as the standard, then indeed the Dixit–Norman result could get reversed (see Schmalensee, 1986).

The other interesting issue concerning advertising is its effect on market structure. Not only are certain market structures prone to encourage promotional activities, but such activities may in turn affect the market structure. As to whether, in general, advertising encourages competition or thwarts it, there is a difference of opinion. It is also similarly controversial whether or not advertising can be an instrument of entry deterrence as suggested at the start of this section (see Schmalensee, 1986).

However, I shall now move away from this back to models of homogeneous-goods industries. We shall next encounter location-type issues in industrial organization only when we turn to the chapter on switching costs.

9

Game Theory: Extensive-Form Games

9.1 INTRODUCTION

An extensive-form game is one in which players make moves in a sequence. Chess is an extensive-form game. So are bridge and the arms race. In most real situations oligopolistic interactions are extensive-form games and, not surprisingly, the theory of such games is widely used in recent studies of oligopoly.

Extensive-form games can be of many different kinds. They can be finite or infinite depending on how long the sequence of moves in a game happens to be. They can take the form of a normal-form game, like the Prisoner's Dilemma, being played repeatedly or they can have a nonrepeated structure like game Γ_1 in chapter 2. Instead of developing the subject in completely general terms, I shall take up some special cases. First, I discuss finite extensive-form games of the kind developed by Selten (1975) and Kreps and Wilson (1982), based on a foundation laid by Kuhn (1950). This is followed by a description of repeated games, finite and infinite. In each case concepts like perfection, subgame perfection, and Nash equilibrium are defined afresh. It is hoped that this will give the reader a grasp of the essential *idea* behind each of these concepts, so that later, in modeling oligopoly, the reader will be able to adapt these concepts suitably for the occasion.

Our first job is to write down a formal description of extensive-form games. (Where confusion is unlikely, I shall drop the cumbersome adjective "extensive-form.") Just as the normal-form game was described by a triple, we want a simple characterization of extensive-form games. Unfortunately, for one of the simplest characterizations eight features (unlike the three of normal-form games) have to be specified.[1] Extensive games, we could say, are octuples!

1   First we have a finite set T of nodes and a binary relation P representing precedence on it. That is, if $x, y \in T$ and $x \, \mathrm{P} \, y$, we shall say that x

precedes y. We shall denote (T, P) by K. It is required that P be a *partial order* (i.e. x P y and y P z implies x P z; and x P y implies not y P x) and K be an *arborescence* (i.e. in English, given any node x, and any nodes y and $z (y \neq z)$ preceding x, either y P z or z P y).

Some notation: a node which has no successor (successor being defined as an antonym for predecessor in terms of P) is called a *terminal node*. An *initial node* is similarly defined. For any nonterminal node x, the set of immediate successors of x will be denoted by $S(x)$.

2   Next we have a finite set A of actions and a function α defined on all nonterminal nodes such that $\alpha(x) \equiv A$ is the first in from taken to reach node x. Note that $\alpha(S(x))$ is the set of all actions open at node x.

3   I is a finite set of players and ι is a function defined on all nonterminal nodes such that $\iota(x) \in I$ is the player whose move it is at x. Unless otherwise specified, we shall write n for #I.

4   H is a partition of all nonterminal nodes. Elements of H are called information sets. If x and y belong to the same information set then $\iota(x) = \iota(y)$ and $\alpha(S(x)) = \alpha(S(y))$. When a player i has to move at a particular information set, he does not know which node in the information set he is at. It is required that information sets satisfy the property of *perfect recall*. This means that if x and y lie in an information set of player i, then it must not be possible for i to deduce whether he is at x or y on the basis of his own earlier actions. That is, he knows what he chose previously and he knows whatever he previously knew. If x is a nonterminal node, we shall denote the information set containing x by $H(x)$. Note that if $y \in H(x), H(y) = H(x)$.

5   For each player i, there is a real-valued function u^i defined on the set of terminal nodes. These describe i's pay-off. We write u for $(u^1, \ldots, u^n)$.

6   There is a probability measure p defined on the set of initial nodes. This captures nature's vagaries.

Any octuple $(K, A, \alpha, I, \iota, H, u, p)$ with the properties specified in (1)–(6) above, is an *extensive-form game*.

In our oligopoly models we shall use this structure. However, the games will be sufficiently simple for it not to be necessary to write out the octuple explicitly. But it will be there for the fastidious to work out. There will be one exception. There are some occasions when we consider *infinite* extensive-form games. But these will usually take the form of repeated games and in section 9.3 infinitely repeated games will be presented formally. The few cases of infinite sequences which will not be composed of repetitions of a one-shot game, that will come up later, will be simple enough for the intuition of this and the next sections to be easily generalizable to these contexts.

In an extensive-form game Γ, a *pure strategy* of player i is a function σ^i defined on all information sets where i has to move. If h is such an information set $\sigma^i(h)$ is one of the actions open to i at h. A *mixed strategy* for player i is a probability distribution on the collection of pure strategies. Given perfect recall we could equivalently think of a mixed strategy of i as a *behavior strategy*, that is, as a specification of a probability measure on the set of actions available at each information set where i has to move (Kuhn, 1953). References to "strategy" in future are references to "behavior strategy."

Given a game Γ, and any node x in Γ, consider all the successors of x along with x itself and let this collection inherit all the structure of the original game Γ. If all the information sets remain intact when the nodes in Γ are partitioned into x and its successors, on the one hand, and all the rest, on the other, then x and its successors along with the inherited structure is known as a *subgame* of Γ. I will denote it by Γ_x.

9.2 THE IDEA OF PERFECTION IN EXTENSIVE GAMES

The Nash equilibrium of an extensive game is defined in much the same way as the Nash equilibrium of a normal-form game already discussed. Consider an extensive game Γ. Given any mixed-strategy n-tuple σ, a probability measure is naturally defined on the collection of terminal nodes of Γ. Using this probability measure and the pay-off function u^i, we can calculate the expected utility $\bar{u}^i(\sigma)$ of each player i.

A *Nash equilibrium* of Γ is a strategy combination σ such that, for all players i,

$$\bar{u}^i(\sigma) \geqslant \bar{u}^i(\sigma/\sigma_i') \text{ for all (mixed) strategies, } \sigma_i' \text{ open to } i$$

In extensive games the idea of Nash equilibrium is susceptible to some special criticisms which were not possible in the normal form. The principal criticism is that the Nash equilibrium may be sustained by threats which are not credible. To see this consider the game Γ_1 (figure 9.1), which is taken from Kreps and Wilson (1982).

A Nash equilibrium of this game consists of 1 playing L and 2 playing l. Check that no player can do better by a unilateral change of strategy. To see why this equilibrium entails the use of incredible threats, suppose we ask 1 why he plans to play L. He will say that he will play L because, if instead he plays R, since 2 has threatened to play l he will be worse off. But is 2's threat credible? Clearly no, because if 2 does *actually* have to play (i.e. *if* node x is reached) he will be better off playing r instead of l.

A first step in weeding out equilibria sustained by incredible threats is to refine the concept of Nash equilibrium to subgame perfect equilibrium.

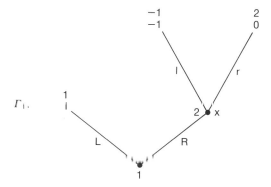

Figure 9.1

For industrial organization theory subgame perfection is one of the most important equilibrium notions, so much so that many authors feel free to omit the qualifying adjective "subgame."

A *subgame perfect equilibrium* of Γ is a strategy combination σ such that σ is a Nash equilibrium of Γ and for every subgame of Γ the restriction of σ to the subgame is a Nash equilibrium of the subgame.

In Γ_1, (L, l) is not subgame perfect because, in the subgame following x, (L, l) entails 2 playing l and that is not a Nash equilibrium of the subgame.

It is not right, however, to suppose that we can identify exactly all subgame perfect equilibria by throwing out the Nash equilibria which involve the use of incredible threats. This is because "credibility" can be an ambiguous concept in some contexts. One should therefore use the direct method of applying the above definition. Consider game Γ_2 (figure 9.2) in which player 1 chooses l or r. After either choice, the two players play the Battle of the Sexes with 1 choosing between the rows. One subgame perfect

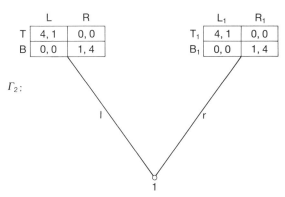

Figure 9.2

equilibrium of Γ_2 consists of 1 playing (r, B, T_1) and 2 playing (R, L_1). What are the other subgame perfect equilibria?

The illustration of Γ_2 is strictly speaking incorrect and may raise some of the questions mentioned in section 2.1. But given the above verbal description, its meaning is clear and it saves space compared with the full extensive-form illustration and that is good reason to use it.

Simple structures like Γ_2 where one agent has to take an initial decision and bases this decision on calculations of the Nash equilibria that would occur as a consequence of his decisions play a very important role in the study of entry deterrence as we shall see later.

Although in discussing extensive-form oligopoly I shall mainly use subgame perfection, it may be useful to sketch the related ideas of perfect and sequential equilibria. These may be motivated with an example. Consider the game Γ_3 illustrated in figure 9.3. This is a game with *imperfect information*. A *perfect information* game is one in which each information set has only one node. Thus Γ_1 is a perfect information game but Γ_2 is not.

This game has no proper subgames (i.e. its only subgame is the game itself). So subgame perfection has no cutting power. In other words, a Nash equilibrium is automatically a subgame perfect equilibrium in Γ_3. Hence 1 playing A and 2 playing r is subgame perfect. But we can intuitively see that 1 playing L and 2 playing l is a much more reasonable outcome. After all, if 2 really had to move, it would be in his interest to play l, no matter whether he believed he was at x or y. If 2 claimed he would move r, it would constitute an incredible threat in the same sense as in the earlier example.

It is worth noting here that the nodes x, y and their successors do not constitute a subgame because the structure inherited from the parent game Γ_3

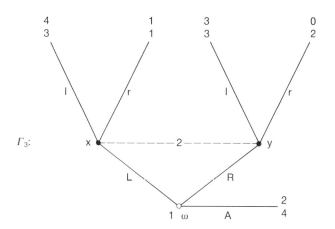

Figure 9.3

does not specify the probabilities of x and y occurring. Since the initial nodes in a game must have an exogenously given probability measure on them (see section 9.1, (6)), x, y, and their successors and the structure inherited on them from Γ_3 do not constitute a game.

The two best-known refinements of subgame perfection which would weed out (A, r) from qualifying as an equilibrium in Γ_2 are trembling hand perfection and sequential equilibrium as developed by, respectively, Selten (1975) and Kreps and Wilson (1982).

To define a sequential equilibrium we need to define "belief." A *belief* is a specification of the probability that each node x is reached given that the information set to which x belongs has been reached. Hence, a belief is a function μ on all nodes such that the restriction of μ to each information set is a probability measure on that set. An *assessment* is a belief and a strategy combination. Given an assessment (μ, σ) and an information set h, we can work out each player's expected utility in the usual way given that h has been reached. Let z be a terminal node. Denote the tth predecessor of z by $p_t(z)$. If $p_n(z) \in h$, then, given (μ, σ), the probability of z being reached is $\sigma(\alpha(z))\sigma(\alpha(p_1(z))) \ldots \sigma(\alpha(p_{n-1}(z))\mu(p_n(z))$. If z has no predecessor in h then the probability of z being reached is zero. The expected utility is now calculated in the standard way by using these probabilities. An assessment is *sequentially rational* if, at each information set h, the player i who has to move there finds that he cannot improve his expected utility based on (μ, σ) by unilaterally changing his strategy.

To go from sequential rationality to sequential equilibrium we merely have to check that μ and σ are consistent (in a Bayesian sense). Given a strictly mixed strategy (i.e. a strategy which attaches a positive probability to each pure strategy) for each player, we can calculate the probability of x being reached given that $H(x)$ has been reached by the usual Bayesian calculation. If this coincides with the belief then we say that the mixed strategy combination and the belief are *Bayes consistent*. An assessment (μ, σ) is *consistent* if it is the limit of a sequence of Bayes-consistent assessments involving purely mixed strategies. Finally, we describe σ as a *sequential equilibrium* if there exists a belief μ such that (μ, σ) is consistent and sequentially rational.

Let us check that (A, r) in Γ_3 is not a sequential equilibrium. This is because no matter what belief 2 holds about the probabilities that x and y occur (remember $\mu(x) + \mu(y)$ must be 1), the rational response of 2 is to play l. It is easy to see that (L, l) is a sequential equilibrium.

Trembling-hand perfection on the other hand makes use of the idea of mistakes in a way that we have already studied in chapter 2. Broadly speaking, we have to consider perturbed games which involve each action a being played with a probability above a minimum amount given by a positive number $\varepsilon(a)$. That is, if $H(a)$ is reached, the probability of a being played

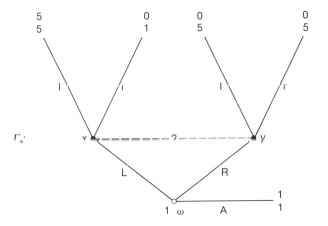

Figure 9.4

exceeds $\varepsilon(a)$. For each such game let $\sigma(\varepsilon)$ be a Nash equilibrium. If σ^* is the limit of a sequence $\sigma(\varepsilon_n)$ where ε_n goes to zero, then σ^* is a *perfect equilibrium*.

In Γ_3, in each perturbed game, 2 will prefer to play l (with as large a probability as permitted) and 1 will prefer L. Hence, in the limit they must play l and L, which is the only perfect equilibrium.

It can be shown that every perfect equilibrium is a sequential equilibrium but *not* vice versa (see Kreps and Wilson, 1982; Van Damme, 1987). This is easy to see. Consider the game Γ_4 (figure 9.4).

The strategy pair (A, r) is a sequential equilibrium. First, check that (A, r) is sequentially rational under the belief μ that, if the information set $\{x, y\}$ is reached, the probability of y being reached is 1. Under μ it is rational for 2 to play r. If 2 plays r, it is rational for 1 to play A.

Next we have to check that the strategy (A, r) and the belief μ are consistent. For this consider the sequence $\{\mu_n, \sigma_n\}$ defined as follows:

$$\sigma_n^1(A) = \frac{n}{1+n} \qquad \sigma_n^1(R) = \frac{1}{1+n}\frac{n}{1+n} \qquad \sigma_n^1(L) = \frac{1}{1+n}\frac{1}{1+n}$$

$$\sigma_n^2(r) = \frac{n}{1+n} \qquad \sigma_n^2(l) = \frac{1}{n}$$

$$\mu_n(y) = \frac{n}{1+n} \qquad \mu_n(x) = \frac{1}{1+n}$$

It is easy to see that, for all n, (μ_n, σ_n) is Bayes consistent; and as n goes to infinity, μ_n converges to μ and σ_n converges to (A, r).

It should be clear from the above discussion that (A, r) is not a perfect equilibrium. After all, if the probabilities of playing L, R, and A are all positive, 2 will not want to play r. Hence, as the perturbations vanish, the probability of playing r goes to zero. This also follows from theorem 2.5. Since r is a dominated strategy, it can never be part of a perfect equilibrium. (L, l), it may be checked, is a perfect and a sequential equilibrium.

9.3   REPEATED GAMES AND TRIGGER STRATEGIES

In this section we shall analyze a special kind of extensive-form games, namely those formed by repeated plays of the same normal-form game.

Let $G = (N, S, P)$ be a normal-form or one-shot game, as described in chapter 2. We denote $\#N$ by n. A *repeated game* (G, T, α), consisting of G being repeated T times (from period 1 to period T) with α as the discount factor, is defined as follows.

Let $H(t)$ be the set of all possible *histories* of play up to period t. That is, for all $t \geqslant 1$,

$$H(t) \equiv S \times \ldots \times S \qquad (t \text{ times})$$

We shall follow the convention of writing

$$H(0) \equiv \{\phi\}$$

In other words, $H(0)$ is the collection of *no* history, that is, history at the beginning of play. Define

$$H \equiv \bigcup_{t=0}^{T-1} H(t)$$

That is, H is the set of all histories of length up to $T - 1$.

A *strategy* of player i in (G, T, α) is denoted by f_i, where $f_i: H \to S_i$. Let F_i be the set of all possible strategies open to player i in the repeated game (G, T, α). Let $F \equiv F_1 \times \ldots \times F_n$.

Given a strategy combination $f \in F$, the *outcome* in game t is denoted by $\sigma(f, t)$ and this is defined by induction as follows:

$$\sigma(f, 1) = (f_1(\phi), \ldots, f_n(\phi))$$

and, for all $t > 1$,

$$\sigma(f, t) = (f_1(\sigma(f, 1), \ldots, \sigma(f, t-1)), \ldots,$$

$$f_n(\sigma(f, 1), \ldots, \sigma(f, t-1)))$$

We shall refer to $\{\sigma(f, t)\}_{t=1}^{T}$ as the *(outcome) path* generated by f.

The *pay-off function* of i in (G, t, α) is denoted by $\hat{P}_i: F \to R$ and $\hat{P}_i$ is defined as follows. For all $f \in F$,

$$\hat{P}_i(f) = \sum_{t=1}^{T} P_i(\sigma(f,t))\alpha^t$$

This completes the definition of a repeated game. If $T = \infty$, then (G, T, α) is called an *infinitely repeated game*. Otherwise it is a *finitely repeated game*.

Let us now introduce the definitions of different kinds of equilibria, that we have encountered earlier, for repeated games.

Given a game (G, T, α), $f^* \in F$ is a *Nash equilibrium* if and only if $\hat{P}_i(f^*) \geqslant \hat{P}_i(f^*/f_i)$ for all $i \in N$ and for all $f_i \in F_i$.

For subgame perfection a little more notation is needed. For all non-negative integers $t < T$, let $F_i(T - t)$ be i's strategy set in the game $(G, T - t, \alpha)$. Clearly, $F_i(T) = F_i$.

Next, we need to show how a strategy n-tuple on the original game (G, T, α) *induces* strategy n-tuples on subgames. Given t such that $0 < t < T$, and for all $h(t) \in H(t)$, for all $i \in N$, and for all $f_i \in F_i$, we define an induced strategy $(f_i | h(t)) \in F_i(T - t)$ as follows:

$$(f_i | h(t)) (\phi) \equiv f_i(h(t))$$

For all $r(k) \in H(k)$, where $k \leqslant T - t - 1$,

$$(f_i | h(t)) (r(k)) \equiv f_i(h(t), r(k))$$

Given a game (G, T, α), $f^* \in F$ is a *subgame perfect equilibrium* if and only if f^* is a Nash equilibrium and for all t $(0 < t < T)$, for all $h(t) \in H(t)$, $((f_1^* | h(t)), \ldots, (f_n^* | h(t)))$ is a Nash equilibrium of $(G, T - t, \alpha)$.

Theorem 9.1 Let $(s^1, \ldots, s^T)$ be a sequence of outcomes such that, for all t, s^t is a Nash equilibrium of G. There must exist a strategy n-tuple f in the game (G, T, α) such that f is subgame perfect and $(s^1, \ldots, s^T)$ is the sequence of outcomes generated by f.

PROOF Let $f_i \in F_i$ be defined as follows: f_i entails playing s_i^t in the tth game, no matter what the history of play is in the first $t - 1$ games. Clearly, then, $\sigma(f, t) = s^t$. Hence $(f_1, \ldots, f_n)$ generates the outcomes sequence $(s^1, \ldots, s^T)$.

To show that $(f_1, \ldots, f_n)$ is subgame perfect, note that if j deviates from this in a particular game then (i) in that game j does not gain since s^t is a Nash equilibrium of G, for all t, and (ii) outcomes in future games are unaffected since all the strategies $f_1, \ldots, f_n$ are history independent. Hence no deviation at no stage is worthwhile. ∎

An immediate and extremely useful corollary of theorem 9.1 is that, if a game G has a Nash equilibrium, then repeated plays of the Nash equilibrium must be a subgame perfect equilibrium. Note that the previous sentence is not strictly correct because it describes a path as an equilibrium whereas what it really means is that the path can be generated (or supported) by equilibrium strategies. This aberration is permitted by convention.

As an exercise, show that if f is a subgame perfect equilibrium of (G, T, α) and $h(t) \in H(t)$, with $t < T$, then $((f_1 | h(t)), \ldots, (f_n | h(t)))$ must be a subgame perfect equilibrium of $(G, T - t, \alpha)$. Show also that the Nash equilibrium has a similar property.

It is well known that a collusive outcome which is not an equilibrium of a one-shot game can nevertheless be supported in a subgame perfect equilibrium of a *repeated* game. This is easily shown in the case of infinitely repeated games; but even in finitely repeated games cooperative behavior can be generated from repeated noncooperative play of the same game (Benoit and Krishna, 1985; Friedman, 1985; Abreu, 1988). At times cooperative outcomes are sustainable in equilibrium only through very complex strategies. However, in many cases, simple "trigger strategies" can be used to support such outcomes. Some of these are easily illustrated following Friedman (1985).

Consider a duopoly game in which each firm can produce a high output H or a low output L. Let the pay-off function be as shown below.

Firm 2

		H_2	L_2
G_1: Firm 1	H_1	4, 4	8, 2
	L_1	2, 8	6, 6

This is the Prisoner's Dilemma game, and the pay-offs shown here are quite plausible in a duopoly if the high output is the Cournot equilibrium output and the low output is below Cournot. G_1 has only one Nash equilibrium (which is in fact a dominant strategy equilibrium) given by (H_1, H_2). If the firms behaved collusively, it would be reasonable to expect them to play (L_1, L_2). What is easy to show is that if G_1 is played infinitely often then, even with each firm playing in its selfish interest, it may be possible to sustain (L_1, L_2). In other words, (L_1, L_2) may be the outcome of each game in a subgame perfect equilibrium of G_1 repeated an infinite number of times.

To demonstrate this consider the following trigger strategies. Each player begins by playing L and continues to do so as long as there is no deviation. Once there is a deviation (it is like a trigger getting pulled) from then on each player plays H. That is, after any history in which H_1 or H_2 occurs even once, player i will play H_i. If both players employ such trigger strategies, then player 1's payoff is $\alpha6/(1 - \alpha)$. It can be shown that, if $\alpha \geqslant 1/2$, then these trigger strategies comprise a subgame perfect equilibrium. If at any point a player deviates from the original path, his pay-off stream will be

8   4   4   4   . . .

The present value of this is $[8 + 4\alpha/(1 - \alpha)]\alpha$. If he does not deviate, his expected present value is $6\alpha/(1 - \alpha)$. If $\alpha \geqslant 1/2$, a deviation is not worthwhile. To complete the proof it has to be shown that, given a history in which a deviation has already occurred, no player benefits from deviating from what the trigger strategies require in the remaining subgame. To see this note that, after a history involving a deviation, the other player (who is playing a trigger strategy) will play *H*. Hence for this player it is best to play *H*, which is exactly what the trigger strategy prescribes. This also follows from theorem 9.1 above.

It may be argued, however, that in reality *finitely* repeated games are more relevant. So the important question is whether collusive outcomes can be supported by subgame perfect strategies in *finitely* repeated games. The answer is: it depends. For a game like G_1 it is easy to check that the answer must be negative. This is true not only under subgame perfection but by the intuitively powerful "backward-induction" argument. This argument consists of noting that in the last game both players will play *H*. The last game's outcome being fixed, in the penultimate game it is best for each player to play *H*. And by an inductive argument one gets that *H* will occur throughout.

This can be the basis of some discomfort with the very notion of subgame perfection (see Rosenthal, 1981; Reny, 1986; Binmore, 1987; Basu, 1990a) but that is not a line I want to pursue just now. Some of these issues will be taken up while discussing entry deterrence and collusion among oligopolists. What will be demonstrated here is that if a game has more than one Nash equilibrium then, even when the game is being played a finite number of times, trigger strategies may be able to sustain the collusive outcome. But trigger strategies are now more complicated than they were in infinitely repeated games.

In order to define trigger strategies in a finitely repeated game, I shall have to introduce some more notation.

Let $G = (N, S, P)$ be a one-shot game. Let $E \subset S$ be the set of Nash equilibria of G. For all $i \in N$, fix

$$s^i \in \operatorname*{argmin}_{s \in E} P_i(s)$$

If player i deviates he is punished by everyone playing s^i. Since a different trigger gets pulled depending on who deviates, what we are about to describe is at times called a *discriminating* trigger strategy.

Next suppose there exists $s^0 \in E$ such that $P_i(s^0) > P_i(s^i)$, for all $i \in N$. If, for instance, one Nash equilibrium strongly Pareto dominates another, then the game will necessarily have the kind of $s^0, \ldots, s^n$ defined above, since s^i need not be distinct from s^j, for $i, j \in N$.

Let $s^* \in S$ be such that $P_i(s^*) > P_i(s^i)$ for all $i \in N$. This s^* need not be a Nash equilibrium. We want to devise a trigger strategy for supporting s^* in the early games. The qualification "in the early games" will of course necessarily be there since in a finitely repeated game a non-Nash outcome can never occur in the last period.

Since we are analyzing *finitely* repeated games very little is lost by setting the discount factor α equal to unity. So consider the finitely repeated game $(G, T, 1)$ and let t^* be a positive integer. Let us denote the (discriminating) trigger strategy for player i based on $(s^0, \ldots, s^n, s^*, t^*)$ by $\hat{\sigma}_i$. Then $\hat{\sigma}_i$ is defined as follows.

If $s(k) \in S$ denotes an outcome in period k, then, as before, $(s(1), \ldots, s(t))$ is a history or a sequence of outcomes. We shall say that $(s(1), \ldots, s(t))$ is a *prescribed sequence* if and only if

$$s(k) = s^* \qquad \text{for all} \qquad k < t^*$$

and

$$s(k) = s^0 \qquad \text{for all} \qquad k \geqslant t^*$$

If $(s(1), \ldots, s(t))$ is not a prescribed sequence, then player i is the *first deviant* if and only if there exists $\hat{t} \leqslant t$ such that $(s(1), \ldots, s(\hat{t} - 1))$ is a prescribed sequence and, for all $j < i$,

$$s_j(\hat{t}) = \begin{cases} s_j^* & \text{if} \quad \hat{t} < t^* \\ s_j^0 & \text{if} \quad \hat{t} \geqslant t^* \end{cases}$$

and

$$s_i(\hat{t}) \neq \begin{cases} s_i^* & \text{if} \quad \hat{t} < t^* \\ s_i^0 & \text{if} \quad \hat{t} \geqslant t^* \end{cases}$$

Now we are in a position to describe $\hat{\sigma}_i$. If $h(t) \equiv (s(1), \ldots, s(t))$ is a prescribed sequence then, for all $i, \hat{\sigma}_i(h(t))$ must be such that $((h(t), \{\hat{\sigma}_i(h(t))\}_{i=1}^n)$ is a prescribed sequence. If $h(t)$ is not a prescribed sequence and j is its first deviant then, for all $i, \hat{\sigma}_i(h(t)) = s_i^j$.

Theorem 9.2 Let G be a one-shot game such that $(s^0, \ldots, s^n, s^*, t^*)$, defined as above, exists. There must then exist a large enough integer T such that in the repeated game $(G, T, 1)$ the trigger strategies based on $(s^0, \ldots, s^n, s^*, t^*)$ comprise a subgame perfect equilibrium.

PROOF Suppose $T > t^*$. If others do not deviate from their trigger strategies, then the best time for player i to deviate is period $t* - 1$ (since $P_i(s^*) > P_i(s^i)$). This way he is penalized for the briefest possible time. The player's maximum net gain from a deviation is therefore

$$D_i \equiv \max_{s_i \in S_i} \{ P_i(s^*/s_i) - P_i(s^*) \} - (T - t^* + 1) [P_i(s^0) - P_i(s^i)]$$

Since $P_i(s^0) - P_i(s^i) > 0$, D_i must be negative for a large enough T. That is, for a large enough T, a deviation from a prescribed sequence is not worth it.

Remember that to complete the proof of subgame perfection we must consider all histories and show that deviations are not worthwhile after them. Hence, consider an $H(t)$ which is not a prescribed sequence. After that, the trigger strategies entail that in each game a one-shot Nash equilibrium is played. It follows from theorem 9.1 that no player can benefit from a unilateral deviation. ∎

From the expression D_i in the proof of theorem 9.2 it is clear that we can calculate the largest t^* for which $D_i \leqslant 0$. This denotes the maximum number of times the collusive outcome s^* can be played without inviting deviations. Also note that if D_i is negative and T and t^* are raised by the same amount, then D_i continues to be negative. In other words, the longer the play, the closer each player's average pay-off (i.e. the total pay-off $\hat{P}_i$ divided by the number of periods) will be to s^*. This suggests that, the longer the play, the larger the set of average pay-offs that can be earned under subgame perfection. Indeed, oral tradition has it that any collusive behavior in a game can be sustained without the need for explicit contract or third-party enforcement if the game is played an infinite number of times and the discount rate is sufficiently small. This so-called *folk theorem* (a term meant to suggest that its authorship is unknown, "folk" being economics' counterpart of "anon" in poetry) has several formalizations. In a sense, the theorem just discussed is a folk theorem for finitely repeated games. More powerful results along these lines are established in Benoit and Krishna (1985). For some examples of actual games and the use of trigger strategies the reader is referred to Friedman (1985). In oligopoly, a wide range of collusive behavior can be explained in terms of trigger strategies as we shall shortly see.

9.4 SIMPLE STRATEGY PROFILES

Trigger strategies make critical use of the Nash equilibria of the relevant stage (or one-shot) game. Punishments take the form of reversion to a Nash equilibrium. But subgame perfection need not always take such a form. It is possible to construct examples – see Abreu (1988, pp. 387–8) for one – where an outcome path can be supported by subgame perfect strategies but *not* by strategies which entail a reversion to a Nash equilibrium. In fact subgame perfect strategies can take a wide range of forms. And looking for subgame perfection can be an arduous task. One gets a hint of this from the fact that, if a two-player game with only two strategies each is repeated an infinite number of times, then in this repeated game each player has (as you ought to check) not just an infinite number of strategies but uncountably so. Fortunately, for most purposes our task can be vastly simplified by focusing attention on "simple strategy profiles" and checking for "simple deviations" only. For a large class of games all outcome paths that can be supported by subgame perfect strategies can be located by this method, as shown by Abreu (1988). In this section I briefly sketch this method. The focus is restricted entirely to infinitely repeated games.

Let $G = (N, S, P)$ be the stage game. Consider now the repeated game (G, ∞, α). Describing the "strategies" in the stage game as "actions," we shall describe an infinite sequence of action n-tuples $\{s(t)\}_{t=1}^{\infty}$ as a *path* or a *punishment*. Let Ω be the set of all possible paths.

Let $Q^0, Q^1, \ldots, Q^n$ be elements of Ω. A *simple strategy profile* based on $Q^0, \ldots, Q^n$ is an n-tuple of strategies $f \in F$ which requires that Q^0 be played until someone deviates individually. And if players are supposed to be on path Q^i, where $i = 0, \ldots, n$, and j deviates individually (j may be i) then from then on Q^j should be played.

It should now be clear that Q^j is a punishment for player j. A simple strategy profile is simple because it entails the use of the same punishment for a deviation no matter *how many times* a player deviates, *when* a player deviates and other such matters of history. If player j deviates repeatedly then Q^j is restarted each time.

What is attractive about simple strategy profiles is that it is very easy to check whether they are subgame perfect or not. Essentially this involves checking that one-shot deviations are not worthwhile from any of the Q^i paths. It will then automatically follow that repeated (even infinite) deviations are not worthwhile. This feature is formalized in the next theorem.

Theorem 9.3 Assume that the game G has bounded pay-off functions, that is, $\{P(s) \mid s \in S\}$ is a bounded set. In the repeated game (G, ∞, α) the simple strategy profile based on $(Q^0, \ldots, Q^n)$ is subgame perfect if and only if, for all $j \in N$, for all $i \in \{0, \ldots, n\}$, and for all $t \in \{1, 2, \ldots\}$, and with $Q^r \equiv \{s^r(t)\}_{t=1}^{\infty}$ for all $r \in \{0, \ldots, n\}$,

$$P_j(s^i(t)/s_j) - P_j(s^i(t)) \leqslant \sum_{k=1}^{\infty} P_j(s^i(t+k))\alpha^k - \sum_{k=1}^{\infty} P_j(s^j(k))\alpha^k$$

for all $s_j \in S_j \setminus \{s_j^i(t)\}$.

PROOF Let the hypothesis of the theorem be true. The inequality condition in the theorem says that, if players are at stage t of path Q^i, then a one-shot deviation is not worthwhile for player j. Hence one-shot deviations are never worthwhile.

Next suppose that m (> 1) deviations are worthwhile for some player j. Consider the situation where $m - 1$ deviations have already occurred. Now the mth deviation in itself cannot be worthwhile since one-shot deviations are never worthwhile. Hence the first $m - 1$ deviations must be worthwhile. But then we can continue arguing in the same way and show that the first of the m deviations must be worthwhile. This contradicts what was proved in the previous paragraph. Hence, no finite number of deviations are worthwhile.

Finally suppose j benefits from an infinite number of deviations. Let the net discounted benefit to j from the kth deviation be D_k^j. Since this is a game with discounting and the stage-game pay-off function is bounded, the gain from the infinite number of deviations is equal to $\Sigma_{k=1}^{\infty} D_k^j$. Hence the first sentence of this paragraph implies that

$$\sum_{k=1}^{\infty} D_k^j > 0$$

This means that there exists $m < \infty$ such that

$$\sum_{k=1}^{m} D_k^j > 0$$

Hence, there exists a finite number of deviations which are worthwhile for player j. But this contradicts what was proved in the previous paragraph. Therefore after every history conformity with the simple strategy profile is each player's best strategy. ∎

Theorem 9.3 provides an easy way of checking whether a simple strategy profile is subgame perfect or not. The utility of theorem 9.3 would be even greater if it were true that, in some sense, it is adequate to focus attention on only the simple strategy profiles of an infinitely repeated game. Abreu has shown that this is indeed true.

Let us make this claim more precise. Assume $G = (N, S, P)$ is such that S is a compact subset of a finite-dimensional Euclidean space and P is continuous. These are clearly reasonable requirements. Given this assumption, if Q^0 is a path in the game (G, ∞, α) such that it can be supported under subgame perfection, then it can be shown that there must exist paths $Q^1, \ldots, Q^n$ and a simple strategy profile based on $(Q^0, \ldots, Q^n)$ which is subgame perfect.

9.5   CRITIQUES, REFINEMENTS AND EXTENSIONS

From the discussion thus far and the remarks on the folk theorem in section 9.3, one may begin to suspect that for many repeated games the set of perfect equilibria may be very large and it may be possible to think of intuitively appealing criteria for further refinements. This is indeed so and in recent times the literature on solution concepts for extensive-form games has proliferated rapidly.

One frequently heard critique of perfection which is related to the kinds of issues discussed above is based on the fact that certain collusive outcomes can be enforced only by the use of punishments which are Pareto suboptimal among the set of perfect equilibria. It seems reasonable to argue that, should such a punishment ever need to be meted out, players could negotiate to treat bygones as bygones and move to a Pareto-superior equilibrium strategy. Since players know this in advance, they may refuse to play the initial equilibrium strategy. This is the broad idea behind the recent literature on "renegotiation-proof equilibria" (see, for example, Bernheim and Ray, 1989; Farrell and Maskin, 1989). While "renegotiation proofness" can be difficult to interpret in infinitely repeated games, it is easy to formalize in finitely repeated games, as discussed, for instance, in Benoit and Krishna's (1989) lucid paper. I shall here confine attention to finitely repeated games. Consider the following game G_2:

			Player 2	
		L	M	R
	T	1, 1	0, 0	5, 0
G_2: Player 1	N	0, 0	3, 3	0, 0
	D	0, 5	0, 0	4, 4

I shall refer to strategies by the pay-offs when this is unambiguous. In G_2, (1, 1) and (3, 3) are the only pure-strategy Nash equilibria. Suppose G_2 is played twice and the discount factor is 1. In other words, we are considering the repeated game $(G_2, 2, 1)$. It is easy to see by applying the method of trigger strategies discussed in section 9.3 that the outcome path ((4, 4), (3, 3)) is subgame perfect. The following discriminating trigger strategy does it. The players decide to play (4, 4) in the first stage. If no deviation occurs in the first stage, they play (3, 3) in the second stage. If any deviation occurs in stage 1, then they play (1, 1) in the second stage.

A card-carrying believer in renegotiation proofness, however, would argue that the above outcome is not reasonable. Suppose player 1 does deviate in game 1 to T. Hence he earns a pay-off of 5. Now suppose that before playing G_2 for the second time he (or, for that matter, player 2) argues that, by carrying out the punishment (1, 1), not only is player 1 hurt but both suffer. So why do they not treat bygones as bygones and play (3, 3) in the second period? This seems reasonable. Since both players can see this they will never try to use a punishment which is vulnerable to this criticism. Hence ((4, 4), (3, 3)) cannot occur.

To apply the renegotiation-proofness criterion more formally we should work backwards. In the last period, Nash equilibria which are not Pareto dominated by other Nash equilibria are *"renegotiation proof."* Hence in G_2 only (3, 3) can occur in the second period. In the penultimate period a strategy (s_1, s_2) is possible under the renegotiation-proofness criterion if it is supportable by threats which are "renegotiation proof" in the last period in the sense just defined. Hence, in G_2 only (3, 3) can occur in the penultimate period since that is the best among the possible. It will be observed by some readers[2] that, if a game G has one Nash equilibrium which Pareto dominates all other Nash equilibria, then the renegotiation-proof outcome of a repeated play of G is unique and consists of playing the dominant Nash equilibrium in each period.

It is interesting to note that, although the *idea* of renegotiation proofness arises from the rejection of Pareto-inferior outcomes, a subgame perfect equilibrium strategy which Pareto dominates other subgame perfect equilibrium strategies may fail to be renegotiation proof. Thus in the above example ((4, 4), (3, 3)) is supported under subgame perfection but is not renegotiation proof, whereas ((3, 3), (3, 3)) is renegotiation proof.

The concept of renegotiation proofness, elegant though it is, highlights some rather troublesome issues concerning common knowledge and, through it, about its own epistemological foundations. Return to the example of G_2 being played twice. Suppose the second-period game is about to be played. Clearly, if it is common knowledge that (3, 3) will be played, then (3, 3) will be played. Likewise for (1, 1). This follows from the fact that (1, 1) and (3, 3) are both Nash equilibria. So how did we agree that negotiation before the play will lead to (3, 3) being played? We argued that all the players would have to do was to talk before the second period's play and *agree that, no matter what conversation had occurred among them earlier*, they will play (3, 3) in stage 2. This seemed to make it common knowledge that (3, 3) will indeed be played.

But now suppose that before the first period's play they talk and *agree that, no matter what conversation occurs among them later*, they will play (1, 1) in stage 2, if in stage 1 anything other than (4, 4) occurs.

If both of the italicized conversations and agreements occur and (4, 4) does not occur in stage 1, what will a player expect to happen in stage 2? The answer is by no means obvious. The renegotiation that occurs before the second game has no effect if i believes in the original agreement or i believes that j believes in the original agreement and so on. Thus suitably worded agreement at the start of the repeated game can jeopardize the effectiveness of subsequent renegotiation. This raises the extremely difficult question: how does anything become common knowledge? The question is usually averted in game theory by treating what is common knowledge as a primitive. Thus it is generally *assumed* that rationality is common knowledge. It is possible that some of the paradoxes of game theory arise from inconsistent primitive assumptions about common knowledge in the same way that some of the early paradoxes of set theory arose from a misuse of the fact that sets are primitives and therefore from an *assumption* that there exists a set of everything.

Turning to matters more mundane, another fascinating refinement of perfection that has been suggested in recent times makes use of the idea of "forward induction" (see, for example, Kohlberg and Mertens, 1986; Cho and Kreps, 1987). Certain moves by players can amount to a signal of their future intentions or expectations and thereby actually narrow down what may happen. This can play a very important role in industrial modeling and I shall illustrate the idea with an example from Kohlberg (1989).

Consider the Battle of the Sexes discussed in chapter 2 (game G_1). But suppose that player 1, the woman, has to make an initial move where she chooses between moving l and earning three dollars or moving r which results in the Battle being played. Thus we have the extensive-form game Γ_5 shown in figure 9.5.

Restricting attention to pure strategies this game has two subgame perfect equilibria: (l, B, R) and (r, T, L). However, in an important sense, (l, B, R) is not self-enforcing. Note that if 1 plays r then in the next stage it is only to be expected that he will play T, because if he is going to follow up r with B he could instead have chosen l and done better for himself. Since choosing

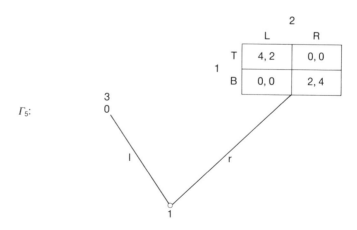

Figure 9.5

r amounts to rejecting a pay-off of 3, it is clearly a signal that the player is hoping to earn more than 3 from the Battle. Since 2 can see this, if 2 is actually called upon to play, 2 will play L. Since 1, in turn, can see this, it is rational for 1 to play r and *not* l. Hence, only (r, T, L) is consistent with both forward and backward induction although (r, T, L) and (l, B, R) are consistent with backward induction alone.

In more complicated games, the forward-induction argument can be difficult to interpret. Thus if before 1's initial move in game Γ_5 player 2 had a move where 2 could end the game and earn 3 units or make a move which leads to Γ_5, the forward-induction argument becomes less persuasive.[3] However, in industrial organization one encounters many situations where an analysis as simple as the one used for Γ_5 can be used to refine the subgame perfection criterion in an intuitively reasonable way.

NOTES

1 The remainder of this section develops a formal description of finite extensive-form games. Since this description, in its full generality, is not used in subsequent chapters, some readers may wish to glance through it quickly and treat it mainly as a manual for referring back to if and when the need arises.
2 I desist from the traditional practice of calling them "discerning readers" because experience suggests that while such readers may indeed be discerning it is more likely that they have read a previous book on the same subject!
3 For a discussion of this case, see Kohlberg (1989).

10

Oligopoly in the Extensive Form: Two Examples

10.1 INTRODUCTION

The purpose of this section is to introduce extensive-form duopoly and the use of subgame perfection and its refinements. This is done by discussing two simple examples. This should be a useful preamble to more complicated arguments involving strategic interaction over time.

There are two ways of bringing interaction over time into our models of oligopoly. One way is to consider an oligopoly game of the kind discussed in, for instance, chapter 3 and then allowing for its repeated play. Models of collusion use this method and we shall see examples of it in later chapters. The second route is to introduce a modicum of temporal considerations into a single round of the Cournot game itself. In the textbook model of Cournot oligopoly, production and sales occur in one instant. In reality production takes time and can rarely be undertaken under complete secrecy. Hence, if a firm plans to flood the market, the other firms would typically get a hint of this and may react to it by producing more or less. In brief, even before the firms offer their output for sale there may be scope for some strategic interaction between them. In this chapter two examples of such modified Cournot oligopolies are presented. I describe the examples without commenting on institutional details because the purpose of this brief chapter is to acquaint the reader with the *techniques* of extensive-form analysis in industrial organization.

10.2 THE TWO FISHERMEN

Suppose two fishermen return from the sea with their catches; they see each other's catch and have an opportunity to go out once again and catch more fish. Then, the next morning, they take their total catches to the market where they sell to the consumers as in the usual Cournot model. This model has very interesting properties as has been shown by Saloner (1987).

More formally, in this model firms 1 and 2 produce output levels (x_1^1, x_2^1) in period 1 and (x_1^2, x_2^2) in period 2. For all t, and $i, x_i^t \geqslant 0$. This last restriction implies that in period 2 each firm can add to its output but not subtract from it.[1] Immediately after period 2, the total output is offered to the consumers. If the inverse demand function is given by $p(\cdot)$ and $x_i^1 + x_i^2 \equiv x_i$, then the market price of the good is given by

$$p = p(x_1 + x_2)$$

If firm i's cost function is linear and is given by $c_i x_i$, then firm i's profit π_i is as follows:

$$\pi_i(x_1, x_2) \equiv p(x_1 + x_2)x_i - c_i x_i \qquad i = 1, 2$$

The *reaction function of firm 1* is defined by

$$\phi_1(x_2) = \operatorname*{argmax}_{x_1} \pi_1(x_1, x_2)$$

Similarly we define

$$\phi_2(x_1) = \operatorname*{argmax}_{x_2} \pi_2(x_1, x_2)$$

These are usual Cournot reaction functions which we encountered before. We are assuming that, for all x_2, $\operatorname{argmax}_{x_1} \pi_1(x_1, x_2)$ is unique (and similarly for firm 2). In other words $\phi_i(x_j)$ is indeed a function (and not a correspondence).

We shall assume throughout this section that the demand function is sufficiently well behaved for the following to be true.

1   For each i, there is a unique Stackelberg output with i as leader. We shall denote this output by S^i. That is, S^i is the pair of outputs by firms 1 and 2 that would occur if the firms were playing the usual Stackelberg game with i as leader. These are illustrated in figure 10.1.
2   For each i, π_i is quasi-concave with respect to x_i.
3   $\partial \phi^i / \partial x^j > -1$. That is, the reaction functions are "stable" in the textbook sense.
4   As we move along i's reaction function from S^j towards the Cournot equilibrium point, j's profit falls. In terms of figure 10.1, as we go from S^1 to N, π_1 keeps falling. A sufficient condition for this is that $\tilde{\pi}_1(x_1)$ be strictly quasi-concave in x_1, where $\tilde{\pi}_1(x_1) \equiv \pi_1(x_1, \phi_2(x_1))$ and likewise for firm 2.

These four conditions would be true under several classes of situations, for example in the case where demand is linear.

At the end of period 1, both firms get to see (x_1^1, x_2^1). So what we now

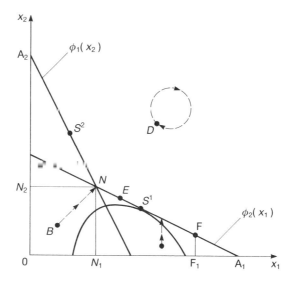

Figure 10.1

have is an extensive-form duopoly game. What are the subgame perfect equilibrium output levels of this model?

The main result of this section is that any output pair that lies on the reaction functions between the two Stackelberg levels (in other words, on the line S^1NS^2) can be the outcome under subgame perfection; and no other output levels are subgame perfect. The remainder of this section is a proof of this theorem.

Let us begin by examining how the duopolists will play in period 2. In other words, let us treat $(x_1^1, x_2^1) \equiv \bar{x}^1$ as given. The analysis is best conducted by partitioning the space shown in figure 10.1 into four segments: the area enclosed between $0N_1NN_2$ (i.e. to the southwest of the Cournot–Nash equilibrium point N); the area N_1NA_1; the area N_2NA_2; and all points northeast of A_2NA_1. It is easy to check that under subgame perfect strategies the following must be true. (i) If $\bar{x}^1$ is in $0N_1NN_2$, in period 2 firms will choose output levels such that aggregate output occurs at N. (ii) If $\bar{x}^1$ is in N_1NA_1, the final output occurs on firm 2's reaction function vertically above $\bar{x}^1$. (iii) If $\bar{x}^1$ is in N_2NA_2, then final output occurs on 1's reaction function horizontally across from $\bar{x}^1$. (iv) Finally, if $\bar{x}^1$ is in the northeast of A_2NA_1, the final output occurs at $\bar{x}^1$. Movements (i)–(iv) are all described in figure 10.1 by broken lines with arrows to indicate direction.

Let me prove (i) as an example. Suppose $\bar{x}^1$ is at B. Since in period 1 firms can only add to their earlier production, the only feasible region in period 2 is the area northeast of B. That is, if we draw a vertical and a horizontal line through B, we could treat these as the axes and the northeast quadrant as the feasible region. If we are considering subgame perfect strategies, then after every history the specified moves must constitute a Nash equilibrium. Hence in the region northeast of B the Nash equilibrium is N. Hence, period 2 strategies must be such that each firm i will produce $N_i - B_i$ in period 2, where $B = (B_1, B_2)$. You should check claims (ii)–(iv) above.

It follows from (i)–(iv) that the final equilibrium (i.e. total output) must be on $A_2 N A_1$ or to the northeast of this line. Suppose it is to the northeast, at a point like $D = (D_1, D_2)$. Given period 2's subgame perfect moves, $\bar{x}^1$ must be at D. But if firm 1 unilaterally changed its period-1 output from D_1 to a lower output D_1' such that (D_1', D_2) is in the northeast of $A_2 N A_1$, then (we know from (iv) above) the final output would remain at (D_1', D_2) and firm 1 would be better off. Hence D cannot be subgame perfect. So now we know that subgame perfect strategies must result in outcomes on $A_2 N A_1$.

Next consider a point like F, to the right of S^1. If the final outcome is at F, we know from (ii) above that the outputs chosen in period 1 must be somewhere on the line segment FF_1. But it is easy to see that if in period 1 firm 1 had produced less – in fact, its Stackelberg output – then the final outcome would be at S^1. Since 1 is better off at S^1 than at F, F cannot be subgame perfect. By the same argument, no point on $A_2 S^2$ can be the outcome of subgame perfect strategies.

Finally, and without loss of generality, consider any point E on the segment NS^1. Let $E = (E_1, E_2)$. Suppose the firms produce (E_1, E_2) in period 1. We already know (see (iv)) that in period 2 no further output will be produced. It is clear that 2 cannot gain by unilaterally changing E_2. If 2 produces more than E_2 in period 1, then 2 will be worse off. If 2 produces less, then the final output would be at E and so 2 will be no better off. It is easy to see, using (i)–(iv) and assumptions (2) and (4), that 1 cannot do better by deviating from E unilaterally.[2]

In some sense what this model allows is similar to the standard Stackelberg duopoly. In a Stackelberg duopoly, one firm gets to see the other's output before choosing its own. In the present model both get to see each other's initial plans. Hence, it is not surprising that the final equilibria are "mixtures" of the Cournot and Stackelberg equilibria.

It is worth noting, however, that the above equilibria have some robustness problems. One extension, which amounts to a robustness check on the Saloner model, is to allow for differences in the costs of production in the two periods of the game. Let us suppose that the per-unit cost of production in period 1 is c_1 and in period 2 is c_2. A recent paper by Pal (1991)[3] shows that the solution just described depends critically on the assumption $c_1 = c_2$.

Consider for instance the case where $c_1 < c_2$. This is not an unreasonable assumption since the second round of production will usually be an activity in a rush, spurred by the other producers' first-round activity. In this case, it is easy to show that the subgame perfect equilibrium collapses to a single point, namely the Cournot equilibrium with the cost function being given by c_1.

To see this, let A'B' be firm 2's reaction function if his cost of production is given by c_2, and let AB be his reaction function if his cost of production is given by c_1. Since $c_1 < c_2$, AB naturally lies to the right of A'B'. The reaction function for firm 1 for firm 2, C'D' and CD, are likewise defined.

Following the same strategy as above, let us first ask what will happen in period 2 if $x^1 = (x_1^1, x_2^1)$ is produced in period 1. Note that, once period 2 commences, the relevant reaction functions are A'B' and C'D'. The reaction functions AB and CD are of no further significance. Hence, following exactly the same reasoning as for figure 10.1, we can use broken lines to indicate what happens in period 2, after x^1. This is indicated in figure 10.2. It immediately follows that the final equilibrium can only occur on or to the right of C'N'B'. Suppose that subgame perfect play entails producing x^1 somewhere inside 0FN'E. Given the second period's play as captured by the pointed arrows, it is evident that each player could do better by deviating from x^1 in period 1. Next suppose x^1 is outside 0FN'E and not at N. Clearly at least one player can benefit through a deviation in period 1: if x^1 is not on AB, 2 will deviate; if it is not on CD, 1 will deviate. Hence only one point could qualify as a subgame perfect equilibrium, namely N. Indeed

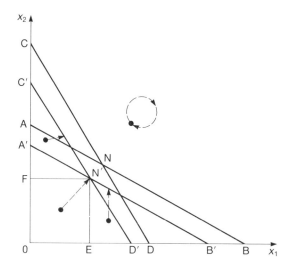

Figure 10.2

N is the only outcome supported by subgame perfect strategies. These require both players to produce at N in period 1.

The case of $c_1 > c_2$ is not very difficult to analyze. As Pal (1991) has shown, if in this case the cost differential is very high, then there is once again a unique subgame perfect equilibrium which involves both firms producing only in period 2. If the cost differential is small, then there are two equilibria: in each of these one firm acts as a leader and produces in period 1 and the other acts as a follower and produces only in period 2.

Before moving to the second example of this chapter, it is worth raising another robustness question which is perhaps of greater conceptual significance. How critical is Saloner's assumption that in period 2 a firm can only add to his output (i.e. he cannot throw away his period-1 output)? Without going into the formal proof here it may simply be suggested that the argument consists of introducing into figure 10.1 reaction functions drawn under the assumption that the cost of production is zero. Clearly if x^1 (i.e. the period-1 output) is to the right of these functions, then these functions are the relevant reaction functions. Using this construct it is not difficult to demonstrate that with free disposal the set of subgame perfect equilibria will shrink, but not to a unique point (Basu, forthcoming).

10.3 TOWARDS COLLUSION

Duopolists under Cournot equilibrium produce more than what would be in their collusive interest. But collusion is not the only reason why duopolists may restrict output to less than what would be predicted by the standard Cournot theory. If before playing the Cournot duopoly game the firms allow themselves one opportunity to "collude," then the subgame perfect equilibrium of this extensive game may entail a much smaller production (and therefore a greater deviation from the efficient competitive solution) than in the Cournot equilibrium. In fact, the production may be smaller than would obtain under effective collusion (Basu, 1990b).

There are two firms producing the same good. In period 1, each firm writes down its proposed output level. That is, firm i writes down a real number x_i^1. In period 2 each firm has to state whether it "accepts" the scheme of production (x_1^1, x_2^1) suggested in period 1 or "rejects" it.

If both accept, then (x_1^1, x_2^1) is put into effect. That is, firm i produces x_i^1 and earns a profit of

$$\pi_i(x_1^1, x_2^1) = p(x_1^1 + x_2^1)x_i^1 - c_i(x_i^1)$$

where $p(\cdot)$ is the inverse demand function faced by the industry and $c_i(\cdot)$ is firm i's total cost function.

If one or more firms reject (x_1^1, x_2^1), then in period 3 each firm i again writes down its production plan x_i^3 and these get implemented. Hence firm i earns a profit of $\pi_i(x_1^3, x_2^3)$.

Note that the game in period 3 is the standard Cournot game. This is the reason why in the introduction it was suggested that the model may be viewed as that of Cournot with one prior attempt at collusion.

The statement of the main theorem is easier if we make the following simplifying (but nonessential) assumptions. It will be maintained throughout that each firm's iso-profit function in $x_1 x_2$ space is quasi-concave and that there is a unique Cournot equilibrium. Let point N (see figure 10.3) be the Cournot equilibrium and let π_{iN} be the iso-profit curve of i which gives i the profit it earns at N. Let M be the other point where π_{1N} and π_{2N} intersect. That is, if the two firms produce at M_1 and M_2 then they will earn the same profits as in the Cournot equilibrium. (We shall also use π_{iN} to denote the amount of profit earned by i at the Cournot equilibrium.)

We may now state the central theorem of this model: in the three-period model of duopoly described in this section the only points in $x_1 x_2$ space which can be supported under perfect equilibrium strategies are N and M.

It ought to be clarified here that the theorem establishes a claim for (trembling-hand) perfect equilibrium. Interestingly, in this model, subgame perfection may result in outcomes which cannot occur under perfection. I explain this after proving the theorem stated above.

To prove the theorem consider stage 3 first. Clearly in period 3 the game is no different from the standard Cournot duopoly. Hence if a rejection occurs in stage 2, the outcome will be N.

Let us now turn to stage 2. Suppose that in stage 1 (x_1^1, x_2^1) has been played. What is the equilibrium in the remaining subgame? It is evident that if $\pi_i(x_1^1, x_2^1) < \pi_{iN}$ then i will move "reject" in period 2 because rejection guarantees that N will occur and firm i will earn π_{iN}. If, on the other hand, $\pi_i(x_1^2, x_2^1) \geq \pi_{iN}$, for $i = 1, 2$, then both players move "accept," since rejection is weakly dominated and cannot be part of a perfect equilibrium strategy (see the discussion of Γ_4 in chapter 9).

In figure 10.3, consider the set of all points where each player earns at least as much as at N. This is described by the area MANBM (including the boundary). So what we have shown is that if (x_1^1, x_2^1) lies outside the area MANBM then it will be rejected. Otherwise it will be accepted.

Finally, let us turn to the first period. From the above discussion it is clear that points outside the area MANBM cannot be supported by perfect equilibrium strategies. So let us turn to points in the area MANBM. Let us partition this area into the set of "corner" points $\{M, N\}$ and the set Z of "non-corner" points (i.e. Z consists of all points in area MANBM except M and N). It will first be shown that no element of Z can be a perfect equilibrium. Let D be an element of Z (see figure 10.1). Suppose in period

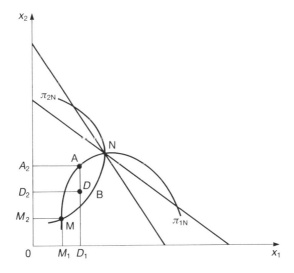

Figure 10.3

1 the two firms choose $(x_1^1, x_2^1) = (D_1, D_2)$. To see that this cannot be a perfect equilibrium, note that for every point E in Z the following property (P) is true.

(P): There exists a point in Z which is vertically above E or horizontally to the right of E.

Without loss of generality let us consider the point A which is in Z and vertically above D. Hence, if starting from D player 2 deviates to point A, then (we know from our analysis of periods 2 and 3) 2 would do better since A is an equilibrium in the subgame following (D_1, A_2) in period 1. (Note that $\pi_2(D_1, A_2) > \pi_2(D_1, D_2)$.) Therefore D cannot be a perfect equilibrium.

Since the points M and N do not satisfy property (P) it is obvious that each of these points is a perfect equilibrium.

In the above game, perfection turns out to be a strict refinement of subgame perfection. It can be shown that all points in the set MANBM can be supported under subgame perfect strategies.

To see this return to the stage 2 analysis above. It was argued there that, if $\pi_i(x_1^1, x_2^1) \geqslant \pi_{iN}$ for $i = 1, 2$, then under perfection both players move "accept." What needs to be noted here is that under *subgame* perfection, both players choosing "reject" is entirely possible. This is because, if the other player rejects, the first player is indifferent between rejecting and accepting.

Now consider any point in the interior of MANBM. Let us consider D. Suppose both players play the strategy that if $(x_1^1, x_2^1) = D$ they will accept; if $(x_1^1, x_2^1) \neq D$, they will reject. It immediately follows that moving D in stage 1 and having it accepted in stage 2 can be subgame perfect. Hence, under subgame perfection, all points in MANBM, including points of perfect collusion (i.e. on the contract curve formed by the tangencies) can be the outcome under subgame perfect strategies in the duopoly game described in this section.

Finally, I make a comment on how the perfection theorem can be generalized. Instead of permitting one attempt at collusion before resorting to the Cournot game as in the above model, we could conceive of a more general game where several such collusive attempts are permitted. Let n be any number. Consider the following n-period generalization of the above three-period game. In period 1 each of the two firms proposes an output level. If both accept this in period 2, it is implemented. Otherwise, in period 3 each of the two firms again proposes an output. If both accept this in period 4, it is implemented. And so on. If by period n no production plan is accepted, then whatever production plan (x_1^n, x_2^n) is proposed in period n gets implemented.

It is easy to see that, no matter what the value of n, the perfect equilibrium of the game consists of only points M and N in figure 10.3.

NOTES

1 It is possible to relax this and allow for "free disposal" but the analysis gets more complicated and only a *variant* of the theorem discussed in this section continues to be valid (Basu, forthcoming).

2 It is interesting to note that, within the continuum of subgame perfect equilibrium outputs, only points S^1 and S^2 can be supported by subgame perfect equilibrium strategies which do not entail the use of weakly dominated strategies. I am grateful to Geir Asheim for bringing this to my attention.

3 For related work see Banerjee and Cooper (1991).

11

Quantities and Prices

11.1 INTRODUCTION

As we have already seen, what happens in an industry depends not only on the market structure but also on the set of strategies open to each firm. This point was evident as early as 1883 when Bertrand showed that if firms chose prices instead of quantities in a duopoly, which is otherwise identical to that of Cournot, the outcome could be dramatically different. This gave rise to the price versus quantity debate. Now with the rise of extensive-form game theory the scope of this debate has become vastly enlarged. After all, firms can now not only select prices or quantities but different variables at different stages. At first there seemed to be a bewildering array of possibilities, but already we can see some consensus emerging. Prices are easier to change than quantities; quantities are easier to cut back than expand, and so on. By using such stylized facts we can create models of great interest and institutional richness.

This chapter begins with a discussion of Kreps and Scheinkman's (1983) seminal paper in which firms first choose quantities, which then form upper limits to what can be sold, and then in the second stage choose prices. That is, the second-stage game is like an Edgeworth duopoly described in chapter 4.

One can go further and push the idea of prices being flexible to the limit by assuming that a firm i can respond to j's price change instantaneously. This gives rise to what is known as a "quick-response" duopoly. A formal model of a quick-response duopoly is presented in section 11.3.

Recent research attempting to resolve the price–quantity problem has led to models where a firm does not choose price or quantity but supply *functions*. That is, it commits itself to selling different amounts at different prices. In other words it has contingent plans. If we think of firms as large organizations instead of simple entities, this is not an unrealistic characterization. After all, different departments of a firm will have to have broad instructions from above as to how to respond to different contingencies that may suddenly arise. Klemperer and Meyer (1989) have explored the nature of Nash equilibria when firms choose supply functions.

Another reasonable line of enquiry is to model inventories explicitly and allow firms to run these up or down depending on market conditions. Judd (1990) has recently modelled oligopolistic equilibria when firms' strategies are enlarged in this manner. These recent developments are commented upon in section 11.4.

11.2   FIRST QUANTITY, THEN PRICE

The main contribution of Kreps and Scheinkman (1983) is that they reinstate the Cournot equilibrium through a different, and more compelling, route than that taken by Cournot himself. Developing the idea that prices are easier to change than quantities, Kreps and Scheinkman consider a two-period model. In period 1, the firms produce outputs. These productions then form the upper limits of what the firms can sell. In period 2, the firms simultaneously choose prices. They then prove that the subgame perfect equilibrium of this game coincides with the Cournot outcome. That is, in period 1 the firms choose the Cournot equilibrium outputs and in period 2 they choose the Cournot equilibrium price.

Following Kreps and Scheinkman, suppose we have a continuous twice-differentiable concave and strictly decreasing demand function given by $d: R_+ \to R_+$. Its inverse is denoted by p, where $p(0)$ is the lowest price at which demand is zero. Two firms confront this demand function. I shall make the simplifying assumption of zero cost of production.

Consider period 2. Assume that the two firms have produced $(x_1, x_2) \equiv x$ in the first period. We shall at times refer to x_i as firm i's capacity because period i's output is what limits period 2's capacity to sell. Each firm i has to choose a price p_i from $[0, p(0)]$. It is useful to write down the rationing rule formally. Suppose $(p_1, p_2) \equiv p$ is chosen in period 2. If $p_1 < p_2$ then firm 1's sales are given by

$$f_1(x, p) = \min\{x_1, d(p_1)\}$$

(i.e. all demand is directed at firm 1 and it sells as much as it can) and firm 2's sales are given by[1]

$$f_2(x, p) = \min\{x_2, \max\{0, d(p_2) - f_1(x, p)\}\}$$

(i.e. broadly speaking, all residual consumers go to firm 2 and it sells to as many as it can given its capacity). The case where $p_1 > p_2$ is treated symmetrically.

If $p_1 = p_2$, then each firm gets half the market share and any spillover from the other firm's failure to supply to its share. Hence, if $p_1 = p_2$, firm 1's sales are given by

$$\bar{f}_1(x,p) = \min\left\{x_1, \frac{d(p_1)}{2} + \max\left\{0, \frac{d(p_1)}{2} - x_2\right\}\right\}$$

Hence given any (x,p), firm 1's sales are equal to

$$z_1(x,p) = \begin{cases} f_1(x,p) & \text{if } p_1 < p_2 \\ \bar{f}_1(x,p) & \text{if } p_1 = p_2 \\ f_2(x_2,x_1,p_2,p_1) & \text{if } p_1 > p_2 \end{cases} \tag{11.1}$$

This is a fairly standard rationing rule (see Kreps and Scheinkman, 1983; Brock and Scheinkman, 1985; Benoit and Krishna, 1987), although not the only possible or even obvious one.

The rationing rule is illustrated in figure 11.1 where $0x_1$ is firm 1's capacity and x_1x_2 is 2's capacity and $p(0)D$ is the demand curve.

Given (x,p), firm 1's profit is given by

$$\pi_1(x,p) = p_1 z_1(x,p)$$

Firm 2's profit function is defined symmetrically.

Now the game is as follows. In period 1 the firms select capacity x_1 and

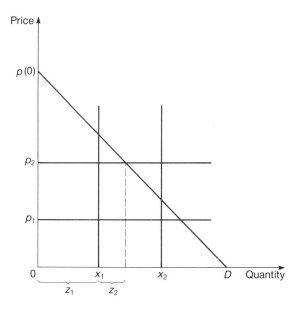

Figure 11.1

x_2 and in period 2 they select price p_1 and p_2. Firms are allowed to use mixed strategies. In particular the use of mixed strategies in prices is important because, as we have already seen in chapter 3, for certain ranges of capacity a pure strategy equilibrium in prices may not exist.[2] This game will be referred to as the *extensive duopoly game*.

Define a function $\bar{\pi}_i(x_1, x_2) \equiv \pi_i(x_1, x_2, p(x_1 + x_2), p(x_1 + x_2))$. Given (11.1), it follows that $\bar{\pi}(x_1, x_2) - p(x_1 + x_2)x_i$. Hence $\bar{\pi}_i$ is the usual "Cournot" profit function.

Let (x_1^N, x_2^N) be the *Cournot equilibrium output*. That is, (x_1^N, x_2^N) is the Nash equilibrium of a game in which, for $i = 1, 2$, firm i chooses x_i in order to maximize $\bar{\pi}_i(x_1, x_2)$. In this model there is a unique and symmetric Cournot equilibrium. Hence, $x_1^N = x_2^N \equiv x^N$. The *Cournot equilibrium price* and *profit* are defined as $p^N \equiv p(2x^N)$ and $\pi^N \equiv \bar{\pi}_i(x^N, x^N)$.

It will now be shown that the Cournot outcome coincides with the subgame perfect equilibrium of the extensive duopoly game described above. This will be proved via the following lemma. Note that, for every $(x_1, x_2) = x$ chosen in period 1, we have a capacity-constrained Bertrand game in period 2. I shall refer to this period-2 game as $G(x_1, x_2)$.

Lemma 11.1 If, in period 1, firm 1 produces x^N and firm 2 produces $x_2 > x^N$, then in the Nash equilibrium of the game $G(x^N, x_2)$ firm 2's expected pay-off is π^N.

The proof of this lemma is not difficult but laborious, sufficiently so for me to omit it here with a reference to Kreps and Scheinkman (1983) or Tirole (1988, pp. 230–1). Actually lemma 11.1 is a special case of the more general result that the firm with the larger capacity earns its minmax pay-off.

Theorem 11.1 There is a subgame perfect equilibrium strategy which results in the firms producing the Cournot equilibrium output and charging the Cournot equilibrium price.

PROOF Suppose firms 1 and 2 produce x^N each in period 1. Then, as we know from chapter 4, the equilibrium price in $G(x^N, x^N)$ is p^N. That is, each firm earns π^N.

Without loss of generality consider deviations by firm 2 in period 1. If 2 produces $x_2 < x^N$, then in $G(x^N, x_2)$ the equilibrium strategy is for both firms to set price equal to $p(x^N + x_2)$. But $p(x^N + x_2)x_2 < p(2x^N)x^N = \pi^N$, by the definition of x^N. Hence such a deviation is not worthwhile for 2.

If 2 deviates to $x_2 > x^N$, the equilibrium in period 2 (i.e. in game $G(x^N, x_2)$) entails the use of mixed strategies. But from lemma 11.1 we know that firm 2's expected pay-off is π^N. Hence the deviation yields no gain.

Therefore the Cournot outcome is supported by a subgame perfect equilibrium strategy. ∎

In fact, as Kreps and Scheinkman show, the Cournot outcome is the unique subgame perfect equilibrium outcome of the extensive duopoly game. Subsequent work (e.g. Osborne and Pitchik, 1986) has demonstrated that this result is robust to certain important relaxations of assumptions, including the troubling concavity of demand used by Kreps and Scheinkman.

The relative flexibility of prices, which is emphasized above, can be modeled in other ways too. An interesting direction is to use "quick-response" games to capture the idea that, as far as price changes go, firms can respond to one another very quickly. This is what I turn to in the next section.

11.3 QUICK-RESPONSE OLIGOPOLY

It is interesting to note that in a Stackelberg game the leader does well for himself (better than if he were a follower) not so much because he is the first mover as because he cannot revise his move after the other player's move. If firm 1 first chooses output x_1, 2 chooses x_2 and then 1 has a chance to revise his output choice of x_1, the outcome would be a Stackelberg one but with 1 as a follower. Viewed in this way, Stackelberg games and even Nash games cause a problem. After all, firms can in reality change their decision variables. This is especially true of a variable such as price which is easy to adjust.

One way of handling this problem is to allow for quick price adjustments until no one wants to make any further adjustments and then to implement the choices. There is a small literature analyzing such price adjustments. The results are extremely interesting. They can explain among other things how collusive outcomes may be sustainable under subgame perfection.

Marschak and Selten (1978) modeled oligopolies as quick-response games. In more recent times several authors have modeled price-setting markets with quick response and have reached the conclusion that the monopoly outcome may be sustained in subgame perfect equilibrium even when there are several firms (Stahl, 1986; Farm and Weibull, 1987; Bhaskar, 1989). Moreover, Bhaskar (1989) has shown that under a reasonable refinement the monopoly outcome is the only equilibrium. I shall consider a slightly modified version of his model.

There are two firms A and B. If both charge the same price p, they share the market equally and each firm earns a profit $R(p)$. Otherwise the firm charging the lower price corners the full market and earns $\pi(p)$ where p is the lower price. Hence $2R(p) = \pi(p)$, for all p.

Both firms have the same linear total cost function, with marginal cost equal to c. Hence, $R(c) = \pi(c) = 0$. We assume that $R(p)$ is strictly concave (i.e. the marginal revenue curve is downward sloping).

Let p^* be the monopoly price. That is,

$$p^* = \text{argmax } R(p)$$

In addition, let $\bar{p}$ be the value of p for which $R(p^*) = \pi(p)$ and $p > p^*$; and $\underline{p}$ be the p for which $R(p^*) = \pi(p)$ and $p < p^*$. These are illustrated in figure 11.2.

The firms announce prices in a sequence. Firm A first announces a price $p(1)$; then B announces $p(2)$; then 1 announces $p(3)$; and so on. The process continues until a time n is reached when $p(n) = p(n-2)$ and $p(n-1) = p(n-3)$. In other words, if A makes the same bid on two consecutive occasions and B makes the same bid on two consecutive rounds, then the bidding stops. Whatever the final bids were at that time is implemented and A and B earn profits accordingly. If the sequence is endless, we shall assume that both earn zero profits. Since no sale occurs until the bidding ends, this suggests that the announcements occur rapidly and no waiting costs are involved. This is why the interaction is called a *quick-response game*.

As before, an n-period history $h(n)$ is a sequence of announcements

$$(p(1), p(2), \ldots, p(n))$$

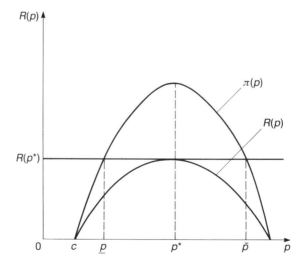

Figure 11.2

A *strategy* σ^A for player A specifies what move A will make initially and after every t-period history, where t is even. Hence $\sigma^A(h(t))$ is a non-negative number. Similarly σ^B specifies what B will move after every odd-numbered history.

The equilibrium notion which I shall employ to start with is subgame perfection. The prices (p_A, p_B) which emerge from the use of subgame perfect strategies will be referred to as the equilibrium outcome.

Theorem 11.2 The shared monopoly outcome, with both firms charging a price p^*, is an equilibrium outcome.

PROOF Consider the following strategies $\hat{\sigma}^A$ and $\hat{\sigma}^B$. Given a history $h(n - 1)$, $\hat{\sigma}^i$ (where $i \equiv$ A, B) specifies the following move.

(a) If i can end the sequence by his next move and earn at least as much as $R(p^*)$, i should do so. (A more formal way of stating this is as follows. Let the last three terms of $h(n - 1)$ be $p(n - 3), p(n - 2)$, and $p(n - 1)$. If $p(n - 3) = p(n - 1) > p(n - 2)$ and $p(n - 2) \in [\underline{p}, \bar{p}]$ or $p(n - 3) = p(n - 1) = p(n - 2) = p^*$, i should set $p(n) = p(n - 2)$.)

(b) If moving p^* means either that the sequence ends here and i earns less than $R(p^*)$ or j can end the sequence in the next move and earn more than $R(p^*)$, then i should move $p(n - 1)$. That is, $p(n) = p(n - 1)$.

(c) If the conditions in (a) and (b) are both false, then i should set $p(n) = p^*$.

Let us first check that $\hat{\sigma}^A$ and $\hat{\sigma}^B$ result in the outcome $(p_A, p_B) = (p^*, p^*)$.

When A makes the first move, there is no history. Hence by (c), $p(1) = p^*$. With this as history $\hat{\sigma}^B$ specifies that $p(2) = p^*$, since the history (p^*) does not satisfy the requirements of (a) or (b). Similarly, $p(3) = p^*$. Finally, by (a), $p(4) = p^*$. Hence the outcome is (p^*, p^*). Next we have to show that $\hat{\sigma}^A$ and $\hat{\sigma}^B$ are subgame perfect. I shall show, without loss of generality, that it does not pay firm A to deviate from $\hat{\sigma}^A$ after any history, given that B is playing $\hat{\sigma}^B$.

Note first that with B playing $\hat{\sigma}^B$ A can never earn more than $R(p^*)$. Hence A can never benefit by deviating from part (a) of $\hat{\sigma}^A$.

Suppose next that the conditions in (b) are valid. That is, either $p(n - 3) = p(n - 1) < p(n - 2) = p^*$ or $p(n - 3) \neq p(n - 1) < p(n - 2) = p^*$ and $p(n - 1) > \underline{p}$ is true. Hence, $p(n)$ is supposed to be $p(n - 1)$. After A's move, check that then B will find himself in category (c). So, he will move p^*. It is easy to see that, if players play $(\hat{\sigma}^A, \hat{\sigma}^B)$, once p^* occurs, either the game stops there or p^* occurs after that. Hence A will end up earning $R(p^*)$. Clearly there is no incentive to deviate. Finally since a play of p^* results in a response of p^*, there is no advantage in deviating from (c).   ∎

Bhaskar (1989) has shown that if we refine subgame perfection by ruling out the use, after any history, of dominated strategies by any player, then the monopoly outcome is the only equilibrium outcome, the word "equilibrium" now being used in this stronger sense. This refinement is in the spirit of trembling-hand perfection, as would be evident from section 2.3. I shall here establish the proposition that non-monopoly outcome can occur in equilibrium.

To prove this, note that no player can earn more than $R(p^*)$ in equilibrium. If someone does so, then the other player must be using a dominated strategy. And for a similar reason no player earns zero or less in equilibrium.

Now consider a history of announcements (p^*, p^*, p^*). Clearly, after such a history, B can ensure a profit of $R(p^*)$, because he can straightaway move p^* and terminate the game. Since for one firm to earn $R(p^*)$ and the other to earn zero implies the use of a dominated strategy by the latter, it follows that in the final equilibrium, after (p^*, p^*, p^*) has occurred, both earn $R(p^*)$ (see figure 11.2).

Hence, after a history (p^*, p^*), A can ensure a profit of $R(p^*)$ for himself. It follows that B can ensure himself $R(p^*)$. Therefore, after (p^*), B can ensure a profit of $R(p^*)$ for himself. Hence A can ensure himself $R(p^*)$. Hence, at the start of play, A can ensure a profit of $R(p^*)$ for himself, because he can always move p^*. For this to happen and B to earn positive profit it is necessary for B to earn $R(p^*)$ as well. Such an outcome is only possible if the strategies are such that the final prices are (p^*, p^*).

There are several other directions of research that can be pursued using the framework of quick response. One line of enquiry concerns the "kinked demand curve."

The kinked demand curve was once staple fare in oligopoly analysis. Born out of the work of Hall and Hitch (1939) and Sweezy (1939), in this theory it is argued that starting from a status quo price, if one of several oligopolists raises the price, others will typically not respond, preferring instead to take a cut in sales. If, however, a single firm lowers price, others would respond by lowering price. This implies a kink in the demand curve confronting the individual firm. The kink in the demand curve in turn suggests a break in the marginal revenue curve. Hence it is possible that, despite small fluctuations in the cost schedule, prices remain unchanged. Thus the kinked demand curve hypothesis can help explain the alleged rigidity of some industrial prices.

However, the theory came under considerable attack (see, for example, Stigler, 1947) both on empirical grounds and for using *ad hoc* assumptions. An interesting attempt was subsequently made by Peck (1961) to present a modified version of the kinked demand curve theory. In Peck's version, the equilibrium price is unique and occurs at a level where a lowering of the price would hurt all the producers and raising would hurt at least one.

Recently, some effort has been made to reinstate the kinked demand curve theory using more sophisticated theoretical techniques. Dreze (1979) has provided an argument based on a model of uncertainty. Bhaskar (1988) has tried to construct a model based on quick-response oligopoly which exhibits some characteristics described by Peck in his study of the aluminum industry.

Another line of research worth pursuing is one which amalgamates the models of this and the previous sections. I feel that the idea of prices being flexible is captured better by thinking of firms as responding quickly to one another than by them choosing prices simultaneously (as in the model of section 11.2). That is the strength of the present model; however, it ignores altogether the existence of capacity constraints, which was central in section 11.2. This suggests a natural course of bringing these two strengths together. This would have us model firms which first choose quantities simultaneously and then, with these quantities defining capacity constraints, play a quick-response game in prices. The quick-response game is complicated by the fact that each firm now has an upper limit on its production capacity. But the equilibria of such a model could yield important insights.

11.4 SUPPLY FUNCTIONS EQUILIBRIA

In reality firms select both prices and quantities. If, however, we suppose that each firm chooses its price and quantity simultaneously, then in a static or one-period model a problem of inconsistency arises. The aggregate demand may not match the aggregate supply. One way of reconciling this is to consider a dynamic model and introduce what in the real world is very important, namely inventories. If in a particular period demand does not match production, consistency can be restored by running down or building up inventories. Such a model has recently been explored by Judd (1990).[3]

Another route to reconciling the price–quantity dilemma is to abandon the notion of firms choosing between *points* in the price–quantity space, the price space, or the quantity space. Instead, we could think of each firm as selecting a supply *function*. Given each firm's supply function, the price is given by the point where the aggregate of all firms' supply intersects the demand function. Given *n* firms, an *n*-tuple of supply functions could be thought of as an equilibrium if no firm could increase its expected profit through a unilateral change of its supply function. Following the early work of Grossman (1981) and Hart (1985), such "supply function equilibria" have been studied in considerable detail by Klemperer and Meyer (1989).

Note first that it is not unrealistic to think of firms as committing themselves to supply functions instead of the more conventional price or quantity. In a large firm with several divisions and departments contingent instructions from the top often play an important role because it may not be possible to refer back to the owners each time a contingency arises. Such contingent instructions could then lock the firms into rules such as "if this is the price then supply this much."

Although this does not involve any extensive-form argument, it is probably the right place to give you some idea of how a supply functions equilibrium works. Consider an industry facing a demand curve

$$x = a - bp \tag{11.2}$$

where $a, b > 0$, x is quantity, and p is price. Given that Klemperer and Meyer anyway assume that the demand function satisfies concavity, the linearity assumption is not particularly strong. Moreover the extension to the concave case is not difficult.

Suppose two firms 1 and 2 confront this demand curve. Firms produce goods costlessly. Firm i's *strategy* consists of choosing a *supply function*

$$s_i = (0, \infty) \to (-\infty, \infty)$$

Given the choice of both firms, the price $\bar{p}$ that will prevail in the market is the one for which demand equals supply. That is

$$a - b\bar{p} = s_1(\bar{p}) + s_2(\bar{p}) \tag{11.3}$$

Hence $\bar{p}$ is defined implicitly by (11.3). Let us assume that such a unique price always exists. We could alternatively assume that whenever there is no unique price satisfying (11.3) firms' profits are zero.

Firm i's profit or pay-off function is defined as follows:

$$\pi_i(s_1, s_2) = \bar{p}s_i(\bar{p}) \tag{11.4}$$

where $\bar{p}$ is defined by (11.3).

A pair of supply functions (s_1, s_2) is a *supply functions equilibrium* (or SF equilibrium, in brief) if (s_1, s_2) is a Nash equilibrium.

For purposes of illustration it is harmless (in this case where there is no uncertainty) to confine attention to linear supply functions. That is, I assume that firm i can only choose a function such as

$$x_i = k_i + d_i p$$

In other words in this special case firm i's strategy is any pair of numbers $(k_i, d_i) \in R^2$.

If the two firms choose (k_1, d_1) and (k_2, d_2) the price that prevails is given by solving (11.4):[4]

$$\bar{p} = \frac{a - k_1 - k_2}{b + d_1 + d_2} \qquad (11.5)$$

Hence, distorting terminology a little, I shall write

$$\pi_i(k_1, d_1, k_2, d_2) = (k_i + d_i\bar{p})\bar{p}$$

An SF equilibrium is illustrated in figure 11.3. Let s_i be firm i's supply function and $s_1 + s_2$ be the horizontal aggregation of 1 and 2's supply functions. What does it mean to say that s_1 and s_2 constitute an SF equilibrium?

Given s_1 the residual demand that firm 2 faces is the gap between the demand curve and s_1. Firm 2 can now effectively choose any price by suitably choosing its own supply curve. If it chooses s_2, price is $\bar{p}$ as shown in the figure and the profit of firm 2 is given by the area ABC$\bar{x}$. For (s_1, s_2) to be an SF equilibrium firm 2 must find that it cannot improve on ABC$\bar{x}$ by changing its supply function, and similarly for firm 1.

An interesting property of an SF equilibrium (in a world of certainty as

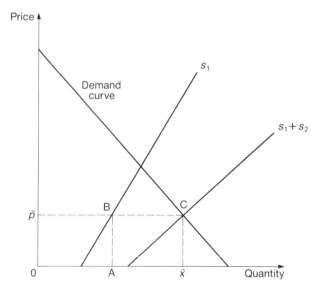

Figure 11.3

assumed thus far) is that, if (s_1, s_2) is such an equilibrium, then each firm is indifferent between an infinite number of supply curves in equilibrium. Thus firm 1 will be indifferent between all supply curves that go through point B. Hence, its specific choice in equilibrium is essentially to ensure that the *other firm* has no incentive to deviate. This is somewhat akin to a mixed-strategy Nash equilibrium, since each firm is indifferent between its equilibrium strategy and any other strategy which uses the same support.

Given this flexibility, it would not be surprising if we had many equilibria associated with any industry. And indeed it can be shown that any point on the demand curve can be supported as an SF equilibrium. This abundant multiplicity collapses rapidly once we introduce uncertainty – for instance demand fluctuations – and that is one of the major themes of Klemperer and Meyer (1989). But first let me illustrate the "abundant multiplicity" claim.

Select any point on the demand curve, for instance $(\hat{x}, \hat{p})$ or E in figure 11.4. Note that $\hat{x} = a - b\hat{p}$. Let firm 1's supply function be one which goes through $(\hat{x}/2, \hat{p})$. Hence, using (11.3) we know that $\hat{x}/2 = k_1 + d_1\hat{p}$, and by using (11.2) we have

$$\frac{\hat{x}}{2} = k_1 + d_1 \frac{a - \hat{x}}{b} \tag{11.6}$$

Given (11.2) and (11.6) firm 2 will want to choose point E if EFAB is the largest rectangle that can be fitted within the triangle aGk_1 with its base on

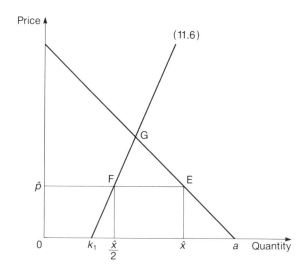

Figure 11.4

the horizontal axis. Clearly this is so if AB is half the distance $a - k_1$. Hence 2 will want to select E if

$$\hat{x} = a - k_1 \tag{11.7}$$

Solving (11.6) and (11.7) we get

$$k_1 = a - \hat{x} \tag{11.8}$$

$$d_1 = \frac{b(3\hat{x} - 2a)}{2(a - \hat{x})} \tag{11.9}$$

Since firms 1 and 2 are symmetrically placed $(k_1^*, d_1^*, k_2^*, d_2^*)$ is an SF equilibrium if $k_1^* = k_2^* = a - \hat{x}$ and $d_1^* = d_2^* = b(3\hat{x} - 2a)/2(a - \hat{x})$. At this equilibrium, each firm produces $\hat{x}/2$ and price is equal to

$$\hat{p} = \frac{a - \hat{x}}{b}.$$

That is, point E in figure 11.4 occurs in equilibrium. Since E was an arbitrarily chosen point on the demand curve, the above exercise proves the abundance claim.

Indeed while I showed that $\hat{x}$ can occur in equilibrium with each firm producing $\hat{x}/2$, it is easy to generalize this and show that, if $\hat{x}_1$ and $\hat{x}_2$ are any nonnegative numbers such that $\hat{x}_1 + \hat{x}_2 = \hat{x}$, then there is an SF equilibrium where firm i produces $\hat{x}_i$.

The number of SF equilibria falls sharply once uncertainty is introduced in the model. Suppose now that the intercept term of the demand function is stochastic. In particular, assume

$$x = a - bp + \varepsilon$$

where ε is a random variable with positive density on an interval D. If $D = [-a, \infty]$, we say that ε has *full support*. If ε has full support, then all positive price–quantity pairs lie on some demand curve with positive density.

In the remainder of the section it will be assumed that firm i's cost of producing x_i units is given by $c(x_i)$ with $c'(x_i) > 0$ for all $x_i > 0$, $c'(0) = 0$, and $0 < c''(x_i) < \infty$, for all x_i. Profits are computed as before but with the obvious modification that costs have to be netted out now since production is no longer costless.

As before, firms choose supply functions s_1 and s_2. It is assumed that these supply functions are twice continuously differentiable. An *SF equilibrium* is a pair of supply functions (s_1^*, s_2^*) such that no firm can increase its expected profit through a unilateral change in its supply function.

If the two firms choose (s_1, s_2) and ε is realized, then price is given implicitly by solving

$$a - bp + \varepsilon = s_1(p) + s_2(p)$$

Let $\bar{p}$ be the solution. Then firm i's profit is given by

$$\pi_i(s_1, s_2, \varepsilon) = \bar{p}s_i(\bar{p}) - c(s_i(\bar{p}))$$

Note that, given a realization of ε and s_i, firm i's residual demand is $a - bp + \varepsilon - s_j(p) \equiv Z$. Hence its profit-maximizing price is given by differentiating $pZ - c(Z)$ with respect to p and setting it equal to zero.

By doing this it is clear that for each ε there is a unique optimal price p for firm i. Let this be written as $p(\varepsilon)$. It follows that given s_j we can trace out firm i's best supply function. The graph of this function is given by points such as $\{p(\varepsilon), a - bp(\varepsilon) + \varepsilon - s_j p(\varepsilon)\}$ with ε varying from $-a$ to ∞. Moreover if ε has full support then, unlike in the case of certainty, each firm's best-response supply function is unique, once the other firm's supply function is fixed.

Klemperer and Meyer (1989) have shown that in this model an SF equilibrium always exists, and if ε has full support the equilibrium supply functions are upward sloping, go through the origin, and are identical for both firms.

Let us end this section by analyzing a special case. Assume that firm i's cost function is given by

$$c(x_i) = \frac{B}{2}x_i^2 \qquad i = 1, 2 \tag{11.10}$$

with $B > 0$. This function is carefully selected to give us a linear marginal cost function, namely Bx_i. I shall also confine each firm i's strategy to a linear supply function, $x_i = d_i p$. Hence firm i's strategy effectively consists of choosing a number d_i.

Without loss of generality, suppose firm 1 has chosen d_1. Let us consider 2's problem. Given a realization of ε, firm 2's profit is given by

$$\pi_2 = [a + \varepsilon - (b + d_1)p]p - \frac{B}{2}[a + \varepsilon - (b + d_1)p]^2$$

By setting $\partial \pi_2 / \partial p = 0$ and rearranging terms we get

$$p = \hat{p} \equiv \frac{(a + \varepsilon)[1 + B(b + d_1)]}{(b + d_1)[2 + B(b + d_1)]} \tag{11.11}$$

Hence *given d_1 and ε*, firm 2 would like to set price equal to $\hat{p}$ and it would be supplying $\hat{x}_2 = a + \varepsilon - (b + d_1)\hat{p}$. By using (11.11) we get

$$\hat{x}_2 = (a + \varepsilon)\left[1 - \frac{1 + B(b + d_1)}{2 + B(b + d_1)}\right] \tag{11.12}$$

Hence if, with d_1 and ε fixed, firm 2 had to select a linear supply function $x_2 = d_2 p$, it would set

$$d_2 = \frac{x_2}{\hat{p}} = \frac{b + d_1}{1 + B(b + d_1)} \tag{11.13}$$

Note that (11.13) is very lucky for us: ε does not figure in it. This means that firm 2's best response "points" on the demand curves (with ε varying and d_1 given) lie on a ray through the origin.

It follows that (d_1^*, d_2^*) is an SF equilibrium if (11.14) and (11.15) are valid:

$$d_2^* = \frac{b + d_1^*}{1 + B(b + d_1^*)} \tag{11.14}$$

$$d_1^* = \frac{b + d_2^*}{1 + B(b + d_2^*)} \tag{11.15}$$

An implication of (11.14) and (11.15) is that the equilibrium must be symmetric, that is, $d_1^* = d_2^*$. To see this note that (11.14) implies

$$d_1^* d_2^* B = b + d_1^* - d_2^* - d_2^* B b$$

Since (11.15) implies a symmetric equation it follows that

$$b + d_1^* - d_2^* - d_2^* B b = b + d_2^* - d_1^* - d_1^* B b$$

Therefore,

$$(d_2^* - d_1^*)(Bb + 2) = 0$$

Since $Bb > 0$, we get $d_1^* = d_2^* \equiv d^*$.

We can therefore describe the SF equilibrium even more simply: (d_1^*, d_2^*) is an SF equilibrium if and only if $d_1^* = d_2^* \equiv d^*$ such that

$$d^* = \frac{b + d^*}{1 + B(b + d^*)} \tag{11.16}$$

Note that this would have no solution if $B = 0$. Hence, the assumption that marginal cost be positive for positive output. is required (in this case with uncertainty) in order to ensure the existence of an equilibrium.

From (11.16) and the usual rule for solving quadratic equations, we get

$$2d^* - -b + \left[b^2 + \frac{4b}{B} \right]^{1/2} \tag{11.17}$$

Hence $d^* > 0$.

It is interesting to compare this equilibrium with the Cournot and Bertrand solutions. Viewed in the present framework a Cournot equilibrium is one in which firms are restricted to choosing vertical supply curves and a Bertrand equilibrium is one where firms choose horizontal supply curves. Since d^* is positive and finite, firms play neither the Cournot nor the Bertrand game.

NOTES

1 Kreps and Scheinkman (1983) use a slightly different-looking but operationally equivalent expression.

2 On the other hand, once we allow players to use mixed strategies, that is, to choose probability measures on $[0, p(0)]$ the existence of a Nash equilibrium is ensured (Kreps and Scheinkman, 1983; Dasgupta and Maskin, 1986).

3 I have not yet studied the model in sufficient depth, and therefore refrain from an elaborate presentation.

4 To rule out negative prices and quantities, we can elaborate on (11.5) by qualifying that (11.5) is valid if $\bar{p}$ and $a - b\bar{p}$ are both positive. If not, then profit is assumed to be zero.

12

Collusion

12.1 INTRODUCTION

The subject of collusion and cartels constitutes one of the most interesting chapters in the emerging field of industrial organization. Collusive efforts on the part of traders and entrepreneurs have been witnessed through the ages and in all fields of commerce and industry. Under monopoly, profits are usually large, but as the number of firms in an industry increases, production tends to rise and profits get frittered away through increased competition. It is natural to expect that even in industries with several firms entrepreneurs will try to collude, overtly or covertly, to curb production, raise price, and thereby earn larger profits.

In the theoretical literature on oligopoly an output (or price) configuration is thought of as comprising a "collusive" outcome if it maximizes the joint profit of all firms or, more generally, if it is the case that there is no other feasible output configuration which gives all oligopolists as much profit as before and at least one oligopolist a larger profit. As has already been seen, in a single-shot oligopoly the collusive outcome may not be sustainable as an equilibrium. Hence the scope for collusion usually arises in a *dynamic* context, and the extensive-form game is the right instrument for analyzing collusive behavior.

Some instances of oligopolistic collusion have already been encountered in the previous three chapters. A more systematic presentation occurs in sections 12.3–12.5. The theoretical literature on collusion is recent but large and I try to provide no more than a brief overview of it. But, before going into that, it is useful to make some observations concerning the "legal problem" of collusion.

12.2 SOME LEGAL ISSUES

Just as collusion is a widespread practice, sentiments against collusive behavior are also pervasive and most nations have grappled with legal provisions designed to control price fixing and restraints of trade. In Europe, unlike in the United States, anti-collusion laws are relatively recent. Consequently Europe provides a rich source of evidence on open collusion. Thus in Switzerland alone in 1953 a government commission found 136 formal price-fixing cartels![1] In the United States most evidence is of covert collusion because the legal strictures against such practices are relatively unambiguous and also older, dating back to the late nineteenth century, specifically the Sherman Act 1890. This has meant that court proceedings provide a rich data source for such industrial practices in the States.[2]

Collusion and cartels are one area of industrial organization where recent advances in theory, especially game theory, have helped us immensely to explain reality and to organize the bewilderingly rich data and experience into an analytical framework. This has been particularly helpful for studying covert and implicit collusion.

It is not surprising that most of the early theoretical work was on cartels with *explicit* price or output agreements. These were also the cases which were the relatively easy ones for the law courts. In such overt cases of trade restraint the court's problem was not about whether there *was* any collusion but whether there were extenuating circumstances to justify some collusive practice. Thus, for example, in the Addyston Pipe and Steel Case, 1899, where six US producers of iron pipe had divided the market area into local monopolies with prices fixed within each, the occurrence of collusion was never in question. The main defense of the producers was that the market condition was such that in the absence of such an agreement there would be ruinous price competition between them. The judge in the Circuit Court of Appeals dismissed the argument of the defendants as unconvincing.

This was soon after the passing of the Sherman Act. It is not surprising that, as more time passed, the firms realized that to collude openly was to fall foul of the law. Gradually the practice was driven underground. In many subsequent cases it became increasingly difficult to decide whether collusion had occurred or not. For instance, what has been described in the courts as "conscious parallelism" (Asch, 1983, pp. 217–18) consists of a set of firms behaving in unison and setting a high price. This can be achieved by the smaller firms following a leader[3] or by all firms following an implicit accord.

The possibility of implicit collusion clearly requires repeated interactions. In a one-shot oligopoly the free-rider problem is too stark to sustain collusion. But once we allow oligopolists to confront one another *repeatedly* through the market place, as they would indeed do in reality, there arises the possibility of "threats" being used to sustain high prices and low production. The value of the theory of extensive-form games in understanding such behavior is obvious. The purpose of the present chapter is to demonstrate several routes for formalizing such arguments.

But before going into these, I want briefly to remark on an interpretational matter which is bound to loom large in any serious legal analysis of "restraints of trade." Most of the repeated-game models show how collusive outcomes can occur under subgame perfection or sequential equilibrium. That is, these outcomes occur without the need for "conversation" or, for that matter, without any "smoking-gun evidence" of cartel-like behavior. As the idea of perfection suggests, such collusive outcomes occur through each firm acting in its self-interest. In such situations it is not clear that a charge of collusion can be brought against the firms in any obvious sense. As Fellner (1950, p. 54) wrote, somewhat prophetically, "The kind of 'collusion' characteristic of oligopolistic market structures does not require direct contacts between rival firms. Consequently, collusion is not a particularly well-chosen word for expressing what we should here have in mind .... *In the real world spontaneous co-ordination shades over into explicit agreement by gradations*" (my italics).[4]

Given this ambiguity, it is natural that attempts to contain collusive practices will encounter political obstacles. Lobbying or using expensive legal counsel to interpret antitrust legislation to the advantage of the firms charged of practising it is widespread. It is therefore not surprising that, while antitrust action has been sluggish in most countries, successful antitrust drives occurred in Japan and Germany after the Second World War. The clue lies in the fact that in these cases the antitrust action came from beyond the borders, from the Allied powers.

A part of the rationale behind the Allied policy of breaking up large industrial houses in Germany and Japan was the belief that these large economic conglomerates were the driving force behind the aggressive behavior of these nations during the War. There has been considerable controversy, however, about the *real* rationale. Several Japanese writers have argued that the policy of the Allied forces to dissolve the *zaibatsus* – the wealthy families with large market shares in multiple industries – was actually a design of Western monopoly capital to expand its market. For an analysis of this controversy I refer you – with the reminder that to refer is not to commend – to Hadley (1970).

Whatever the rationale, the upshot is that the antimonopoly rules that the Allied powers drew up and implemented would not have been politically feasible in these countries if they were left entirely to themselves. And though, it is true, some of the *zaibatsus* had reassembled themselves by the mid-1950s, the new laws had unleashed greater industrial competition (see

Caves and Uekusa, 1976, chapter 4). It is somewhat ironic that the forces from "outside" unwittingly turned out to be a blessing in disguise for the Japanese economy.

While on this topic, and given that I shall not return to it anymore in this book, it is worth remarking that theory can contribute a lot to some of these debates. First, the modeling of the *zaibatsus* could be of some inherent interest. As a first step, this would consist of modeling agents (which could be families or groups) which control large firms in several oligopolistic industries. When such agents confront one another, the appropriate equilibrium to study is the one among the *agents*, that is, an equilibrium in several industries simultaneously. It has been suggested that this kind of interaction helps collusion and lies at the core of Japanese industrial behavior. This claim concerning collusion, however, is not obvious and hence its *a priori* plausibility can be a subject of theoretical investigation. I suspect this will be quite a difficult exercise and therefore adopt the strategy of leaving it to the reader, and turn now to models of greater transparency.

12.3   INFINITELY REPEATED OLIGOPOLY

The possibility of implicit collusion in an infinitely repeated play of an oligopoly game is obvious in the light of the discussions in chapter 9. Let me illustrate this with a simple trigger-strategy argument which was developed by Friedman (1971).[5]

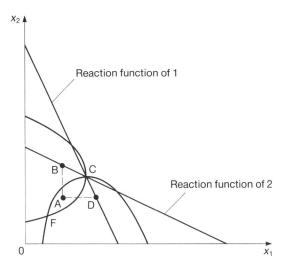

Figure 12.1

Consider a symmetric duopoly with reaction functions and iso-profit curves as shown in figure 12.1. The Cournot equilibrium point is given by C. Let us see how a point like A can be sustained under subgame perfection. Let A be a point where joint profits are maximized and the two firms produce the same level of output. I shall denote the profits earned (in each period) by the two firms at A by (π^A, π^A). If the firms produce the Cournot equilibrium outputs (i.e. at point C), their profits are (π^C, π^C). If firm 1 deviates optimally from A, let the two firms' profits be (π^D, π^N). Thus (π^D, π^N) represents the profits earned by firms 1 and 2 at point D. Since the firms are identical, the profits earned at B are (π^N, π^D).

Consider now the trigger strategies whereby the firms produce at A as long as no deviation occurs but they revert to a repeated play of the Cournot outcome if ever a deviation occurs. Then, if firm 1 never deviates, it expects to earn $\pi^A/(1 - \delta)$, where δ is the discount factor. To check whether these strategies are subgame perfect it is enough to check that a one-shot deviation is not worthwhile. If a firm deviates, it expects to earn $\pi^D + \pi^C\delta/(1 - \delta)$. Hence, a deviation is not worthwhile if

$$\frac{\pi^A}{1 - \delta} \geq \pi^D + \frac{\pi^C\delta}{1 - \delta}$$

or

$$\delta \geq \frac{\pi^D - \pi^A}{\pi^D - \pi^C} \tag{12.1}$$

Since $\pi^D > \pi^A$ and $\pi^A > \pi^C$, the right-hand term in (12.1) lies in the interval (0, 1). Hence, what we have illustrated is that as long as the discount factor is sufficiently large, in particular greater than $(\pi^D - \pi^A)/(\pi^D - \pi^C)$, "collusive behavior," i.e. a repeated play of A, is supportable under subgame perfection.

The range of behavior supportable under subgame perfection can be shown to be quite large if we are willing to consider strategies which are more complicated than trigger strategies. For a lucid, if somewhat theorem-intensive, venture in this direction, see Abreu (1986). I shall refrain from pursuing such a line here, however, and instead consider some more mundane problems.

Note that in the above model of collusion aggregate output is constant from period to period, and hence price also never changes. Price wars, which are so much a part of reality, can never occur. An ingenious model for explaining price wars within the ambit of equilibrium analysis was developed by Green and Porter (1984).[6] The central feature of their model is a repeated Cournot game *with imperfect monitoring*. The repeated games discussed thus far involve perfect monitoring in the sense that, when a player is called in to make a move in a stage game, he can base his choice on the entire history of play up to that stage. An imperfectly monitored game, however, is one in which players are not allowed to base all moves on the entire history of play. In Green and Porter's model, in each period firms choose output but cannot observe each other's choices. Hence, a firm in period t cannot base its output decision on the history of outputs chosen by the other firms. Firms do observe price but from this they cannot deduce how much was produced because the inverse demand function has a multiplicative risk term. In particular, let the inverse demand function be given by

$$p = \theta p(x)$$

where $p'(x) < 0$, as usual, and θ is a random number with mean equal to 1. Hence θ is the multiplicative risk term.

For simplicity suppose that there are two identical firms and let figure 12.1 illustrate their reaction functions and iso-profit curves, where all calculations are based on *expected* profit maximization. Hence, the "Cournot game" consists of firms choosing quantities and the pay-off functions are the same as the expected profit functions. I shall denote the (expected) profit of a firm in a Cournot equilibrium by π^C. Let p^C be the (expected) price when firms produce their Cournot equilibrium outputs.

Now suppose the Cournot game is played an infinite number of times. Let x^* be a point on the 45° line through the origin somewhere between F and C. Hence, both firms earn higher profits at x^* than at C. Now we shall consider a "collusive strategy" based on three parameters $(x^*, T, \bar{p})$ where T is a positive integer and $\bar{p}$ is a price below p^C. The strategies are as follows: both firms produce at x^* (i.e. firm i produces x_i^*) and continue to do so as long as price is at least as great as $\bar{p}$. The first time price drops below $\bar{p}$, firms produce the Cournot equilibrium outputs (i.e the firms produce so as to be at point C in figure 12.1) and do so for $T - 1$ periods. In the Tth period after the stage when price dropped below $\bar{p}$, firms go back to producing x^*. They do so until price drops below $\bar{p}$ again and then again they punish themselves for $T - 1$ periods by producing the Cournot outputs. Such periods are called "reversionary episodes." I shall denote such a strategy combination by $s(x^*, T, \bar{p})$.

For arbitrarily specified $(x^*, T, \bar{p})$, the strategies $s(x^*, T, \bar{p})$ need not be subgame perfect. But if we can restrict $(x^*, T, \bar{p})$ suitably, subgame perfection may be ensured. To see this, let us denote the per-period expected profit of a firm when they produce at x^* by π^*. Let q^* be the probability that $\theta p(x_1^* + x_2^*) < \bar{p}$, and let δ be the discount factor. Without loss of generality, suppose that firm 2 adheres to the above strategy specification and that we are at a stage where in the previous stage price was at or above $\bar{p}$, or that the reversionary episode ended in the previous period. Then if V^* is the present value of firm 1's pay-offs by adhering to the above strategy, we have

$$V^* = \pi^* + (1 - q^*)\delta V^* + q^*[\pi^C(\delta + \ldots + \delta^{T-1}) + \delta^T V^*]$$

$$= \pi^* + (1 - q^*)\delta V^* + q^*\left(\pi^C \frac{\delta - \delta^T}{1 - \delta} + \delta^T V^*\right) \qquad (12.2)$$

By rearranging terms, (12.2) can be written as

$$V^* = \frac{\pi^* - \pi^C}{1 - \delta + q^*(\delta - \delta^T)} + \frac{\pi^C}{1 - \delta} \qquad (12.3)$$

Let us now consider one-shot deviations. When firms are in a reversionary episode and playing Cournot, there is clearly nothing to be gained from a deviation. So consider a deviation from $x^* = (x_1^*, x_2^*)$. Suppose firm 1 produces x instead of x_1^*. Let $V(x)$ be the present value of 1's payoffs given such a one-shot deviation. Let $q(x)$ be the probability that $\theta p(x + x_2^*) < \bar{p}$. Let $\pi(x)$ be firm 1's profit in one period if it produces x and 2 produces x_2^*. Hence,

$$V(x) = \pi(x) + [1 - q(x)]\delta V^* + q(x)\left(\pi^C \frac{\delta - \delta^T}{1 - \delta} + \delta^T V^*\right) \qquad (12.4)$$

The strategy based on $(x^*, T, \bar{p})$ is subgame perfect if $V(x) - V^* \leqslant 0$, for all x. Note that (12.2) and (12.4) imply

$$V(x) - V^* = [\pi(x) - \pi^*] - [q(x) - q^*]\left(V^* - \frac{\pi^C}{1 - \delta}\right)(\delta - \delta^T)$$

$$= [\pi(x) - \pi^*] - [q(x) - q^*]\frac{\pi^* - \pi^C}{1 - \delta + q^*(\delta - \delta^T)}(\delta - \delta^T)$$

by substituting (12.3).

Since $q(x) - q^* > 0$ and $\pi^* - \pi^C > 0$, it follows that, even though $\pi(x) - \pi^* > 0$, $V(x) - V^*$ may be negative. Hence, if the right-hand side of the above equation for $V(x) - V^*$ is less than or equal to zero for all x, we have a subgame perfect equilibrium strategy.[7]

Let $(x^*, T, \bar{p})$ be such that per-period profit at x^* exceeds the Cournot profit, T is finite, $\bar{p}$ is less than the Cournot price, and $s(x^*, T, \bar{p})$ is a subgame perfect equilibrium. This is an interesting equilibrium.[8] Here firms will normally play collusively and produce x^*. But occasionally price wars get triggered. Then low prices last for $T - 1$ periods and the collusive phase resumes once again.

Note, however, that the price wars are never actually triggered by deviations. Instead they occur when prices naturally drop very low. Deviations never occur in this model. This is of course obvious since the model is one of subgame perfection.

The Green–Porter model has roots in Stigler's (1964) work on collusion in oligopoly. Stigler had explicitly discussed the problem of enforcement and pointed to the problem caused by "secret price-cutting" by individual firms.

Hence, Stigler was also suggesting a model where the strategies pursued by other firms cannot be observed and can only be deduced from market indicators. Note, however, that in Stigler's discussion price is the strategic variable whereas in the Green and Porter model firms choose quantities. It is possible to construct game-theoretic models using either of these two assumptions.[9]

Porter (1983) has applied the above analysis to a case of collusion in the late nineteenth century. The study pertains to the period 1880–6, and since it precedes the enactment of the Sherman Act 1890 it is not surprising that the collusion was explicit. It involved an agreement among railroads for the pricing of freight. Porter argues that the collusive agreement entailed the use of trigger strategies where firms responded to low prices by having wars; and, moreover, that the price wars "were caused by unpredictable disturbances."

12.4   FINITELY REPEATED OLIGOPOLY

It is arguable that, even if the predictions of the models of the previous section perform well, they are not dependable, because the assumption of infinite repetition is unrealistic. In reality firms may meet repeatedly over long stretches of time but the length of interaction is nevertheless finite, and firms know this. Moreover, in a typical Cournot oligopoly there exists only one Nash equilibrium and we know that for such games finite repetitions, no matter how long, need not result in the set of equilibria converging to the set of equilibria in the infinite-repetition case. It is therefore important to analyze the possibility of collusion in finitely repeated oligopolies separately.

The main problem is well known. Consider a Cournot oligopoly with a unique Nash equilibrium. It is easy to see, and follows from theorem 9.1, that if the Cournot oligopoly is played a finite number of times then there is a unique subgame perfect equilibrium which consists of the Cournot outcome in each stage game.

Introspection, experiments with related problems such as repetition of the Prisoner's Dilemma (Rappaport and Chammah, 1965) and the experience of industries suggest that it is unrealistic to expect firms to produce the Cournot outcome year after year without striking up some implicitly collusive behavior. How can we formally explain collusion in a finite-time-horizon framework? One interesting possibility is to relax the assumption that rationality is common knowledge. This has been done in many different ways in the literature (see, for example, Radner, 1980; Kreps et al., 1982). I shall illustrate it here with Rosenthal's (1981) game, although, strictly speaking, it is not a repeated game.

Suppose there are two firms which make moves in a sequence. When it is firm *i*'s turn to move, it can choose to collude (C) or defect (D). If it defects it earns 3 units, the other firm earns zero and the game ends there. They refuse to interact again, that is. If the firm chooses to collude, both firms earn 2 units each and it is then the other firm's turn to move. And so on. Let firm 1 have the first move. Thereafter they alternately make moves. After the hundredth move the game ends no matter whether the last move was C or D. What I have just described is Rosenthal's centipede game, which is illustrated in figure 12.2 as game Γ_1. It seems intuitively clear that in such a game each firm should play C in the early moves. However, all standard game-theoretic arguments (for instance, backward induction, sequential equilibrium, rationalizability) imply that firm 1 will move D in the very first move and the game will end with the two players earning a paltry pay-off of $(3, 0)$. It can be argued (Basu, 1990a) that attempts to predict behavior in games such as this are bound to be flawed for some fundamental reasons. Without going into this here, let me follow the cue of Kreps et al.'s (1982) paper and show how, if one player has doubts about the other's rationality, collusive behavior can be explained in terms of equilibrium analysis.

To keep the analysis simple consider a three-period version of Rosenthal's game described above. Let us suppose further that firm 2 believes that 1 is a "habitual tit-for-tat player" (i.e. 1 will play C if 2 has played C in the previous move). I introduce this idea formally by supposing that there is a probability *p* that 1's pay-off differs from Rosenthal's game in a way which makes it reasonable for 1 to play tit-for-tat. In particular consider the imperfect information game Γ_2 described in figure 12.3.

The section on the left is a three-period analog of Rosenthal's game. The "game" on the right is different. Let the probability that the game on the right is chosen by nature be *p*. Suppose now that the "game" on the left (i.e. Rosenthal's game) is being played. That is, nature has chosen the node ω. The way the information sets are constructed means that 1 knows that Rosenthal's game is being played but 2 does not know this.

Γ_1:

Figure 12.2

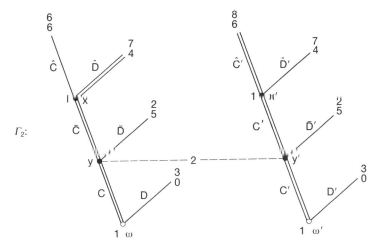

Figure 12.3

An alternative way of viewing Γ_2 is that there is a probability p that 1 is "irrational" and "irrationality" takes the form of 1 *believing* that 1 will earn 8 instead of 6 if they play collusively throughout.

If $p > 1/2$, then in Rosenthal's game (i.e. if nature picks the left panel) we shall find that under a sequential equilibrium player 1 will play C and $\hat{D}$, and 2 will play $\bar{C}$. Hence, collusion in the early moves can be explained.

To see this assume $p > 1/2$. It can now be checked that the double-line moves constitute a sequential equilibrium. For this suppose 2 believes that if the information set $\{y, y'\}$ is reached the probability of being at y' is p. Given such a belief, if 2 plays $\bar{C}$, 2 expects $p6 + (1 - p)4$, and if he plays D, he expects 5. Since $p > 1/2$, he plays $\bar{C}$. It is obvious that 1 should play as indicated by the double lines if 2 adheres to the double lines. The consistency of 2's belief with the specified strategy is obvious. Hence the double lines do depict a sequential equilibrium. Such an argument would be possible with weaker restrictions on p if the number of periods of the game were more.

It is interesting to note that to explain collusion in Rosenthal's game it is not necessary for player i to believe that j is irrational. It may be enough to assume that j believes that i believes that j is irrational. Without going into details, I describe such a case in Γ_3 (figure 12.4).

Let p_1 be the probability that nature chooses ω_1. Note that the two right-hand segments together constitute exactly the game Γ_2. Suppose, now, nature picks ω_1. So they will play Rosenthal's game. However, in playing this game, 1 does not know if 2 knows that nature has picked ω_1. That is, 1 thinks that 2 may think that 1 is "irrational" (i.e. 1 is actually playing the game at ω_3). It is left to the reader to check that for suit-

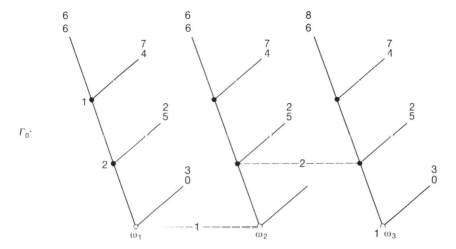

Figure 12.4

able values of p_1, p_2, and p_3, 1 will play collusively at ω_1 in a sequential equilibrium.[10]

12.5 EXTENSIONS

There is a third line of analysis which is available for oligopoly models but which seems to have been ignored in the large amount of literature on collusion. This involves giving some more structure to the Cournot *stage* game. Usually the Cournot stage game is conceived of as a one-shot inter-action. But of course, in reality, even the stage game has some temporal dimensions. Once we allow for this, collusive behavior becomes explicable without having to sacrifice the assumption of *finite* length of interaction and full rationality (in fact, common knowledge) among the firms.

Production takes time and it seems reasonable to suppose that production cannot be undertaken in complete secrecy. That is, oligopolists can observe whether other competitors are planning to produce a lot or a little; and they can respond to this by adjusting their own production plans before the product is finally made available on the market. If one is willing to take a somewhat stylized view of this one does not have to start from scratch. The models described in chapter 10 offer a good starting point. This entails think-ing of each stage as a game broken up into two substages. In the first substage, each firm produces some amount. The firms observe this and in the second substage produce more or dispose of any amount of the output produced in the first substage. Then their total production is offered on the market and price and profits are determined in the usual Cournot style. I shall refer to this game, described in detail in section 10.2, as the *extensive Cournot game*. Note that the extensive Cournot game is an extensive-form game.

If the extensive Cournot game is played a finite number of times, collusive behavior becomes possible under subgame perfection. Of course, we have to be careful in defining "subgame perfection" since the full game consists of repetitions of an extensive-form game. Hence we shall have to consider histories of not just *n* stage games but also *n* stage games and a half of the (*n* + 1)th stage game (Babu, forthcoming).

The analysis consists of constructing a discriminating trigger strategy of the kind developed in chapter 10 which supports collusive behavior in all but the last few games. Since the number of final games where collusion is not possible is fixed independently of the number of times the stage game is being repeated, the average pay-off (i.e. the pay-off per stage) can be made to approach the joint profit-maximizing solution by extending the length of play. In fact, by using more sophisticated punishment strategies – of the kind used in Benoit and Krishna (1985) – more general results, like limit folk theorems, can be established.

The oligopoly models discussed so far can be classified as having the structure of either a finite or an infinite supergame. Yet it seems reasonable to argue that in reality oligopolists interact in a way that cannot be described as either. This is because in finite repetition games it is implicitly assumed that the number of repetitions is common knowledge among players. Consider the owner of a firm who knows that he will meet his rival each year in the market place until one of them dies. The game he is playing is clearly not a game of infinite repetition. But neither is it a finite repetition game in the formal sense. Therefore the most reasonable assumption seems to be that among oligopolists in an industry it is common knowledge that the "game" will be played a finite number of times but it is not common knowledge how many times the game will be played.

One way of handling uncertain termination is to assume that for each firm *i*, and each stage *t*, there exists a real number $p_i(t)$ in the open interval (0, 1) which denotes the probability according to *i* of the game continuing after the *t*th stage. Such an assumption is easy to handle within the framework of infinitely repeated games by adjusting the discount factor by the probability of termination at each stage. Then, by using the adjusted discount factors instead of the real discount factors to compute pay-offs, we could proceed in the usual fashion.

However, it seems reasonable to argue that the finiteness and uncertainty of repetitions occur in a more troublesome way than described above. In particular, it seems that in reality, at the start of the supergame, each player *i* can write down an integer T_i such that *i* believes that the game will not last for more than T_i years. A full description of the supergame may now require writing down these termination beliefs of the players and may also require writing down i's belief about when j thinks that the game will end. There are several ways of modeling repeated games of this kind[11] and this may be a direction well worth pursuing in future.

NOTES

1 See Scherer (1980, p. 169). Scherer's chapter 6 provides a brief but useful discussion of "experience" in price-fixing from several industrialized nations.

2 According to Mason (1957, chapter 2), among the various aspects of antitrust legislation the anti-collusion provisions have been the most effective. Several successful prosecutions under the Sherman Act are discussed by Asch (1983).

3 For a recent model of this see Rotemberg and Saloner (1990). Examples of various kinds of collusion, including price matching, can be found in the Indian motor tire industry: see Mani (1985).

4 Stepping back further in time, one finds Adam Smith (1776, pp. 66–7) writing about the role of implicit "combinations" which help employers to keep wages low: "Masters are always and everywhere in a sort of tacit, but constant and uniform combination, not to raise the wages of labour above their actual rate. To violate this combination is everywhere a most unpopular action, and a sort of reproach to a master among his neighbours and equals. We seldom, indeed, hear of this combination, because it is usual, and one may say, the natural state of things which nobody hears of."

5 For extensions of this to the case where the dominant firms face a price-taking fringe, as in chapter 3, see Martin (1990).

6 For empirical work related to this model see Porter (1983), Levenstein (1989), and Town (1991). For discussion and extensions see Fudenberg and Tirole (1986) and Abreu et al. (1986).

7 If $x^* = x^C$, then $s(x^*, T, \bar{p})$ is subgame perfect for the obvious reason that the strategies entail a repeated play of the Cournot equilibrium. Hence, existence, in a trivial sense, is assured.

8 Green and Porter (1984) also characterize the $(x^*, T, \bar{p})$ which gives the optimal (from the industry's point of view) equilibrium strategies.

9 Brock and Scheinkman (1985) discuss collusion in markets where firms set prices but face capacity constraints of the kind described in chapter 4. An interesting empirical exercise based on the gasoline market in Vancouver where firms choose prices occurs in Slade (1987).

10 It is possible to continue with more elaborate constructions of "1 thinks that 2 thinks that 1 thinks . . . ." But, following Bertie Wooster's advice, I stop here. The following quote is from Sir P. G. Wodehouse's *Right Ho Jeeves*, where Gussie Fink-Nottle tells Bertie of his love for Madeline Basset. The narrator is Bertie.

"I wish I were [a male newt] . . ."
"But if you were a male newt Madeline Basset wouldn't look at you. Not

with the eye of love, I mean."

"She would if she were a female newt."

"But she isn't a female newt."

"No, but suppose she was."

"Well, if she was, you wouldn't be in love with her."

"Yes, I would if I were a male newt."

A slight throbbing about the temples told me that the discussion had reached saturation point.

11 One avenue is explored in Basu (1987c).

13

Entry Deterrence

13.1 INTRODUCTION

Firms compete not only with other existing firms, as is transparent, but also with nonexistent firms. An important part of most firms' strategy is to ensure that new firms, and therefore competitors, do not come into existence or, in other words, "enter" the industry. Several existing institutions and practices in industry would be beyond our comprehension if we did not recognize that entry deterrence is a major concern of incumbent firms. Entry deterrence strategies can take many forms, including lobbying the government, lowering prices, brand proliferation (see section 8.3) and building up excess capacity. In recent years the subject has spawned a very large literature straddling practical issues concerning industrial legislation and antitrust, on the one hand, and abstract matters such as the meaning of rationality and solution of games, on the other.

Entry deterrence is a topic in which the empirical and descriptive literature had a head start in the work of Bain (1956). Recent impetus for theoretical investigation arose out of the work of Modigliani (1958), Bhagwati (1970), Spence (1977), Selten (1978), and Dixit (1979, 1980). Whereas the Spence-Dixit work went into details of firm structure and usually took the form of an extensive-form but nonrepeated game, Selten's (1978) paper triggered off a rigorous literature where the firm and its strategy set is simple and abstract but interest arises from the fact that the firm is involved in a game which has a repeated or "near" repeated structure. We shall look into both kinds of models in this chapter.

The normative and legislative literature on entry deterrence is open ended and ambivalent, however. And as the theoretical literature has advanced, doubts about the social consequences of the use of deterrent strategies have grown. In a way this is natural since the early views were so categorical. It had seemed natural to suppose that, since entry deterrence fostered monopoly or, at any rate, high industrial concentration, it worked against the interest of the consumer. There is probably some validity in this and antitrust laws in most countries have forbidden the use of a wide range of strategies that have been thought of as inimical to the entry of potential competitors.[1] Problems arise, however, from the fact that, in order to deter entry, firms are often compelled to make large concessions to the consumer. Limit pricing is an example of this. But, if in order to block entry an incumbent has to keep prices so low as to drive (super-normal) profit down to zero,[2] it is not clear that entry deterrence is particularly harmful to the consumer. Hence, the legal position with a good bit of these uses of such strategies is not as obvious as may appear to lawyers.

Another complication that has been brought out with the rise of extensive-form reasoning in oligopoly emanates from the fact that incredible pre-entry threats are unlikely to play much part in reality. What matters to the potential entrant is his view of what the incumbent *will* do after he enters. What he does before entry is important only because of what it suggests about post-entry behavior. A recognition of this weakens some of the traditional limit pricing analysis and shifts the focus to the concept of "predatory pricing," that is, the incumbent's use of pricing so as to drive out new entrants. It also means that entry deterrence may not have clear behavioral manifestations in a pre-entry situation. In one case discussed in Basu and Singh (1990) entry deterrence requires no special effort on the part of the incumbents in the pre-entry scenario and only an optimal response in the event of entry. It is not at all clear what the law can do in such cases. This is discussed in section 13.2.

Finally, if we allow for the fact that there are typically *many* potential entrants and they do not always take simultaneous decisions regarding entry, it can be shown that legislation which makes deterrence more difficult may end up causing less entry (Bernheim, 1984). The reasoning is simple. If deterrence is made more difficult, a potential entrant would realize that after he enters he will find it difficult to block the *next* entrant. Hence it may not be worthwhile for him to enter because future competition will drive his profits down. Related arguments raise some interesting issues regarding the classical belief that profits will be driven down to zero if there is perfect competition with free entry. We investigate such themes in section 13.4.

As elsewhere in the book, no detailed suggestions on policy and legal matters are made in this chapter. That is, no attempt is made to assert what the "correct" laws concerning the use of entry deterrence strategies are. But, as should be transparent from remarks made in this section and also the theoretical models that follow, I believe that the existing laws are not the "correct" ones. This is the theme that occurs between the lines of this book in several chapters. The laws of industry were drafted in most countries at a time when industrial organization theory was in its nascency and by people who probably had no familiarity even with that. Consequently legislation usually varies from being ambiguous to counterproductive. It is a frequent complaint in India that the Monopolies and Restrictive Trade Practices Act 1969 has not been implemented. As one develops an understanding of industrial organization and looks back one cannot escape the feeling that may well be the Act's saving grace. Its intention and concern with "common detriment," as suggested in the preamble to the Act, is extremely appealing. But it is doubtful whether the specific controls and prohibitions outlined in the Act are capable of attaining its ultimate objectives. In brief, there is much more that needs to happen in the terrain which lies between law and economics.

13.2 CAPACITY, INVESTMENT AND DETERRENCE

As mentioned in section 13.1 a firm contemplating entry into an industry is not as concerned about what the incumbents are doing now as about what the incumbents would do once the firm actually enters. This means that lowering prices before entry is in itself no serious threat to the entrant. Since the incumbents know this, limit pricing in the standard textbook sense is unlikely to be a widely used instrument. The technical way to circumvent this problem is to use what has come to be known as the *Sylos postulate*, its original suggestion being associated with Sylos-Labini.

The Sylos postulate is an axiom which states that incumbents have to choose their level of production before entry occurs and they cannot alter this whether or not entry occurs. With the Sylos postulate in place, limit pricing by incumbents makes sense. But the postulate is an extremely strong assumption and much of the interest in this subject arises out of its abandonment.

Fixed costs and entry as a signal

To inject formalism consider a case with two firms: 1, the incumbent, and 2, the entrant. Let us first assume that there are no fixed costs in production. In this case, for a large class of parameters, the firms will have reaction functions as shown in figure 13.1, CM for firm 1 and AF for firm 2, where x_i is the volume supplied by firm i.

Now, suppose firm 2 has a fixed cost $K > 0$, and apart from this everything else underlying AF and CM is the same. In other words, if $c = c(x_2)$ was the cost function with no fixed costs, then now the cost function is being assumed to be $c(x_2) - K$ if $x_2 > 0$ and zero if $x_2 = 0$. This will change firm 2's reaction function from AF to AEBF, where B is somewhere to the left of F. In other words, B indicates that level of supply of firm 1

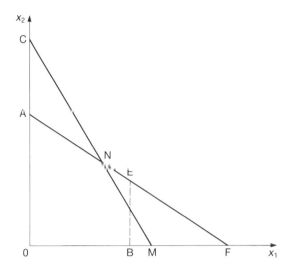

Figure 13.1

which makes firm 2 indifferent between producing (and in particular, producing EB units of output) and not producing. We shall assume that if x_1 is at B, firm 2 will set $x_2 = 0$.

To start with, assume that, if firm 2 enters, then after its entry the two firms play a Cournot game. It is easy to see what happens. If B is to the right of M, there is only one equilibrium, at N. If B is to the left of M but to the right of N, then, as observed by Dixit (1979), there are two equilibria, at N and at M. This is the case illustrated in figure 13.1.

Before moving on to the case of deterrence *à la* Spence (1977) and Dixit (1979), it is worth noting that there may be an easy refinement of the two equilibria at N and M discussed above. Suppose the actual act of entry entails a small cost d on the part of the entrant. We assume $\pi_{2N} > d > 0$, where π_{2N} is 2's profit at point N (assuming no entry cost). If firm 2 does not enter, his profit is zero. However, if he enters and the post-entry game is Cournot and we have the case illustrated in figure 13.1, then at the two possible post-entry Nash equilibria firm 2 earns, respectively, $\pi_{2N} - d$ and $-d$. If the equilibrium settles at N, 2 earns $\pi_{2N} - d$, and if the equilibrium settles at M, 2 earns $-d$, since d is the cost of entry. In this case entry is a signal of what 2 expects in the post-entry game. If 2 were heading for point M in the figure, clearly he would not enter. Hence, by the argument of forward induction discussed in chapter 9, we see that the post-entry play must lead to N. This is so no matter how small d is, as long as it is positive. It follows that using the refinement of forward induction the outcome of the game will consist of 2 entering and the equilibrium settling down at point N. Hence,

Dixit's (1979, p. 23) observation, made in the context of the case illustrated in figure 13.1, that "when there are multiple Nash equilibria, we cannot point to a deterministic outcome" would cease to be valid once we recognize the role of signals and forward induction.

The above discussion highlights two ideas. First, forward induction can be a powerful refinement in a model of entry deterrence. Indeed this has already been recognized, and a small literature is beginning to emerge (see Bagwell and Ramey, 1990; Mishra, 1991). Second, there may be a case for distinguishing between fixed costs associated with the commencement of production and fixed costs associated with entry. We shall see the role of this later.

The Sylos postulate and Bain's taxonomy

Before abandoning the Sylos postulate for good, it may be valuable briefly to sum up its role in a deterrence model. I do this via Dixit (1979) wherein it is shown that Bain's taxonomy of deterrence can be given a neat formal characterization by using the Sylos postulate. Consider a duopoly where in period 1 firm 1 has to choose x_1. In period 2 firm 2 chooses whether to enter or not and, if the former, x_2. In keeping with the Sylos postulate the move does not return to firm 1 and so after period 2 the game ends. As before, firm 2 has some fixed costs of production so that there is a critical output of firm 1, defined by B in figure 13.1. If B is to the left of M, it is easy to see that in a subgame perfect equilibrium x_1 is at M and firm 2 will not enter. This corresponds to Bain's case of entry being *blocked* and is a case of *natural* monopoly.

The case where B lies to the right of M can be further subdivided into two categories. Mark the traditional Stackelberg equilibrium point with 1 as leader as S. Through this draw 1's iso-profit curve. The point where this curve touches the horizontal axis is called Z. All this is illustrated in figure 13.2. If B lies between M and Z, in equilibrium firm 1 will produce at B and 2 will not enter. This is Bain's case of entry being *effectively impeded* and corresponds to the case of limit pricing. Here in the final equilibrium there will be only one firm but this firm will not be producing the monopoly output at M. Instead it produces more than the monopoly output and has a lower price than in a standard monopoly.

Finally, if B lies to the right of Z (figure 13.2 illustrates this case), then in equilibrium firm 1 will produce S_1 units and 2 will enter and produce S_2 units. To see this consider firm 1's options. If it decides to deter entry, the best it can do is produce at B. If it decides to produce less than B, the best it can do (knowing that firm 2 will enter and respond optimally) is to produce S_1. Hence by deterring entry the incumbent is on the iso-profit curve that goes through B. Otherwise it is on the iso-profit curve going through S.

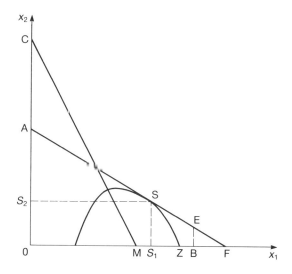

Figure 13.2

Therefore it allows entry. This is the case of entry being *ineffectively impeded* – a convoluted expression which is, I hasten to add, not mine but that of Bain.

The above classification was developed by Dixit (1979) as a precursor to a Spence (1977) type model in which investment or capacity build-up is used by an incumbent firm to deter entry. The appeal of these models is limited, however, because of their somewhat cloudy characterization of the post-entry game. In particular it would be interesting to see what would happen to the entire interaction if the Sylos postulate is abandoned and the incumbent is permitted to change its output decision in the event of entry. Dixit (1980) models this elegantly, assuming that the post-entry game is Cournot. In the next section, I briefly sketch Dixit's argument (the brevity being a response to the fact that Dixit's model has been extensively discussed elsewhere) and then extend it along some important directions.

Capacity commitment as an instrument of deterrence

Let $p = p(x)$ be the inverse demand function confronted by an incumbent firm. We call it firm 1. There is one potential entrant called firm 2.

Firm 1's marginal cost of production is v_1. To understand Dixit's notion of commitment, suppose $\bar{r}_1 (< v_1)$ is the part of v_1 spent on capacity, for instance machinery. That is, to produce 1 unit of the good, firm 1 has to spend $\bar{r}_1$ units of money on machinery and $v_1 - \bar{r}_1$ on other things. Let k_1 be the number of units of output for which the machinery input is bought in advance and let x_1 be the amount of good sold by the incumbent firm. Then its total cost of production is given by

$$\bar{c}_1(k_1, x_1) = f_1 + (v_1 - r_1)x_1 + r_1 \max\{k_1, x_1\} \tag{13.1}$$

where $r_1 = \bar{r}_1$ and f_1 is a fixed cost.

Equation (13.1) is exactly the cost function specified in Dixit (1980). By making k_1 larger, firm 1 can enhance its capacity. What this essentially does is to present an altered marginal cost function for the incumbent. This is clarified in figure 13.3. The line through v_1 is firm 1's marginal cost curve. Let $\bar{r}_1$ be given by the length v_1A. Now once firm 1 has set k_1 at the level shown in figure 13.3, this simply means that the shaded area is committed expenditure. Hence if $x_1 < \bar{k}_1$, the marginal cost of production is effectively given by the height 0A. If $x_1 > \bar{k}_1$, the marginal cost is v_1. Thus once machinery for producing $\bar{k}_1$ units of output has been produced, the incumbent's marginal cost curve is given by ABCD. Therefore by choosing k_1 before the entrant comes in, firm 1 can partly influence the equilibrium in the post-entry game.

Dixit analyses the following game:

$$\Gamma_1 = [k_1; D; x_1, x_2]$$

This is shorthand for saying that in stage 1 firm 1 chooses k_1; in stage 2 firm 2 chooses $D \in \{0, 1\}$ where $D = 0$ means that 2 stays out and $D = 1$ means that 2 enters; and in stage 3 the two firms simultaneously choose x_1 and x_2 (keeping in mind that, if $D = 0$, then x_2 *has* to be 0). Therefore a semicolon separates stages, but if there is a comma between two variables, as between x_1 and x_2, then these are chosen simultaneously. By this notation, $[k_1; D; x_1; x_2]$ is a duopoly in which the post-entry game is Stackelberg with 1 as leader.

To characterize the subgame perfect equilibrium of Dixit's model, first draw firm 1's reaction function assuming that the marginal cost of production is v_1 and then the same assuming that the marginal cost of production

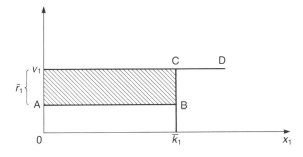

Figure 13.3

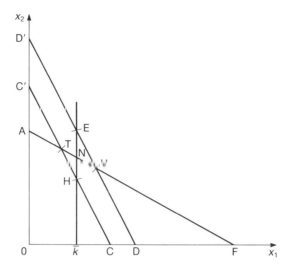

Figure 13.4

is $v_1 - \bar{r}_1$. Let these be C'C and D'D respectively in figure 13.4. If firm 1 sets k_1 at $\bar{k}$ as shown in figure 13.4, then it follows that 1's reaction function will be D'EHC, since if $x_1 < k$ it is *as if* the marginal cost is $v_1 - \bar{r}$. Now on this same figure superimpose 2's reaction function AF. It follows that if $k_1 = \bar{k}_1$ and 2 enters, then in stage 3 the Nash equilibrium occurs at N since N is the point of intersection of D'EHC and AF.

Now turn to stage 1. By choosing k_1 suitably the incumbent can ensure that the final equilibrium will occur anywhere on TV (assuming for the time being that 2 has no fixed costs). Hence the subgame perfect equilibrium is at that point in TV where 1's profit is at its highest. It is interesting to observe that this is a kind of limited Stackelberg solution. In the pure Stackelberg case 1 chooses his highest profit point on the entire line AF, whereas now 1 chooses his highest profit point on the line segment TV. It is not difficult to see that excess capacity (i.e. k_1 exceeding the final production x_1) never occurs in equilibrium.

If now we introduce the fact that the entrant incurs a fixed cost K associated with entry, then 2's reaction function will not be AF but a broken line such as in figure 13.3. Depending on where the break (B in figure 13.3) occurs, 1's decision concerning the commitment k_1 will vary. The taxonomy can be worked out as in the above section and is also carefully described in Dixit (1980, section II). Instead of dwelling on that, let me move to two modifications of the above model as developed in Basu and Singh (1990).

Note that in reality the entrant's fixed cost will have two components, one associated with the act of entry and one associated with the commencement of production. Hence, firm 2's cost function may be written as

$$\bar{c}_2(x_2, D) = \begin{cases} 0 & \text{if } D = 0 \\ K & \text{if } D = 1 \text{ and } x_2 = 0 \\ K + f_2 + v_2 x_2 & \text{if } x_2 > 0 \end{cases}$$

As before $D \in \{0, 1\}$ is the entry decision and $D = 0$ implies $x_2 = 0$. Implicit in Dixit's and Spence's work is the assumption that $f_2 = 0$ but $K > 0$. As shown in Basu and Singh (1990), interesting possibilities arise if we allow for $f_2 > 0$. Traditionally the case where the post-entry game is Stackelberg with the incumbent as leader has been ignored as uninteresting, although there is something natural about the incumbent retaining first-mover advantages.[3]

Once we distinguish between these two kinds of fixed costs some interesting cases arise in the Stackelberg model. To take up one such case, let us suppose $K > 0$ and $f_2 > 0$. It follows that once firm 2 enters its reaction function will be like AEBF where the location of B depends on the size of f_2. Note that K does not affect the reaction function, since once entry has occurred K is in the classic category of bygones.

Suppose now that the sequence of moves is as follows. First 1 chooses how much to produce, then 2 decides where to enter or not, then 1 gets a chance to revise his output and finally 2 chooses how much to produce. Consider the case illustrated in figure 13.5, where B lies between M and Z. The following is the subgame perfect equilibrium outcome. Firm 1 produces at M, and 2 does not enter. If 2 did enter (i.e. $D = 1$), then *following this* it is optimal

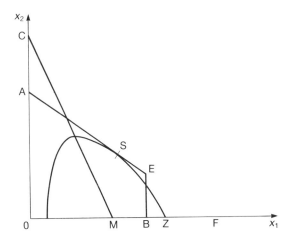

Figure 13.5

for 1 to produce at B and 2 to produce zero. Since entry is costly this implies that 2 does better by not entering.

This is an interesting possibility which stands in sharp contrast with the case of entry being effectively impeded discussed by Dixit (1979) and in the last section. There, if the configuration described in figure 13.5 arose (i.e. B between M and Z), 1 would use limit pricing, that is, it would produce at B and that would deter entry. But now entry is being deterred without the incumbent having to lift a finger. The incumbent simply ignores the entrant and produces at M (i.e. its monopoly output). But the entrant nevertheless does not come in because if it did come in the incumbent would adjust its behavior in such a way that 2 would be forced to stop production. This contrasts rather sharply with what happens under the Sylos postulate.

A second possible modification of Dixit's (1980) model pertains to his notion of commitment. In Dixit's model in equation (13.1) above r_1 is fixed at a level $\bar{r}_1$. The only form of commitment for the incumbent is to choose k_1. But the fixity of r is a strong assumption. Production does not consist of only machinery and labor. There are usually several factors. Thus if factor 1 is bought in advance for producing k_1 units of output, r_1 will be at a certain level. If factors 1 *and* 2 are bought in advance for producing k_1 units of output, r_1 will be at another (and higher) level. Moreover there is no reason why the incumbent cannot actually undertake a certain level of production and hold a part of it as stocks to threaten a potential entrant. This amounts to setting $r_1 = v_1$ and $x_1 < k_1$. One polar case is to treat r_1 as a variable in $[0, v_1]$. With this generalization and with two kinds of fixed costs we have a richer institutional framework for studying deterrence. We have seen some of its possibilities with the examples above. It is useful to give a brief formal statement of the model and the next section, based on Basu and Singh (1990), is devoted to this.

Stackelberg perfect equilibria

Let x_1 and x_2 be the sales (to be distinguished from output) of firms 1 and 2 and $p(x_1 + x_2)$ the inverse demand function. Firm 1's cost function is like (13.1) above but now r_1 is a variable lying in the domain $[0, v_1]$. Hence,

$$c_1(r_1, k_1, x_1) = f_1 + (v_1 - r_1)x_1 + r_1 \max\{k_1, x_1\} \tag{13.2}$$

Firm 2's cost function is

$$c_2(x_2) = \begin{cases} 0 & \text{if } x_2 = 0 \\ f_2 + v_2 x_2 & \text{if } x_2 > 0 \end{cases} \tag{13.3}$$

Hence f_2 is the cost of commencing production. It will in addition be assumed that when a firm is indifferent between entering and not entering it chooses the latter. This captures the idea of there being a "small" entry cost over and above the production commencement cost of f_2. I could have used the more general function $\bar{c}_2(x_2, D)$ described above but the extra complication is unnecessary since it is enough here to capture the presence of a positive entry cost by the lexicographic assumption that entry is rejected in the event of indifference between entry and nonentry.

The game that is being played here may be summed up, using the above terminology, as

$$\Gamma_2 - [r_1, k_1; D; x_1; x_2]$$

In stage 1 (r_1, k_1) is chosen; in stage 2 the entrant decides whether to enter or not; in stage 3 firm 1 chooses x_1; and in stage 4 firm 2 chooses x_2. The pay-off or profit functions of the two firms are

$$\pi_1(r_1, k_1, D, x_1, x_2) = \begin{cases} p(x_1 + x_2)x_1 - c_1(r_1, k_1, x_1) & \text{if } D = 1 \\ p(x_1)x_1 - c_1(r_1, k_1, x_1) & \text{If } D = 0 \end{cases}$$

and

$$\pi_2(x_1, x_2) = p(x_1 + x_2)x_2 - c_2(x_2)$$

It will be assumed throughout the remainder of this section that

(a) $\pi_2(x_1, x_2)$ is strictly concave in x_2,
(b) $\pi_1(r_1, k_1, 0, x_1, 0)$ is strictly concave in x_1 and
(c) $\tilde{\pi}_1(r_1, k_1, x_1) \equiv \pi_1(r_1, k_1, 1, x_1, R(x_1))$ is strictly concave in x_1, where $R(x_1)$ is firm 2's reaction function.

Assume also that

(d) firm 2 will not produce (enter) if, by producing (entering), it can at best earn the same as or less than what it earns by not producing (not entering).

The subgame perfect equilibrium of Γ_2 will be referred to as a *Stackelberg perfect equilibrium*.

For reasons of aesthetics, I shall from hereon drop the '1' subscript when speaking of the incumbent, where this is unambiguous.

Now we define

$$\phi(r) \equiv \operatorname*{argmax}_{x} p(x)x - (v - r)x$$

$$M(r, k) \equiv \operatorname*{argmax}_{x} \pi(r, k, 0, x, 0)$$

and

$$S(r, k) \equiv \operatorname*{argmax}_{x} \tilde{\pi}(r, k, x)$$

Therefore, $\phi(r)$ is the output level a monopolist would choose if his marginal cost of production was $v - r$, $M(r, k)$ is the monopoly output of the incumbent firm with a commitment of (r, k), and $S(r, k)$ is its Stackelberg equilibrium output if entry occurs and commitment is at (r, k).

In characterizing the Stackelberg perfect equilibrium of Γ_2 it is useful first to characterize the incumbent's monopoly output in the presence of precommitment.

Lemma 13.1 For all r in $[0, v]$ and all $k \geq 0$,

$$M(r, k) = \begin{cases} \phi(0) & \text{if } k < \phi(0) \\ \phi(r) & \text{if } k > \phi(r) \\ k & \text{otherwise} \end{cases}$$

PROOF Suppose $k > \phi(r)$. For any $x > 0$,

$$\pi(r, k, 0, \phi(r), 0) - \pi(r, k, 0, x, 0)$$
$$= [\theta(\phi(r), r) - rk] - [\theta(x, r) - r\max\{x, k\}]$$
$$= \theta(\phi(r), r) - \theta(x, r) + r\max\{x, k\} - rk$$
$$\geq 0$$

where $\theta(x, r) \equiv p(x)x - (v - r)x$, since $\phi(r) = \text{argmax}_x \theta(x, r)$. Hence $\phi(r) = M(r, k)$.

Suppose $k < \phi(0)$. For any $x \geq 0$,

$$\pi(r, k, 0, \phi(0), 0) - \pi(r, k, 0, x, 0)$$
$$= \theta(\phi(0), 0) - \theta(x, 0) + r[\max\{x, k\} - x]$$
$$\geq 0$$

Hence $\phi(0) = M(r, k)$.

Finally, suppose $\phi(0) \leq k \leq \phi(r)$. If $x < k$, then $\pi_x(r, k, 0, x, 0) = \theta_x(x, r)$. Since $\theta_x(\phi(r), r) = 0$ and $x < \phi(r)$, hence $\pi_x(r, k, 0, x, 0) > 0$, by assumption (b) above. If $x > k$, then $\pi_x(r, k, 0, x, 0) = \theta_x(x, 0)$. Since $\theta_x(\phi(0), 0) = 0$ and $x > \phi(0)$, hence $\pi_x(r, k, 0, x, 0) < 0$, by assumption (b). Therefore, $M(r, k) = \text{argmax}_x \pi(r, k, 0, x, 0) = k$. ∎

As an aside, note that $\phi(0) = M(0, 0)$ and that (b) implies that $\phi(r)$ is strictly increasing in r. Hence, by lemma 13.1, $M(r, k)$ is nondecreasing in k. Reasoning analogous to lemma 13.1 yields a similar characterization for $S(r, k)$. In particular, $S(r, k)$ is nondecreasing in k.

Theorem 13.1 If $(r_1^*, k_1^*, D^*, x_1^*, x_2^*)$ is a Stackelberg perfect equilibrium, then either (i) $x_1^* = M_1(r_1^*, k_1^*)$ and $D^* = 0$ (and by implication, $x_2^* = 0$) or (ii) $x_1^* = S_1(0, 0)$ and $x_2^* = R(x_1^*)$.

PROOF As a first step, it will be proved that, given any r,

$$k > k' \rightarrow S(r, k) \geqslant S(r, k') \tag{13.4}$$

Suppose $k > k'$ and let $x' \equiv S(r, k')$. Then

$$p(x' + R(x'))x' - (v - r)x' - r \max\{k', x'\}$$
$$> p(\hat{x} + R(\hat{x}))\hat{x} - (v - r)\hat{x} - r \max\{k', \hat{x}\} \qquad \text{for all } \hat{x} < x' \tag{13.5}$$

The strict inequality in (13.5) is because $S(r, k')$ is unique by virtue of assumption (c). It is easily checked that, if k' is replaced by k, inequality (13.5) remains unchanged. Thus, even with k, firm 1 finds that x' earns a greater profit than all $\hat{x} < x'$. Hence as k' is replaced by k, firm 1 will not choose a smaller output, thereby establishing (13.4).

Let Q be the set of commitments of firm 1, given which, 2 prefers to stay out of the industry:

$$Q = \{ (r, k) \mid S(r, k) \geqslant B \}$$

where $B = \min\{x_1 \mid R(x_1) = 0\}$.

First, consider the case where $(r^*, k^*) \in Q$. If $D = 1$, $x_2 = 0$ and firm 2 earns no profit. If $D = 0$, $x_1 = M(r^*, k^*)$ and 2 earns zero profit. By assumption (d), firm 2 chooses $D^* = 0$, and $x_1^* = M(r^*, k^*)$.

Next suppose $(r^*, k^*) \notin Q$. If $D = 1$, then $x_1 = S(r^*, k^*) < B$. Firm 2 earns positive profit. Hence $D^* = 1$, $x_1^* = S(r^*, k^*)$ and $x_2^* = R(x_1^*)$. Furthermore, $\tilde{\pi}$ is decreasing in k for $k > x$. This, together with (13.4) – which implies that $(r^*, k) \notin Q$ for $k < k^*$ – implies $k^* \leqslant x_1^*$. But then,

$$\tilde{\pi}(r^*, k^*, x_1^*) = p(x_1^* + R(x_1^*))x_1^* - v_1 x_1^* = \tilde{\pi}(0, 0, x_1^*)$$

Suppose now that for some x_1

$$\tilde{\pi}(0, 0, x_1) > \tilde{\pi}(0, 0, x_1^*) \tag{13.6}$$

Since $(0, 0) \notin Q$, (13.6) implies that firm 1 can do better by commiting $(0, 0)$, that is, nothing. Hence, (r^*, k^*) cannot be part of a perfect equilibrium outcome. This contradiction establishes (13.6) as false. Thus

$$x^* = \operatorname*{argmax}_{x} \tilde{\pi}(0, 0, x) \equiv S_1(0, 0) \qquad \blacksquare$$

Theorem 13.1 may be illustrated. In figure 13.6 AEBF is the reaction curve of firm 2. CC' and DD' are 1's reaction curves with $r = 0$ and $r = v$ respectively. Lemma 13.1 implies that CD is the segment within which the monopoly equilibria of firm 1 with different commitment levels must lie. S is the usual Stackelberg point. Theorem 13.1 therefore asserts that the Stackelberg perfect equilibrium must be either at S or at some point on CD.

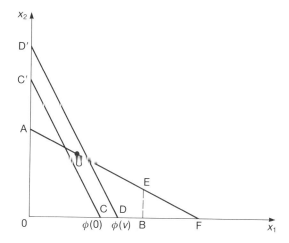

Figure 13.6

This theorem provides a partial characterization of Stackelberg perfect equilibria.

The intuitive argument behind theorem 13.1 is clear: if entry is not to be deterred, then there is no point in making a costly commitment. Hence $x = S(0, 0)$. If entry is deterred, the firm is a monopolist, with the precommitment (r, k) necessary to deter entry. Hence, $x = M(r, k)$. This theorem is interesting for what it excludes. All configurations of output and strategies, apart from those just described, are ruled out as possible candidates for equilibria. By using this theorem we can describe some special kinds of equilibria which can arise and which highlight the constrasts and similarities of our model with other work on entry barriers including the pioneering work of Bain (1956) and Sylos-Labini (1956).

One case has already been seen in the previous section where B lies to the right of the monopoly output, the incumbent produces the monopoly output and yet entry is deterred.

Another interesting corollary asserts that there exists Stackelberg perfect equilibria where the incumbent produces more than it sells (i.e. $r_1 = v_1$ and $k_1 > x_1$). In other words, not only is excess capacity used as a deterrent but actual excess stocks could be used in equilibrium to thwart newcomers. This can be demonstrated by constructing suitable examples but I shall be content to leave this as an exercise for the reader. Other outcomes of interest which can be explained by Stackelberg perfect equilibria are discussed in Basu and Singh (1990, section 4).

13.3 CHAIN STORES AND REPUTATIONS

Another line of investigation into the problem of entry deterrence was triggered by a parable of Selten (1978) called the Chain Store game. While in terms of institutional details this is sparse terrain it raises important game-theoretic questions.

A chain store 0 has branches in 20 towns, called 1, 2, . . ., 20. In each town k it faces a potential competitor or entrant k. First, in town 1 the potential competitor has to decide whether to enter or stay out. If he enters, 0 has to decide between two possible pricing strategies, predatory pricing or accommodative pricing. The accommodation strategy yields a higher profit than predatory pricing for both 0 and the competitor. The purpose of predatory pricing is essentially to drive down the profit of the entrant. It is punishment to the competitor for entering. The pay-offs are as follows. If entrant 1 does not enter, 0 gets 5 and the entrant gets zero. If he enters and 0 uses predatory pricing, both get −1, and if 0 is accommodative they both get 2. After this interaction, it is competitor 2 who has to decide whether to enter or not. Once again, exactly the same options and pay-offs are open to 0 as was the case in town 1. Interactions in towns 3, 4, . . . occur exactly in this fashion, in sequence. Hence, the "game in town k" may be described as in figure 13.7, where the lower numbers are entrant k's pay-off and the upper numbers are the incumbent's (i.e. 0's) pay-off.

It is straightforward that in a single town considered in isolation (or, equivalently, if instead of 20 towns and 20 entrants there was only one town and one entrant, with the game being described by Γ_k) the outcome will be for the entrant to enter and for 0 to play accommodation after that. But what would we predict in the 20-town case? At first it may appear that

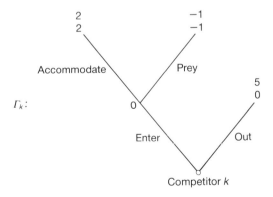

Figure 13.7

0 has an interest in playing aggressively (i.e. in using predation) in the early towns, in order to establish a threatening reputation which would deter future entrants. However, as will be obvious to today's reader, this will not happen under subgame perfection, because a simple backward-induction argument suggests that what happens in the last town must happen in all towns.

It can be seen that the Chain Store game raises similar issues to the finitely repeated Prisoner's Dilemma or Rosenthal's game (see chapters 9 and 12). Selten used it to raise some very deep questions concerning the notion of rationality and the role of psychology, which suggest that backward induction need not be the sacred cow that it is often made out to be. Although the Chain Store paradox is now well known and has generated a considerable technical literature, some of the conceptual issues raised by Selten have received less attention than they deserve. Given the nature of this book, I cannot here make amends for this. My interest is to see how the role of reputation can be modeled formally. Reputations play an important function not only in international relations and politics but in oligopoly as well. As we know from the influential work by subsets of Kreps, Milgrom, Roberts, and Wilson, to model reputation we need imperfect information. Hence the clue to understanding why firms may use predatory pricing in situations like the Chain Store game lies in the modeling of imperfect information.

Before going into that I want briefly to address some epistemological matters concerning our *knowledge* of rationality. While it is true that cooperation in the early stages of the finitely repeated Prisoner's Dilemma or predation in the early stages of the Chain Store game can be explained by abandoning the "rationality is common knowledge" assumption and for models of oligopoly this is the right route, introspection tells us that even without abandoning such an assumption we should be able to explain such behavior. After all, even if two experts in game theory play the Prisoner's Dilemma several times, it seems reasonable to expect cooperation in the early games. So such play ought not *necessarily* to be dependent on the irrationality of players or the expectation on the part of one player of another's irrationality. In Basu (1990a) I start not with any definition of rationality but with some extremely plausible axioms which ought to be satisfied by a definition of rationality. It is then shown that no solution concept satisfies these axioms. Broadly speaking the source of the problem is this.

In strategic environments where moves occur in a sequence, it is possible to come across a move m with the following property: (i) if other players treat m as irrational, it influences their future play in a way which makes the move m a rational one, and (ii) if other players treat m as rational, then it influences their future play in a way which makes move m irrational. I have no precise response as to what is the way out of this impasse; my view at this stage is not sufficiently well articulated to be inflicted on the reader, and so I shall move on leaving this as an open issue.

One route to explaining predation, as mentioned above, is to make room for imperfect information. Milgrom and Roberts (1982) and Kreps and Wilson (1982) achieve this by allowing for asymmetric information. In particular, the incumbents can be of different types but, like the consumers in chapter 5, they are faceless. So the entrant knows that there can be different types of incumbent but does not know who is who. He can try to make informed guesses about the kind of incumbent he is confronting on the basis of the history of moves made by the incumbent, and therein lies the importance of reputation.

I shall illustrate this by a simplified version of the Kreps–Wilson explanation that occurs in Ordover and Saloner (1989). Suppose we have a Chain Store type of game but with only two towns and therefore two entrants, instead of 20. The incumbent called firm 0 can now be of two types: "tough" or "weak." If he is tough he would prefer to prey even if there were only one entrant and if he is weak he would prefer to accommodate if there were only one entrant. Hence, the weak incumbent is like the incumbent in Selten's Chain Store game. Thus toughness here could be thought of as a surrogate for irrationality (a case, for instance, where the incumbent misreads his pay-off function). Let p be the probability that the incumbent is tough. Instead of using numbers for pay-offs I shall here use algebraic expressions. This information is summed up in the pay-off matrices below (though the moves occur in sequence).

		Entrant			Entrant	
		Enter	Out		Enter	Out
Incumbent	Prey	P_0^T, P	$M, 0$	Prey	P_0^W, P	$M, 0$
	Acc	A_0, A	$M, 0$	Acc	A_0, A	$M, 0$
		Probability p			Probability $1 - p$	

M is monopoly profit. P_0^T and P_0^W are the incumbent's pay-offs for preying given that he is, respectively, tough and weak. It is assumed that $P_0^T > A_0 > P_0^W$. Since P and A have no subscripts, it is clear that both entrants 1 and 2 have the same pay-offs. Of course, $P < 0 < A$. It will be assumed that if the incumbent, weak or tough, believes that by using predatory strategy on the first entrant he can ensure that the second entrant will not enter, he would prefer that to playing accommodation to both entrants:

$$P_0^W + \delta M > (1 + \delta)A_0 \tag{13.7}$$

where δ is the discount factor.

It is also assumed that if the entrant uses the prior probability p to assess the likelihood of encountering a tough incumbent, he would prefer to enter:

$$pP + (1 - p)A > 0 \qquad (13.8)$$

Relation (13.8) implies that the entrant would certainly enter in a single-town game. In illustrating the extensive form of the game, we can economize on space a little by simple considering what happens to the incumbent and the second entrant, with the first entrant's entry being taken as a *fait accompli*. This is illustrated in Γ_3 (Figure 13.8). Ignore for now the fact that some actions have double lines in Γ_3. Only some of the pay-offs are given in the figure. The top number is firm 0's pay-off and the bottom one that of firm 2.

It will be shown that this game has no pure strategy equilibrium. To prove this by negation, first suppose that 0 decides to play Prey if he is weak. Then, when it is 2's move, he has no extra information regarding the type of player 0 is. Hence 2 will enter, because of (13.8). But if preying does not deter entry, the weak incumbent is better off playing Accommodation (Acc). Next suppose that the weak incumbent plays Accommodation. Then, if 2 sees that predation has occurred he knows that the incumbent is tough. So he will not enter. But in that case the weak incumbent should go for predation since we have assumed (13.7).

There is a mixed strategy, however, which constitutes a sequential equilibrium and in which even the weak incumbent makes use of the predatory strategy. The sequential equilibrium is described by doubling up the actions

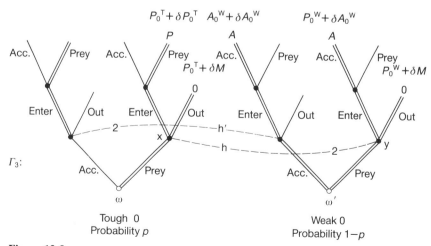

Figure 13.8

which are taken with a positive probability in Γ_3. Hence at information set ω the incumbent chooses Prey and at information set h firm 2 uses a mixed strategy.

That the pure strategies described in Γ_3 are part of a sequential equilibrium is obvious. To see how 2 mixes between the actions Enter and Out at information set h and 0 mixes Accommodate and Prey at ω', let the probability of playing Accommodate at ω' be a and the probability of playing Enter at h be e.

Firm 0 will be indifferent between Accommodate and Prey at ω' (which is essential for him to agree to mix actions) if and only if

$$A_0^W + \delta A_0^W = e(P_0^W + \delta A_0^W) + (1 - e)(P_0^W + \delta M)$$

That is,

$$e = 1 - \frac{A_0^W - P_0^W}{\delta(M - A_0^W)} \qquad (13.9)$$

Remembering that 2's belief as to whether he is at x or y must be Bayes consistent with the probability priors and firm 0's strategy, it follows that 2 will be indifferent between Enter and Out at h (and therefore willing to mix) if and only if

$$\frac{pP}{p + (1 - p)(1 - a)} + A - \frac{pA}{p + (1 - p)(1 - a)} = 0$$

or

$$a = 1 + \frac{pP}{(1 - p)A} \qquad (13.10)$$

Hence if at ω' and h actions are mixed using probabilities as specified in (13.9) and (13.10), the mixed strategies just described constitute a sequential equilibrium for Γ_3.

Recall that Γ_3 is a game *assuming* that 1 chooses Entry. To describe a sequential equilibrium in which 1 actually enters, we simply need to append the following assumption to (13.7) and (13.8):

$$[p + (1 - p)(1 - a)]P + (1 - p)aA \geqslant 0 \qquad (13.11)$$

where a is given by (13.10).

Hence given (13.7), (13.8) and (13.11) the strategies described in Γ_3 by doubling the actions and (13.9) and (13.10), *plus* the specification that firm 1 will enter, constitute a sequential equilibrium.

Hence, the weak incumbent (who is like Selten's Chain Store) uses predatory pricing with some probability. This is to create the reputation that it may be a tough firm (someone who prefers predation for its own sake). Note that in a model with more periods, a reputation for toughness is even more rewarding. Thus in such a model the probability p of the incumbent being tough or irrational can be very small but even then the weak incumbent would use predation in equilibrium.

13.4 SEQUENTIAL ENTRY

There are two important ways in which we can generalize the above models of entry deterrence. First, we could allow for there being more than one incumbent firm; and second, we could allow for more than one entrant waiting to enter the same market.

If there are several incumbent firms, the new twist to the problem arises from the fact that entry deterrence is now like a public good. All incumbents benefit from the action of any incumbent which deters entry. However, it has been shown (Gilbert and Vives, 1986) that, despite this, there will be no under-investment in entry deterrence and there may actually be some over-investment.

The other problem, where there are several entrants waiting to enter the same market, also raises interesting questions and may constitute a more general framework since it requires taking into consideration what happens when some entrants gain entry but others stay out (so that several incumbents confront several entrants). Before proceeding further note that the Chain Store model just described does not fall into this category because although there are several entrants they do not enter into the same market but are located in completely separate towns.

If we consider multiple entrants, who cannot all enter or stay out at once but make sequential decisions, we can reverse some age-old wisdom on industry. Let us begin with perfect competition. It has long been taken as axiomatic that if there is free entry and firms are identical then entry will occur up to the point where profits are driven down to zero. A first hint as to why this may be troublesome can be found by pure intuition.

Suppose you are outside an industry where firms are earning positive profit. Conventional wisdom says that

1   you will enter and
2   others will also enter until profit goes to zero.

But now, because of (2), there may be good reason for you not to bother to enter. If everyone reasons this way, positive profit can persist without causing entry.

To study this more formally let us assume that there is a countably infinite number of identical firms given by the set $N = \{1, 2, 3, \ldots\}$. All firms have to decide whether to enter or stay out. They get their choice in a sequence –

first firm 1, then 2, etc. If n firms enter the industry, then each firm in the industry earns $\pi(n)$. We assume that $\pi(n)$ decreases with n, and that there exists an integer n^* such that $\pi(n^*) = 0$. A firm that does not enter the industry earns zero.

Standard theory says that n^* firms will enter the industry and profit will be zero. But now carefully using the extensive-form structure just described it can be shown that any number m of firms entering where $m \leqslant n^*$ is a subgame perfect equilibrium strategy.

To see this suppose $m \leqslant n^*$. Consider the following strategy. If $k \leqslant m$, firm k enters. Firm $m + 1$ does not enter. If $k > m + 1$, firm k will enter if and only if fewer than n^* firms have entered so far and firm $k - 1$ has entered. These strategies are clearly subgame perfect and they support m entries.[4]

It is now interesting to observe that if a licensing law is enacted which prevents entry after k firms have entered where $k < n^*$, in equilibrium k firms will enter. Since, without such a law, we may have had less than k firms in the industry, a law guaranteeing to deter entry beyond a certain number may actually encourage entry.

Closely related to this is a proposition that emerges from Bernheim's (1984) model. Bernheim's model assumes that if there are n firms which spend nothing on deterrence, each firm's profit is given by $\pi(n)$. As before, $\pi(n)$ is strictly decreasing in n. However, now a firm can invest in what is loosely called a "deterrence technology." If these n firms invest $I_1, \ldots, I_n$ in the deterrence technology then an entrant incurs a cost of $D(\Sigma_{i=1}^{n} I_i)$ when entering. The function $D(\cdot)$ is increasing, continuous, and unbounded and $D(0) = 0$. It sums up the efficiency of investment in deterrence.

It is assumed that there exists N such that $\pi(N) \geqslant 0$ and $\pi(N + 1) < 0$. Hence, once N firms have entered, no further entry will occur.

The game is played as follows. To start with there is firm 1 in the industry – the monopolist. He has to decide how much to invest in deterrence. After that firm 2 has to decide whether to enter or not. If he decides not to enter, the game ends with 1 earning $\pi(1)$ minus what he spent on deterrence and all other firms earning zero. If he decides to enter, each of the two firms in the industry decides how much to invest in deterrence. Then it is firm 3's decision whether to enter or not. If he chooses not to enter, firm 1 earns $\pi(2) - I_{12} - I_{13}$, where I_{ij} is what firm i spends to deter firm j; firm 2 earns $\pi(2) - D(I_{12}) - I_{23}$; and all other firms earn zero. If firm 3 enters the three of them now have to decide how much to invest to deter firm 4. And so on.

Given the assumption of the existence of N as defined above it is clear that entries can only be finite. Hence even if there is an infinite number of potential firms, the equilibrium can be solved for by using the standard backward-induction argument.

It may appear at first that because of the public-good character of entry deterrence (whenever the number of incumbents exceeds one), there will be under-investment in the deterrence technology. This is not so because of the discontinuity in the benefits of investment in deterrence, because deterrence will be successful if D is critically above a certain level. This would imply that even when decisions are taken by firms individualistically, either there will be zero investment in deterrence or just enough investment to ensure that deterrence is effective.[5] In keeping with Bernheim (1984), let us assume that whenever deterrence is in the interest of the incumbent firms the second outcome will occur, that is, there will be just enough investment in the deterrence technology to deter entry. In addition, it will be assumed that all incumbents contribute equally to deterrence.

This information is summed up in figure 13.9, assuming that $N = 3$. Note that the figure resembles a game tree but is not one. To understand the figure, note that, if all three firms are being allowed to enter, it is best not to waste anything on deterrence technology. So each firm earns $\pi(3)$. This explains the pay-off at the bottommost terminal node. Now suppose that firms 1 and 2 are in the industry and they are opting to deter entry. The lowest investment I in the deterrence technology by each firm that would deter firm 3 from entering is given implicitly by

$$\pi(3) - D(2I) = 0$$

Therefore,

$$I = D^{-1}(\pi(3))/2$$

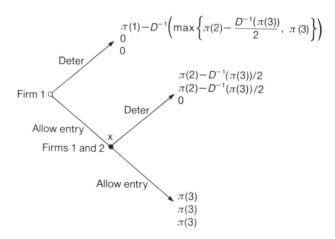

Figure 13.9

This explains the pay-offs at the terminal node where firms 1 and 2 deter further entry. It follows that at node x each of the two incumbents can be sure of earning

$$\max\{\pi(2) - D^{-1}(\pi(3))/2, \pi(3)\} \equiv V(2)$$

since they will choose to deter entry if and only if that is worthwhile.

Therefore when firm 1 is the only incumbent the minimum investment $\bar{I}$ which deters entry is given by

$$V(2) - D(\bar{I}) = 0$$

or

$$\bar{I} = D^{-1}(V(2))$$

which explains the pay-off at the top terminal node.

This model can yield different kinds of insights (see Bernheim, 1984). Here I shall simply recount what is perhaps its most important implication: that legislative bans on the use of certain kinds of deterrence strategies can be counterproductive.

Suppose $\pi(1) = 18$, $\pi(2) = 7$, $\pi(3) = 1$, and $\pi(4) < 0$. Firms have two potential deterrence technologies: holding excess capacity (as described earlier in this chapter) or choosing a unionized labor force which implies a commitment to compensation for workers who are laid off.[6] Let the effectiveness of the latter technology be given by

$$D^u(I) = I/15$$

and the effectiveness of the excess-capacity technology be given by

$$D^c(I) = I/10$$

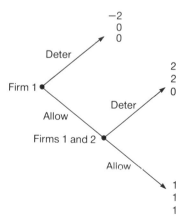

Figure 13.10

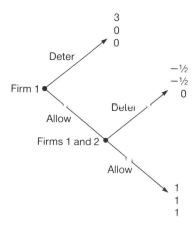

Figure 13.11

Clearly in an environment without legal restrictions the unionization technology will not be used because it is more expensive. In such a case it can be checked that in equilibrium there will be two firms in the industry, with firm 3's entry being deterred. To see this, all we have to do is compute the pay-offs in figure 13.9 using the numbers given for $\pi(1)$, $\pi(2)$, $\pi(3)$, and $D^c(I)$. This gives us figure 13.10 and the above claim is immediate.

Now consider an alternate scenario where a well-meaning government, concerned about the excessive industrial concentration, legislates against the use of excess capacity to deter entry. Firms will now be forced to use the more inefficient deterrence technology $D^u(\cdot)$. Computing the pay-offs under $D^u(\cdot)$ once again, we get figure 13.11. It follows that the monopolist will now deter entry right from the start and only one firm will be in the industry in equilibrium. Hence, deterrence having been made more expensive results in a greater industrial concentration.

NOTES

1 An important related topic, into which I shall not venture here however, is "contestability": see Baumol et al. (1982, 1986). For a discussion of the assumptions underlying contestability, see Jacquemin (1987).
2 The essential idea behind "limit pricing" is that low prices or large supplies can be used to keep profitability low and deter entry (Bain, 1956; Sylos-Labini, 1956). However, it should be clarified that limit pricing does not necessarily mean that the incumbents' profit will be driven to zero: see the numerical example in Areeda and Turner (1975, p. 705).
3 The case where the post-entry game is Stackelberg but with the entrant taking up leadership has been analyzed (Salop, 1979). While this is not the most realistic case,

its analysis is probably prompted by its being interesting. In any case, in theoretical work, without any prior empirical information, it is perhaps right to analyze all plausible cases.

4 It is true that this result hinges on the existence of an n^* which fits the above description. If such an n^* does not exist, that is, there exists an integer $\bar{n}$ such that $\pi(n) > 0$ and $\pi(n + 1) < 0$, then this result will break down. But note that in such a case even in the textbook model free entry would not drive profit to zero. Indeed the equilibrium argument just given is fragile in other ways too. For instance, the iterated deletion of dominated strategies could also be used to motivate criticism against it. However, I want to stress that the importance of my argument is contextual. It shows that the ubiquitous assumption of zero profit in competition is not as compelling as has been made out in standard texts.

5 This is akin to what happens in what Sen (1967) has described as an "Assurance Game."

6 An argument for deterrence along this line occurs in Saha and Sen (1990).

14

Managerial Incentives

14.1 INTRODUCTION

It has been known for some time that in game-theoretic environments a principal may gain extra benefit by hiring an agent and giving her incentive to maximize something other than the principal's pay-off function because this creates strategic advantages (D'Aspremont and Gerard-Varet, 1980; Katz, 1986). This new angle on principal–agent models, which was first noted by Vickers (1984) and was subsequently modeled by Fershtman (1985), Fershtman and Judd (1987), and Sklivas (1987), provides a new rationale for the existence of managers. As an agent of the owner or principal, the manager takes decisions to maximize his own welfare and in the process helps the owner to earn a larger profit than he would if he were without a manager and taking all decisions himself. Of course, if all owners hire managers, they may all be worse off as a consequence of the heightened competition. But that need not change the fact that each owner may nevertheless prefer to have a manager.

The purpose of this chapter is to introduce the reader to models of managerial incentives in oligopoly. In section 14.2, I present a simple model drawing on Fershtman and Judd (1987) and Sklivas (1987) – indeed it is not possible to draw on one of these papers and not the other – and more tangentially on Vickers (1984). What is interesting about these models is the intuitive idea underlying them. There are problems with the formalization, however. It can be shown, for instance, that small expansions of the strategy sets of the owners can lead to an enormous multiplicity of equilibria. In section 14.3 we discuss some of these problems and suggest directions for future investigations.

14.2 THE INCENTIVE EQUILIBRIUM

In keeping with the existing literature, let us consider a duopoly facing the following linear inverse demand function:

$$p = a - b(x_1 + x_2)$$

where $a, b > 0$, p is price, and x_i is firm i's output. Let the firms have linear cost functions with firm i's marginal cost being c_i, which we assume is less than a. Firm i's profit function $\pi_i(\cdot)$ and sales function $S_i(\cdot)$ are defined as follows:

$$\pi_i = \pi_i(x_1, x_2) = (a - b(x_1 + x_2) - c_i)x_i \tag{14.1}$$

$$S_i = S_i(x_1, x_2) = (a - b(x_1 + x_2))x_i \tag{14.2}$$

In other words, "sales" refers to the value of the amount sold or revenue earned.

In this model, which I shall refer to as the FJS model, the owner earns π_i minus whatever he pays to his manager. The owner can set his manager's objective function to be any weighted average of profit and sales. Hence manager i, that is, the manager of firm i, maximizes

$$R_i = R_i(\alpha_i, x_1, x_2) = \alpha_i \pi_i + (1 - \alpha_i)S_i \tag{14.3}$$

where α_i is chosen by the owner or shareholders of firm i.

Actually manager i's salary is given by

$$A_i + B_i R_i(\alpha_i, x_1, x_2)$$

where A_i and B_i are constants. Clearly maximizing this is equivalent to maximizing (14.3) given that the manager's control variable is x_i. The terms A_i and B_i are chosen by owner i to ensure that the manager's participation constraint is satisfied; that is, if $(\bar{\alpha}_i, \bar{x}_1, \bar{x}_2)$ is the equilibrium value, then A_i and B_i are chosen such that $A_i + B_i R_i(\bar{\alpha}_i, \bar{x}_1, \bar{x}_2)$ is equal to the manager's reservation income or opportunity cost Y.

In the FJS model the formal game is as follows. In period 1, the two owners simultaneously choose α_1 and α_2. In period 2, the managers choose x_1 and x_2. Manager i maximizes R_i and owner i maximizes π_i. Actually he maximizes π_i minus the cost of having a manager but, since the latter is constant, this is equivalent to maximizing π_i. The model then characterizes the subgame perfect equilibrium of the above game.

Before proceeding with the formal analysis, let us explore some basic ideas intuitively. Consider period 2 and suppose that (α_1, α_2) is fixed. Let us first derive firm 1's *managerial reaction function*, that is, a function that gives manager 1's choice of x_1, given any value of x_2. Clearly then 1's managerial reaction function is

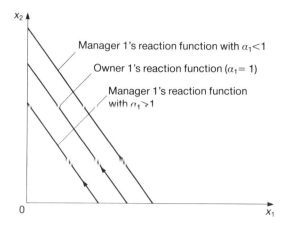

Figure 14.1

$$\phi_1(\alpha_1, x_2) = \underset{x_1}{\operatorname{argmax}} \, R_1(\alpha_1, x_1, x_2)$$

This may be derived from the first-order condition $\partial R_1 / \partial x_1 = 0$ using (14.1), (14.2), and (14.3). A little labor reveals that

$$\phi_1(\alpha_1, x_2) = \frac{a - bx_2 - \alpha_1 c_1}{2b} \tag{14.4}$$

$\phi_2(\alpha_2, x_1)$ is defined symmetrically.

If $\alpha_i = 1$, then manager i's objective is to maximize profit. Hence (14.4) with $\alpha_1 = 1$ is the usual Cournot reaction function – I shall refer to this as the *owner's reaction function* – which we have encountered repeatedly in earlier chapters. Note now that by varying α_1 the owner of firm 1 can ensure that his manager's reaction function will be any line parallel to the owner's reaction function, as shown in figure 14.1.

As a digression, suppose neither firm has a manager. Hence the relevant reaction functions of the two firms are the owner's reaction functions and the equilibrium will presumably be at point N in figure 14.2, where AB and CD are the owners' reaction functions.

Now suppose that firm 1 considers hiring a manager. What is the incentive that owner 1 would like to set for his manager? In other words, what will α_1 be, given that owner 1 knows that firm 2 is run by its owner? Clearly α_1 will be such that 1's managerial reaction function A'B' goes through point S, which is the usual Stackelberg equilibrium point with 1 as leader. The curved line through S is 1's iso-profit curve. Hence, by hiring a manager, owner 1's net profit is the profit earned by him as a Stackelberg leader minus the cost of hiring a manager. If the latter is small, then it follows that it is worth hiring a manager if no one else does. Thus the FJS model provides a

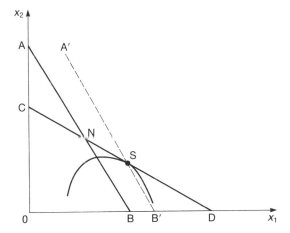

Figure 14.2

strategic-advantage-based rationale for the institution of managers.

Let us now return to the formal FJS framework and assume that both firms have managers. To characterize the subgame perfect equilibrium, we first characterize the Nash equilibrium in period 2 with (α_1, α_2) treated as fixed. Clearly, (x_1, x_2) comprise a Nash equilibrium given (α_1, α_2) if and only if

$$x_1 = \phi_1(\alpha_1, x_2)$$

and

$$x_2 = \phi_2(\alpha_2, x_1)$$

We shall denote such an x_i as $x_i(\alpha_1, \alpha_2)$. Using (14.4), we get

$$x_1(\alpha_1, \alpha_2) = \frac{a - 2\alpha_1 c_1 + \alpha_2 c_2}{3b} \tag{14.5}$$

and $x_2(\alpha_1, \alpha_2)$ is defined similarly.

Now turn to period 1. Remembering that x_i will be equal to $x_i(\alpha_1, \alpha_2)$ in period 2, we could think of profit π_i as a function of (α_1, α_2). For this we have to substitute (14.5) into (14.1). Define a function f_i as follows:

$$\pi_i = \pi_i(x_1(\alpha_1, \alpha_2), x_2(\alpha_1, \alpha_2)) \equiv f_i(\alpha_1, \alpha_2)$$

Clearly $(\bar{\alpha}_1, \bar{\alpha}_2, \bar{x}_1, \bar{x}_2)$ is a subgame perfect equilibrium if

$$\bar{\alpha}_1 = \operatorname*{argmax}_{\alpha_1} f_1(\alpha_1, \bar{\alpha}_2)$$

$$\bar{\alpha}_2 = \operatorname*{argmax}_{\alpha_2} f_2(\bar{\alpha}_1, \alpha_2)$$

$$\bar{x}_i = x_i(\bar{\alpha}_1, \bar{\alpha}_2) \qquad i = 1, 2$$

Following Fershtman and Judd, I shall refer to $(\alpha_1, \alpha_2, x_1, x_2)$ as an incentive equilibrium. It is easy to solve for these explicitly. We get

$$\bar{\alpha}_i = \frac{8c_i - a - 2c_j}{5c_i} \qquad i = 1, 2, \; j \neq i \tag{14.6}$$

$$\bar{x}_i = \frac{2a - 6c_i + 4c_j}{5b} \qquad i = 1, 2, \; j \neq i \tag{14.7}$$

It is easy to check that the total output produced in an incentive equilibrium always exceeds production under the usual Cournot equilibrium and hence price in an incentive equilibrium is lower than price in the Cournot model.

Let us check this in the symmetric case, that is, with $c_1 = c_2 = c$. Clearly, (14.6) and (14.7) reduce to $\bar{\alpha}_i = (6c - a)/5c$ and $x = (2a - 2c)/5b$. Hence,

$$\bar{\alpha}_i = 1 - \frac{a - c}{5c}$$

This is less than unity since $a > c$. Hence, figure 14.1 shows us that the managerial reaction function in equilibrium lies to the right of the owner reaction function. Hence, as illustrated in figure 14.3, the incentive equilibrium point E must lie to the northeast of the Cournot equilibrium point

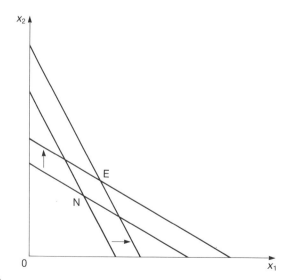

Figure 14.3

N. In the asymmetric case, however, all we can assert is that the sum of all firms' output in the FJS model exceeds that in the Cournot model.

It is possible to do a similar analysis in the case where managers set prices instead of quantities. Consider a model identical to the above in all respects except that the products of the two firms are differentiated and, in particular, are strategic substitutes and managers choose prices. In the subgame perfect equilibrium of such a model, prices actually exceed the prices that would prevail under the usual "Bertrand" equilibrium, that is, the equilibrium in which managers maximize profits (see Fershtman and Judd, 1987).

14.3 EXTENSIONS AND CRITIQUES

Many different questions can be raised about the FJS model, pertaining to its robustness with respect to generalizations of the strategy space.

Consider a simple problem. Suppose instead of restricting managerial incentives to the class defined by (14.3), we allow for any arbitrary specification in (x_1, x_2) space. In other words, let manager i's income $\bar{R}_i$ be any function

$$\bar{R}_i = \bar{R}_i(x_1, x_2) \tag{14.8}$$

This in turn implies that manager i's reaction function is given by

$$\bar{\phi}_i(x_j) = \operatorname*{argmax}_{x_i} \bar{R}_i(x_1, x_2) \tag{14.9}$$

Now consider what may be called the *generalized FJS model*. In this each owner i specifies a function $\bar{R}_i$ in period 1. Then the managers choose x_1 and x_2 in order to maximize $\bar{R}_1$ and $\bar{R}_2$. As before, the owners maximize profit. Which points in (x_1, x_2) space can be supported under subgame perfection? The answer turns out to be: all points! Clearly "incentive equilibrium" is not a very discriminating solution concept once we generalize the space of managerial incentives.

To prove this, note that instead of thinking of owner i as choosing a function $\bar{R}_i$, we could equivalently think of him as choosing a reaction function $\bar{\phi}_i$ by which his manager has to abide. Now take an arbitrary point P in figure 14.4. Draw the two iso-profit curves of the two owners which pass through P. These are shown as π_1 and π_2. Now through P draw two lines which are tangential to the two iso-profit curves. Thus I_2 is a tangent to π_1 and I_1 is a tangent to π_2. Now assume that owner i sets I_i as the reaction function of manager i. It is easy to show that we have just described a subgame perfect equilibrium which supports point P.

Given managerial reaction functions I_1 and I_2, the two firms will

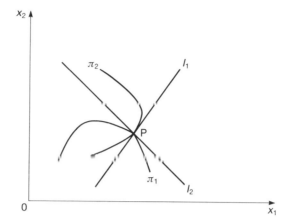

Figure 14.4

obviously produce at P. Now consider, without loss of generality, owner i's decision problem. Can he do better by changing his manager's reaction function from I_1 to something else? Clearly not, because with firm 2's manager having reaction function I_2 the only points that owner 1 could ever hope to achieve (by varying his manager's incentives) are those that lie on line I_2. Of these P is the best from owner 1's point of view since π_1 is tangential to I_2 at P. Hence, owner 1 cannot do better by changing I_1. It follows that P is subgame perfect. Since P was an arbitrary point, this proves that all outputs can occur under subgame perfection.

In the light of this problem one possible direction to pursue is to restrict $\bar{R}_i$ to somewhere between the full generality just described and the extreme restrictiveness of the FJS model. Daripa (1991) has analyzed one such class. But given the richness of the field there should be scope for much more investigation here.

Another very different form of generalization of the strategy space is to bring explicitly into the model the owner's decision whether to have a manager or not. Let us suppose that we have a three-period model in which, in period 1, firm i chooses $m_i \in (0, 1)$, where $m_i = 0$ means owner i does not hire a manager and $m_i = 1$ means owner i does hire a manager. In period 2, if $m_i = 1$ then owner i selects α_i, as before. If $m_i = 0$ the owner himself manages his company and hence there is no question of choosing α_i, although we could equivalently suppose that $\alpha_i = 1$ whenever $m_i = 0$. In period 3 firm i chooses x_i. If $m_i = 1$, then the manager takes this decision; otherwise the owner takes this decision.

Viewed in this manner it becomes clear that the FJS model is simply an analysis of the subgame of the model just described, given that in period 1 $(m_1, m_2) = (1, 1)$ has already occurred. That is, in the FJS model it is implicitly assumed that firms invariably have managers.

Once the model is generalized in this manner it turns out that under certain parametric configurations (m_1, m_2) could be $(1, 0)$ or $(0, 1)$ in equilibrium. As already demonstrated in section 14.2, if $m_i = 1$ and $m_j = 0$ then the equilibrium that occurs coincides with the usual Stackelberg equilibrium with firm i as leader. In other words, generalizing the FJS model so as to model explicitly the decision of owners to hire managers provides an endogenous explanation of Stackelberg leadership (Basu, 1991b).[1]

Finally, to end on a somewhat open note, observe that Fershtman and Judd's critique of the standard duopoly models, where no managers are used, applies at a different level to their model as well. In particular, it is easy to see that the same motivation which makes an owner want to hire a manager in the FJS model would make the manager want to hire a deputy manager. That is, manager i can typically do better if she in turn can hire a deputy manager and set him an objective function R_i' (different from R_i) $= \alpha_i' \pi_i + (1 - \alpha_i')S_i$. It follows that the deputy manager could serve his own ends better if he can hire a sub-deputy manager. And so on. Presumably the process would terminate where the opportunity cost of having managers and submanagers became, in some sense, untenable. This is a line of enquiry which could provide us with a new explanation of organizational heirarchies within firms.

Finally, and this is pure speculation, the models of Vickers (1984) and Fershtman, Judd, and Sklivas may give us some insight into the controversial subject of share tenancy. The existence of share tenancy has, for long, puzzled economists.[2] The problem stems from the fact that the share tenant has an objective function which is different from that of the landowner and it therefore appears unreasonable for a landowner to rent out his land on a rent-sharing basis. In the light of the above discussion, however, it seems that, if it is accepted that landowners operate in strategic environments, it can no longer be considered irrational for a landowner to appoint an agent and give him an objective function different from that of the landowner. Thus there seems to be some possibility here of building up a new explanation of rent-sharing arrangements, especially in the case where the control variables are strategic complements.

NOTES

1 In most conventional treatments a Stackelberg solution is either assumed or deduced directly from an exogenously imposed temporal structure. In recent times, however, several interesting contributions have appeared which explain the Stackelberg outcome endogenously (see, for example, Gal-Or, 1985; Boyer and Moreaux, 1987; Mailath, 1988).

2 See, for instance, Stiglitz (1974), Newbery (1977), Allen (1985), and Basu (1992). For an excellent survey, see Singh (1989).

15

Switching Costs

15.1 INTRODUCTION

For certain goods and services switching brands can be costly for the consumer. If a person uses a particular computer program to do her word-processing, then even if a better program becomes available she may be reluctant to switch over to the new one because of learning costs. A person who flies by the same airline for some time and accumulates frequent flyer mileage may be reluctant to switch over to a new airline.[1] A cook who works in a household for some years may have a preference for continuing with the same household because of a disinclination to adjust to the ways of a new one. These are all examples of "switching costs" or "lock-ins." Given the pervasiveness of such costs, it is not surprising that we have seen a considerable effort to model and analyze this aspect of markets (von Weizsacker, 1984; Summers, 1986; Klemperer, 1987; Farrell and Shapiro, 1989; Basu and Bell, 1991).

In the early literature on industry, the desire of firms to acquire larger market shares was widely noted and discussed but it was never really clear why firms were concerned so particularly about market shares. This new literature on switching costs sheds light on this. If those who buy from you now have an increased desire to buy your product next year, it is natural that increasing your market share now is in your interest. This allows us to understand better why firms adopt strategies like giving cheap introductory offers to new consumers of their products and why newspapers and magazines offer a lower rate to young readers.

While the pervasiveness of switching costs, whether arising naturally (the cook and the household example) or as an outcome of firm strategy (for example, frequent-flyer programs), is quite evident, what has not yet been adequately appreciated in the literature is their special relevance to backward agrarian markets.

It has been argued for a long time that markets in backward agrarian areas tend to be "fragmented" (Rudra, 1982, chapter 4; Bardhan, 1984). The fragmentation is allegedly sharpest in credit markets. When it has come to the modeling of such markets, however, the tendency has been to treat a "fragmented market" as equivalent to a market which is broken up into several isolated monopolies. But it has been felt by some (see Bhaduri, 1983) that such a characterization misses out on the institutional complexity of the phenomenon of fragmentation. This is where the new switching-cost literature can play a very useful role by providing a theoretical base for a more sophisticated modeling of market fragmentation. I comment on this in section 15.3.

15.2 A FORMAL MODEL

The basic idea of lock-ins and switching costs can be modeled in many different ways. I shall here present an adaptation of Klemperer (1987).

Consider a duopoly consisting of firms 1 and 2, in a two-period world. In period 1 each consumer buys goods from either firm 1 or firm 2. Once he has done so, he tends to get locked in or, in other words, if he decides to switch to the other firm's product in the next period he has to incur a "switching cost." The switching cost can differ from consumer to consumer – after all, not all human beings are equally adaptable – but, in this model, it is exogenously given. That is, the producers cannot raise or lower switching costs and use them as strategic variables.

It will be shown that switching costs can make markets monopolistic in the sense that in period 2 the Nash equilibrium price can be equal to the monopoly price. As one would expect, in a model with switching costs a firm has an interest in selling to a larger set of consumers in period 1 than in traditional models because this enlarges his "captive segment" of the market in the next period. It can be shown that this heightened competition in period 1 can more than offset the firm's gain from the higher prices attained in period 2.

Let us assume that there are n (*ex ante*) identical consumers with each consumer's demand function for the good in each period being given by

$$x = x(p) \tag{15.1}$$

where p is price and x is quantity. I assume that $x(\cdot)$ is continuous, differentiable, and downward sloping at any price p where $x(p) > 0$. The inverse demand function is written as

$$p = p(x) \tag{15.2}$$

I shall here only consider price-setting firms. Klemperer (1987) has discussed both price-setting and quantity-setting firms. I discuss quantity-setting behavior in a different context in the next section.

It is assumed that in period 1 each consumer buys all goods from one firm. The cost to a consumer of switching from one firm in period 1 to another in period 2 is, I shall assume, independent of the number of units of the good bought. Let $G(w)$ be the fraction of consumers whose switching costs are less than or equal to w. I shall ignore the fact that G will in reality be non-differentiable and treat $g(w) = \partial G/\partial w$ as the density function of switching costs. It is assumed that $G(0) = 0$.

Turning first to an analysis of period 2, suppose that n_i is the number of consumers who had bought from firm i in period 1. In this model we suppose that there are no uncommitted consumers in period 2. Thus

$$n_1 + n_2 = n$$

Without loss of generality, assume $p_1 \leqslant p_2$ in period 2. Based on usual consumer's surplus calculation, it is reasonable to treat the (gross) benefit to a consumer of buying from firm 1 instead of firm 2 as[2]

$$\int_{p_1}^{p_2} x(p) \, dp$$

Hence, we take the demand q_1 faced by firm 1 in period 2 to be

$$q_1(n_1, p_1, p_2) = n_1 x(p_1) + n_2 G\left(\int_{p_1}^{p_2} x(p) \, dp\right) x(p_1) \tag{15.3}$$

Note that since $n_2 = n - n_1$ there is no need to write n_2 as an argument in the function $q_1(\cdot)$. Since $p_1 \leqslant p_2$, all consumers who earlier bought from firm 1 will now buy from firm 1 and, from among those who bought from firm 2 earlier, the fraction whose switching cost is less than or equal to the benefit of buying the good at p_1 instead of p_2 will buy from firm 1. Actually those whose switching cost is equal to the benefit of buying at p_1 instead of p_2 will be indifferent between firms 1 and 2. Hence it is our *assumption* that they will buy from 1. This explains (15.3) and also (15.4), below.

$$q_2(n_1, p_1, p_2) = n_2 \left[1 - G\left(\int_{p_1}^{p_2} x(p) \, dp\right)\right] x(p_2) \tag{15.4}$$

Hence, firm i's profit in period 2 is given by

$$(p_i - c)q_i(n_1, p_1, p_2)$$

where c is the cost of producing 1 unit.

Firm i's first-order condition if $p_i \leqslant p_j$ is given by (where $j \neq i$)

$$n_i x(p_i) + n_j G\left(\int_{p_i}^{p_j} x(p)\,dp\right) x(p_i) + (p_i - c)$$

$$\times \left[n_i x'(p_i) + n_j x(p_i) \frac{\partial G}{\partial p_i} + n_j x'(p_i) G\left(\int_{p_i}^{p_j} x(p)\,dp\right) \right] = 0 \quad (15.5)$$

and firm i's first-order condition if $p_i > p_j$ is given by (where $j \neq i$)

$$n_i \left[1 - G\left(\int_{p_j}^{p_i} x(p)\,dp\right) \right] x(p_i) + (p_i - c)$$

$$\times \left\{ n_i \left[1 - G\left(\int_{p_j}^{p_i} x(p)\,dp\right) \right] x'(p_i) - n_i x(p_i) \frac{\partial G}{\partial p_i} \right\} = 0 \quad (15.6)$$

Let us check what happens in the symmetric case. Setting $p_1 = p_2 = p$, $n_1 = n_2 = n/2$ in (15.5) and recalling that $G(0) = 0$ we get

$$x(p) + (p - c)\{x'(p) - [x(p)]^2 g(0)\} = 0 \quad (15.7)$$

Note that inserting $p_1 = p_2 = p$ and $n_1 = n/2$ in (15.6) also yields (15.7). Hence (15.7) does define a stationary point. Recall that (15.7) is merely the first-order condition. The global optimum may or may not occur at the p which satisfies (15.6).

It is interesting to consider two special cases. First, suppose that $g(0) = 0$. Then (15.7) reduces to

$$x(p) + (p - c)x'(p) = 0 \quad (15.8)$$

which is the standard *monopoly solution* arising out of maximizing $(p - c)x(p)$ and assuming that $(p - c)x(p)$ is strictly concave.

Next, consider the limit as $g(0) \to \infty$. Then from (15.17) it is evident that $p \to c$, that is, the solution converges to the *competitive solution*.

An important special case of the above model is where all consumers face the same positive switching cost. Then there exists $\bar{w}$ such that $G(w)$ takes a value of zero at all $w < \bar{w}$ and $G(w) = 1$ for all $w \geqslant \bar{w}$. Clearly in this case $g(0) = 0$, and therefore (15.7) reduces to (15.8). If $\bar{w}$ is sufficiently large it will also be a global solution and therefore a Nash equilibrium for the duopolist in period 2.[3]

To visualize this special case, assume $c = 0$ and let the line AB in figure 15.1 be the aggregate demand curve for the n consumers.

Let p^m be the monopoly solution. That is, p^m satisfies (15.8). Since $n_1 = 1/2$, firm 1 faces half the demand if $p_1 = p_2$. Hence, AC is the relevant demand curve for 1 if $p_1 = p_2$. Therefore, if both firms charge the monopoly price firm 1's (and, by symmetry, also firm 2's) profit equals the

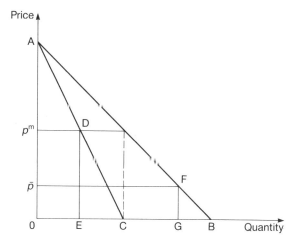

Figure 15.1

area p^mDE0. Now if firm 1 considers a "small" unilateral deviation in its price it cannot do better because it will operate on AC (in the vicinity of D) and D is the profit-maximizing point on AC. If p_1 is lowered sufficiently, however, then all the consumers who had bought from 2 previously would switch to firm 1, and hence 1's profit would rise discontinuously. Let $\bar{p}$ be such a price. In this case, if 1 sets price at $\bar{p}$, 1's profit is given by area $\bar{p}$FG0. If area $\bar{p}$FG0 $\leqslant$ area p^mDE0, then $p_1 = p_2 = p^m$ is a Nash equilibrium.

To take an example, assume that

$$x = 1 - p \tag{15.9}$$

$c = 0$, $n_1 = n/2$, and all consumers have the same switching cost w. In this case,

$$p^m = \frac{1}{2}$$

and the gross benefit to a consumer of a price fall from $1/2$ to p is $(1 - p)^2/2 - 1/8$. Therefore, if firm 1 deviates from a situation where both firms are charging p^m and begins to charge a lower price p, the largest lower price at which 2's consumers come to him is denoted by $\bar{p}(w)$ and this is given by

$$\bar{p}(w) = 1 - \left(2w + \frac{1}{4}\right)^{1/2} \tag{15.10}$$

Since a negative price is meaningless, restrict attention to $\bar{w} \in [0, \frac{3}{8}]$. Therefore if 1 deviates to $\bar{p}(w)$ 1's profit is

$$n\left[1 - \left(2w + \frac{1}{4}\right)^{1/2}\right]\left(2w + \frac{1}{4}\right)^{1/2}$$

Before deviation 1's profit was $n/8$. Hence, a deviation would not be worthwhile if and only if

$$\frac{n}{8} \geqslant n\left[1 - \left(2w + \frac{1}{4}\right)^{1/2}\right]\left(2w + \frac{1}{4}\right)^{1/2}$$

As w varies from 0 to 3/8 the right hand term goes continuously from $n/4$ to 0. Hence there must exist a critical switching cost $\bar{w}$ which makes the right-hand side equal to $n/8$. Hence, if the switching cost is greater than or equal to $\bar{w}$, the equilibrium for the duopoly is the same as the monopoly equilibrium.

Hence, switching cost may help sustain the collusive outcome as a non-cooperative equilibrium. If, after period 1 and before the start of period 2, the two firms decide to announce that each firm will give concessions to those who bought from it earlier, then, far from the consumers benefiting from this, they would actually be worse off. It is interesting to note here that it is not actually necessary for firm i to offer benefits to those who previously purchased from firm i. The concession could just as well be only for those who had bought from firm $3 - i$ or only for those belonging to a certain caste group.

The analysis gets more complicated, however, once we model period 1 as well. Let us return once again to the assumption of exogenous switching costs (from which I had deviated in the previous paragraph). A simple point which emerges without having to enter into formalism is this. Given the reasonable assumption that a rise in n_i raises firm i's equilibrium profit in period 2,[4] in period 1 each firm will play more aggressively, trying to capture a larger share of the market. In the end of course market shares need be no different. So the firms will dissipate some of their profits in period 1; and aggregate profits over the two periods may or may not be greater than in the case without switching costs.

To demonstrate this without going into details let us suppose that in period 1 firm i chooses a strategy v_i where v_i is a real number. A higher v_i suggests a more aggressive play in the sense that, if v_i increases with v_{3-i} constant, then n_i rises.

Given any n_1, suppose in period 2 that firm 1's expected profit in a Nash equilibrium is uniquely given by $\pi_2^1(n_1)$. Since n_1 depends on (v_1, v_2), that is, on how aggressively the two firms play in period 1, we could write firm 1's total profit as

$$\tilde{\pi}^1 = \pi_1^1(v_1, v_2) + \pi_2^1(n_1(v_1, v_2))$$

where π_1^1 is firm 1's profit in period 1. Let me assume that π_1^i is strictly quasi-concave in v_i. This would be a fairly standard assumption if v_i was quantity or the inverse of price.

The first-order condition is given by

$$\frac{\partial \pi_1^1}{\partial v_1} + \frac{\partial \pi_2^1}{\partial n_1} \frac{\partial n_1}{\partial v_1} = 0$$

Since $\partial \pi_2^1/\partial n_1 > 0$ and $\partial n_1/\partial v_1 > 0$, it follows that $\partial \pi_1^1/\partial v_1 < 0$. That is, firm 1 raises v_1 past what it would do if it was not concerned about period 2, since in the latter case it would set $\partial \pi_1^1/\partial v_1 = 0$. So excessive competition in period 1 results in the dissipation of some profit.[f]

15.3   SWITCHING COSTS AND RURAL CREDIT

In rural markets where the hand of law is weak, a moneylender usually agrees to lend only to people over whom he has some control in order to ensure that the borrower does not abscond with the money. Thus, for instance, the village merchant 1 may agree to lend money only to the set of people S_1 who frequent his shop, and the village landlord 2 may lend only to the set S_2 who work on his land. Suppose 1 and 2 are the only two moneylenders in a village.

There is no reason to believe that $S_1 = S_2$ which would make the credit market a standard duopoly. Neither is there reason to suppose $S_1 \cap S_2 = \phi$ which would amount to there being two isolated monopolies. As has been argued in Basu (1990c) and Basu and Bell (1991), the more realistic assumption is that neither $S_1 = S_2$ nor $S_1 \cap S_2 = \phi$; and this is what we take to be a formal description of the pervasive phenomenon of fragmented markets.

Let me be somewhat abstract and move away from the story of the merchant and the landlord and think instead of 1 and 2 as two moneylenders and S_i as the set of people outside of which i will refuse to lend money. Define $N_1 = S_1 \backslash S_2$, $N_2 = S_2 \backslash S_1$ and $N_3 = S_1 \cap S_2$. Let $\#N_i = n_i$. If n is the total number of potential borrowers in the village, then $n_1 + n_2 + n_3 = n$. We could think of N_1 and N_2 as the "captive segments" of, respectively, moneylenders 1 and 2. Let us also assume that the borrowers or customers are identical and each has a demand function given by (15.1) above.

What we now have is a model as in section 15.2 but with infinite switching cost for some customers $(N_1 \cup N_2)$ and zero switching cost for others (N_3). Hence, the assumption $G(0) = 0$ is now being dropped.

If we assume that firm (or moneylender) i cannot price-discriminate between its customers, then if the two firms' supply (q_1, q_2) to the "floating" segment N_3, firm i's profit is given by

$$\pi_i(q_1, q_2) = \begin{cases} \max_{x} [p(x/n_i) - c]x & \text{if } q_i = 0 \\[2ex] \left[p\left(\dfrac{q_1 + q_2}{n_3}\right) - c \right] \left[q_i + \dfrac{n_i}{n_3}(q_1 + q_2) \right] & \text{if } q_i > 0 \end{cases}$$

The first line is explained by the fact that firm i can always choose to withdraw from the floating segment and supply only to its captive segment N_i. If it supplies $q_i > 0$ to the floating segment, price is $p((q_1 + q_2)/n_3)$ and demand from his captive segment is $n_i(q_1 + q_2)/n_3$. This explains the second line of the profit function.

For every (n_1, n_2), a Nash equilibrium (q_1^*, q_2^*) is defined in the usual way. Let $N(n_1, n_2)$ be the set of Nash equilibria, given (n_1, n_2), and let $N(\cdot)$ be called the *Nash equilibrium correspondence*. Properties of the Nash equilibrium and comparative statics results are discussed in Basu and Bell (1991).

A more interesting problem is to recognize that before playing the above game the moneylenders may be able to choose n_1 and n_2. How does one characterize the subgame perfect equilibria of this two-period "game" and what are its properties?

To get an understanding of the problem suppose that $R_i(n_i)$ is the first-period profit of firm i when it has n_i exclusive borrowers. If we suppose that a village landlord can lend to all villagers but can stop his own employees n_i from going elsewhere for credit and that the employees work on land in period 1 and borrow in period 2, then $R_i(n_i)$ could be thought of as $X_i(n_i) - wn_i$, where $X_i(\cdot)$ is the production function and w the wage.

Now for every *selection f* from the Nash equilibrium correspondence N,[6] we can define each firm's total profit from the two periods as a function of (n_1, n_2) as follows:

$$\Omega_i(n_1, n_2, f) = R_i(n_i) + \pi_i(f(n_1, n_2))$$

A triple (n_1^*, n_2^*, f^*) is a *subgame perfect equilibrium* if, for all n',

$$\Omega_1(n_1^*, n_2^*, f^*) \geq \Omega_1(n', n_2^*, f^*)$$

and

$$\Omega_2(n_1^*, n_2^*, f^*) \geq \Omega_2(n_1^*, n', f^*)$$

The subgame perfect equilibrium of a fragmented duopoly turns out to be a very useful formal instrument for analyzing standard topics in agrarian economics such as interlinkage and disguised unemployment. These are focused on in Basu and Bell (1991). While it would be a digression to go into such themes here, note that if the two moneylenders were landlords and $R_i(n_i)$ was the net profit $x_i(n_i) - wn_i$ from land, then we would have $X_i'(n_1^*) < w$. That is, landlords would employ more laborers than in textbook models. This conforms to the idea of "disguised unemployment" and is a direct analog of Klemperer's (1987) theory of heightened competition for market shares.

More recently, Mishra (1991) has examined how moneylenders may try to deter entry of other lenders into the floating segment of the market. His analysis makes use of "fixed costs" of entry and refines subgame perfection by an interesting use of forward induction of the kind described in chapter 9.[7]

15.4 CAPTIVE SEGMENT CONDITIONS AND PROFIT

An interesting and paradoxical example discussed by Bulow et al. (1985) is worth discussing here. This involves a variant of the above model. Instead of assuming that all consumers are identical, suppose that firm 1 has a captive segment where price is fixed at 50. In the floating segment inverse demand is given by

$$p = 200 - q_1 - q_2$$

where q_i is the amount sold by firm i in this segment. If x is the amount sold by firm 1 in its captive segment then firm 1's cost of production is

$$c^1 = \frac{1}{2}(q_1 + x)^2$$

and firm 2's cost of production is[8]

$$c^2 = \frac{1}{2}(q_2)^2$$

Firm 2 has no captive segment. Hence,

$$\pi_1 = (200 - q_1 - q_2)q_1 + 50x - \frac{1}{2}(q_1 + x)^2$$

$$\pi_2 = (200 - q_1 - q_2)q_2 - \frac{1}{2}q_2^2$$

It is easy to check that in the Nash equilibrium $x = 0, q_1 = q_2 = 50$, and $\pi_1 = 3750$.

Now consider an exogenous shock in the captive segment which raises price from 50 to 55. If firm 2 does not change its decision to produce 50 units, firm 1 would certainly gain from this "beneficial" change in its captive segment. But let us see what happens in the Nash equilibrium after the shock. It is easy to calculate that $x = 8, q_1 = 47, q_2 = 51$, and $\pi_1 = 3721$. Firm 1 ends up a loser!

In order to isolate the conditions under which this paradoxical-seeming result occurs it is necessary to develop a general algebraic model.

Let me suppose that the two firms produce differentiated goods and if they produce, respectively, q_1 and q_2 units for the floating segment they earn gross revenues equal to, respectively, $R^1(q_1, q_2)$ and $R^2(q_1, q_2)$. Firm 2's cost of production is zero and it has no captive segment. Firm 1 has a captive segment where price is exogenously fixed at p. If it sells x units to the captive segment and q_1 to the floating segment, its cost of production is $c(q_1, x)$. Hence the two firms' profit functions are given by

$$\pi^1(x, q_1, q_2, p) = R^1(q_1, q_2) + px - c(q_1, x)$$

and

$$\pi^2(q_1, q_2) = R^2(q_1, q_2)$$

At the Nash equilibrium the following must be true:

$$\frac{\partial \pi^1}{\partial x} = p - c_2 = 0 \tag{15.11}$$

$$\frac{\partial \pi^1}{\partial q_1} = R_1^1 - c_1 = 0 \tag{15.12}$$

$$\frac{\partial \pi^2}{\partial q_2} = R_2^2 = 0 \tag{15.13}$$

Since we want to analyze the effect of changes in p on π^1, note that

$$\frac{d\pi^1}{dp} = \frac{\partial \pi^1}{\partial x}\frac{\partial x}{\partial p} + \frac{\partial \pi^1}{\partial q_1}\frac{\partial q_1}{\partial p} + \frac{\partial \pi^1}{\partial q_2}\frac{\partial q_2}{\partial p} + x$$

$$= \frac{\partial \pi^1}{\partial q_2}\frac{\partial q_2}{\partial p} + x$$

by (15.11) and (15.12).

If x is very large, the sign of $d\pi^1/dp$ will obviously be positive because the captive segment will then swamp all other effects. Hence, in order to consider the interesting case, assume that at the Nash equilibrium x is "small." In addition I assume that the two goods are conventional substitutes (see section 6.3), that is, $\partial \pi^1/\partial q^2 < 0$. Hence

$$\text{sign}\left(\frac{\partial \pi^1}{\partial p}\right) = \text{sign}\left(-\frac{\partial q_2}{\partial p}\right)$$

In order to find the sign of $\partial q_2/\partial p$, differentiate through (15.11)–(15.13) with respect to p:

$$1 - c_{21} \frac{\partial q_1}{\partial p} - c_{22} \frac{\partial x}{\partial p} = 0$$

$$(R_{11}^1 - c_{11}) \frac{\partial q_1}{\partial p} + R_{12}^1 \frac{\partial q_2}{\partial p} - c_{12} \frac{\partial x}{\partial p} = 0$$

$$R_{21}^2 \frac{\partial q_1}{\partial p} + R_{22}^2 \frac{\partial q_2}{\partial p} = 0$$

or, equivalently,

$$\begin{pmatrix} c_{22} & c_{21} & 0 \\ -c_{12} & R_{11}^1 - c_{11} & R_{12}^1 \\ 0 & R_{21}^2 & R_{22}^2 \end{pmatrix} \begin{pmatrix} \partial x/\partial p \\ \partial q_1/\partial p \\ \partial q_2/\partial p \end{pmatrix} = \begin{pmatrix} 1 \\ 0 \\ 0 \end{pmatrix} \tag{15.14}$$

Hence,

$$\frac{\partial q_2}{\partial p} = \frac{c_{12} R_{21}^2}{c_{22}(R_{12}^1 R_{21}^2 - \theta R_{22}^2)}$$

where

$$\theta \equiv R_{11}^1 - c_{11} + \frac{c_{12}^2}{c_{22}}$$

The determinant in (15.14) is $(R_{22}^2 \theta - R_{12}^1 R_{21}^2) c_{22}$. If this determinant is assumed to be negative, as Bulow et al. suppose is the case (and justify it as a necessary condition for local stability), then

$$c_{22}(R_{12}^1 R_{21}^2 - R_{22}^2 \theta) > 0 \tag{15.15}$$

Given this condition,

$$\text{sign}\left(\frac{d\pi^1}{dp}\right) = \text{sign}(-c_{12} R_{21}^2) \tag{15.16}$$

It follows from (15.16) that the paradoxical case would arise whenever the amount sold on the captive segment is small, (15.15) is satisfied and one and only one of the following two is valid:

(a) $c_{12} > 0$, that is, there are joint diseconomies in production;
(b) $R_{21}^2 < 0$, that is, the goods are strategic complements.

In other words, if there are joint diseconomies in production, then an improvement in firm 1's captive segment hurts firm 1 if the goods are strategic complements and benefits firm 1 if the goods are strategic substitutes.

NOTES

1 A "frequent flyer program" is an airline's offer of greater concessions to passengers who have traveled more by this airline in the past. Indeed some of the early motivation for research in this area was in response to the various frequent-flyer programs being offered by airlines.

2 To keep out controversy about the relevant measure of consumer's surplus it may be assumed that the income effect is zero for the good in question.

3 If the switching cost is small, there may not exist any pure-strategy Nash equilibrium. However, mixed-strategy equilibria would exist.

4 This is not unequivocal, though. It is possible that a rise in n_1 makes firm 2 more aggressive and firm 1 to be affected negatively.

5 In a more elaborate model we would have to decide whether to treat consumers as players who choose firms bearing in mind that they will get locked in and taking into account what will happen in the subgame in period 2 or as mechanical agents who in each period go to the firm that makes a better offer in that period.

6 This means that f is a function defined on all pairs (n_1, n_2) such that, for all $(n_1, n_2), f(n_1, n_2) \in N(n_1, n_2)$.

7 For the use of forward induction in the context of entry deterrence, see also Bagwell and Ramey (1990).

8 I assume that firms cannot set up multiple plants.

16

Government Intervention

16.1 INTRODUCTION

The state or government is one of the least understood and most influential agents in an economy. For a long time the internal structures of both the state and the firm were treated as black boxes in the economics literature. This has been changing rapidly in the case of the firm. Its internal organization has been the subject of considerable theoretical investigation and our understanding of it has advanced rapidly.[1] The same cannot be said of government. This is somewhat ironical because in many ways economics owes its origin to early human efforts at understanding the nature and role of the state. Yet, and this must in part be a reflection of the inherent intractability of the subject, economists have very little to say on it.[2] But with the recent rise in game theory and, more importantly, game-theoretic analysis, it should be possible to make a serious effort to dissect the state and construct realistic and usable models.

The plan for this last chapter is not nearly as grandiose as that, however. For instance, I shall ignore the fact that the government in reality comprises a multitude of individuals, each endowed with a will and a preference. In other words, I shall retain the view of the government as a monolithic agent, and shall consider recent developments that have occurred within the confines of such a concept of government. This route evades the really philosophical issues but even so one has to take on some issues of intricacy and interest.

In the traditional literature government intervention is modeled as a nonstrategic activity. For instance, the government uses its (alleged) knowledge of the behavior of firms and consumers and sets taxes, subsidies, etc. to maximize some objective function. There are indeed more sophisticated models in which governments are, more realistically, assumed to be not fully informed of each agent's behavior. The more recent literature on, for instance, optimal income taxation and nonlinear pricing – of the kind discussed in chapter 5 – allows for such asymmetry of information among agents. But in terms of strategic characterization it is no different from the textbook models in the sense that the government is as aloof as in the more traditional models.

The line I take here is the more modern one of treating the government as no different from other agents in strategic terms. Its objective function may be different from that of private firms, but it is just another agent in a strategic environment. This slight shift in perspective can give us some novel theorems and insights.

There are two broad classes of models which fit this description. Of these, the traditional class is one where the government tries to regulate by choosing taxes, subsidies, and quotas (e.g. Stern, 1987; Konishi et al., 1990; Anant et al., 1991). Following Stiglitz (1990), I shall call these "Pigouvian interventions." The other class is one in which the government intervenes by actually participating in production. There has been a burst of research on this in recent years (e.g. Beato and Mas-Colell, 1982; Sertel, 1988; De Fraja and Delbono, 1989; Cremer et al., 1989, 1991; Fershtman, 1990; Ireland, 1990; Sen, 1990) following the early work of Merrill and Schneider (1966). A part of this surge is probably in response to the recent debate on privatization in East Europe and the Third World; but it is also partly supply induced in the sense that game theory has made it *possible* for us to analyze the issues with rigor.

In sections 16.2 and 16.3 we discuss oligopoly equilibria where some firms are partly or wholly state owned or nationalized. Section 16.4 comments on Pigouvian government interventions, and is followed by a brief concluding section.

16.2 MIXED OLIGOPOLY

The general idea behind modeling a mixed oligopoly is simple. It is essentially an industry in which both private and nationalized firms coexist. In the simplest form we could think of an industry consisting of n private firms and m nationalized or public-sector firms. A private firm maximizes profit, whereas a public firm maximizes something else. The solution would vary depending on what objective we attribute to the public firm. In the literature cited above, it is usual to assume that a public firm maximizes social welfare, defined as the sum of consumers' surplus, producers' surplus, and profit. One can then characterize the Nash equilibrium of the industry and it is possible to do a variety of comparative statics exercises concerning some very relevant issues. For instance, if public firms are privatized what will happen to total output or to aggregate welfare? What are the consequences of nationalizing the entire industry? Exercises of this kind abound in the literature and will in general be quite easy for the reader to work out independently. Let me here simply give a flavour of the argument.

Let the industry have n private firms, $1, \ldots, n$, and m public firms, $n + 1, \ldots, n + m$, and face the following inverse demand function:

$$p = p(x_1 + \ldots + x_{n+m}) \tag{16.1}$$

This is downward sloping and differentiable and generates a marginal revenue curve which is also downward sloping.

Each firm i's total cost curve is given by

$$c_i = c(x_i) \tag{16.2}$$

where c is nondecreasing and differentiable and generates a marginal cost curve which is also nondecreasing.

For a private firm, that is, for $i \in \{i, \ldots, n\}$, the pay-off function is

$$\pi_i(x) = p\left(\sum x_r\right) x_i - c(x_i) \tag{16.3}$$

where $x = (x_1, \ldots, x_{n+m})$ and $\Sigma x_r = x_1 + \ldots + x_{n+m}$.

For a public firm, that is, for $j \in \{n + 1, \ldots, n + m\}$, the pay-off function is

$$W_j(x) = \int_{t=0}^{\Sigma x_r} p(t)\,dt - \sum_{r=1}^{n+m} c(x_r) \tag{16.4}$$

As before, x^* is an equilibrium if, for all $i \in \{1, \ldots, n\}$, $\pi_i(x^*) \geqslant \pi_i(x^*/x_i)$, for all x_i, and for all $j \in \{n + 1, \ldots, n + m\}$,

$$W_j(x^*) \geqslant W_j(x^*/x_j) \qquad \text{for all } x_j$$

Let us first consider the interesting special case where the total cost function is linear. That is, (16.2) takes the special form

$$c_i = mx_i \tag{16.5}$$

where m is the (constant) marginal cost. In this case in equilibrium the total industry output is equal to the competitive output with the private sector producing nothing and the public-sector firms sharing the market in any arbitrary fashion.

To see this, suppose x^* is an equilibrium; then $p(\Sigma x_r^*) = m$. Otherwise a public-sector firm could do better by altering its production level. It follows that for every private-sector firm i, in equilibrium, $\pi_i(x^*) = p(\Sigma x_r^*)x_i^* - mx_i^* = 0$. If $x_i^* > 0$, then by cutting back production firm i could raise price and earn a positive profit. Hence x_i^* must be zero.

If in the above case we introduce a small fixed cost in the cost function
(16.5), we would get an equilibrium where only one public firm will exist and
produce the amount produced in a competitive equilibrium, and all other
firms, private and public, will close down.

The result that the efficient outcome will always occur is a consequence
of the assumption of a linear cost function. More general results obtain if
we consider cost functions with rising marginal cost. De Fraja and Delbono
have considered the case where the cost function (16.2) takes the following
form:

$$c_i = c + \frac{k}{2} x_i^2 \tag{16.6}$$

To keep other kinds of unnecessary complications away, let us assume
that inverse demand is linear and, in particular, (16.1) takes the special
form

$$p = a - \sum_r x_r \tag{16.7}$$

Finally, we shall assume that there is only one public firm, that is, $m = 1$.
This is a harmless simplifying assumption.

As De Fraja and Delbono (1989) show, in this special case, in equilibrium,[3] the public-sector firm produces

$$x_{n+1}^* = \frac{a(k + 1)}{(1 + k)^2 + nk}$$

and

$$x_i^* = \frac{ak}{(1 + k)^2 + nk} \qquad \text{for all } i \in \{1, \ldots, n\}$$

It is easy (though somewhat labor intensive) to obtain that the aggregate
social welfare in equilibrium is given by

$$W^* = \frac{a^2(1 + k)^3 + nk(nk + 2 + 4k + k^2)a^2}{2[(1 + k)^2 + nk]^2} - (n + 1)c$$

One can raise interesting questions such as what will happen if this public
firm is privatized. To answer this one would simply have to consider the case
where firm $n + 1$ (like all other firms) maximizes *profit* and compute the
Nash equilibrium of the industry.

Expending some more labor one can check that in the Nash equilibrium
every firm $i \in \{1, \ldots, n + 1\}$ produces

$$\tilde{x}_i = \frac{a}{2 + k + n}$$

and aggregate welfare in equilibrium is

$$\tilde{W} = \frac{a^2(3 + k) + a^2(4 + k)n + a^2n^2}{2(2 + k + n)^2} - (n + 1)c$$

Using the expressions for W^* and $\tilde{W}$ it is simple to analyze the consequences of privatization. Check that as n becomes smaller W^* must exceed $\tilde{W}$. Hence, the nationalization of one firm is worthwhile if it is a very concentrated industry.

Of course, this is a rather limited exercise where cost conditions and managerial incentives are taken to be unaffected by the nationalization or privatization of firms. Depending on the context and the problem one is trying to analyze, one can build in more sophistication. I shall not in general go into such details here but take up one special case in the next section mainly by way of illustration.

16.3 PARTLY STATE-OWNED FIRMS AND ENTRY BARRIERS

In India, much more ubiquitous than nationalized firms are firms which are partly state owned. These are firms in which a sizable fraction of equity is owned by government-run financial institutions. Hence, the state exerts partial control in the decision-making of such firms. Interestingly, partly state-owned firms have been the subject of some recent investigation – Fershtman (1990). Fershtman's model is closely related to the framework developed in the previous section and therefore can be easily presented here.

Let us suppose that there are two firms, 1 and 2, confronting a linear inverse demand function like (16.7),

$$p = a - x_1 - x_2 \tag{16.8}$$

and endowed with affine cost functions consisting of a fixed cost and a constant marginal cost. Let firm 1 be the partly state-owned firm. Given the nature of the analysis that follows, firm 1's fixed cost can be ignored without loss of generality. Hence, I take its cost function to be

$$c_1 = mx_1 \tag{16.9}$$

It is easy to check that, if this firm were private, its reaction function would be

$$x_1 = \hat{x}_1(x_2) \equiv (a - x_2 - m)/2 \tag{16.10}$$

and if it were completely state owned, maximizing social welfare as defined by (16.4), its reaction function would be

$$x_1 = \tilde{x}_1(x_2) \equiv a - x_2 - m \qquad (16.11)$$

Given that firm 1 is partly state owned, its reaction function can be modeled in many different ways. One simple route – and this is the one that Fershtman (1990) takes – is to treat 1's reaction function as a weighted average of $\hat{x}_1(\cdot)$ and $\tilde{x}_1(\cdot)$. In particular, we assume that there exists $\theta \in [0, 1]$ such that 1's reaction function is

$$x_1 \equiv \phi(x_2, \theta) = \theta\tilde{x}_1(x_2) + (1 - \theta)\hat{x}_1(x_2) = (a - x_2 - m)(1 - \theta)/2 \qquad (16.12)$$

An increase in θ suggests a greater voice for the state in the firm's decision-making. The three reaction functions (16.10), (16.11), and (16.12) are illustrated in figure 16.1, where 0M is the (profit-maximizing) monopoly output and 0C is the competitive output.

The equilibria that would arise if (i) firm 2 were also partly state owned, (ii) firm 2 were private or (iii) firm 2 were fully nationalized is simple to work out and can be omitted here. What is interesting and one of the central concerns of Fershtman's paper is the relation between state-ownership and entry deterrence.

Suppose firm 1 is an incumbent and 2 is a potential entrant which happens to be a private firm. Following the discussion in chapter 13, suppose that firm 2's cost function is

$$c_2 = K + mx_2$$

and 1 can commit itself to purchasing a certain level of capacity in advance. Hence, 1's cost function is

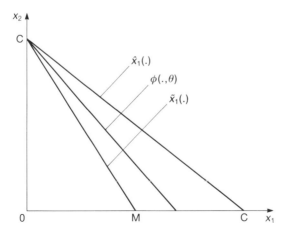

Figure 16.1

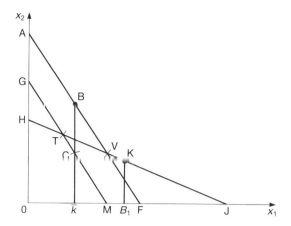

Figure 16.2

$$c_1(k_1 x_1) = \begin{cases} (m - r)x_1 + rk_1 & \text{if } x_1 < k_1 \\ mx_1 & \text{otherwise} \end{cases}$$

Following the analysis of chapter 13 we see that if $\theta = 0$ and firm 1 sets $k_1 = \bar{k}_1$, then its reaction function is given by line ABCM in figure 16.2, where AF is the reaction function assuming that marginal cost is equal to $m - r$ and GM is the reaction function assuming that marginal cost is equal to m. As in chapter 13, B_1 is the critical level of 1's output where 2 prefers not to produce. Hence 2's reaction function is HKB_1J.

As before consider a two-period model where 1 first chooses k_1 and then in period 2 the two firms simultaneously choose x_1 and x_2. We look at the subgame perfect equilibrium of this game.

As seen earlier, such an equilibrium must lie on the line segment TV or at B_1. If B_1 lies to the left of M, in equilibrium 1 produces 0M units and 2 produces zero. Hence if B_1 is less than or equal to the output at M we have a case of *natural monopoly*.

Let us extract parts of figure 16.2 and put them in figure 16.3. To start with assume $\theta = 0$ and let GM be firm 1's "full-cost" reaction function and AF be its "variable-cost" reaction function. Now if θ becomes greater than 0, that is, 1 becomes a partly state-owned firm, its two reaction functions would shift to lines $GM(\theta)$ and $AF(\theta)$ as shown in figure 16.3. Suppose the output at M is less than or equal to $B_1 < M(\theta)$. Hence, if firm 1 were purely private it would not be a natural monopoly whereas by being partly state owned it becomes a natural monopoly.

What this demonstrates is the important point that state-ownership tends to create natural monopolies and has a deterrent effect on potential entrants.

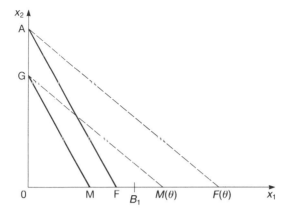

Figure 16 3

16.4 PIGOUVIAN INTERVENTIONS

In the above sections government intervened in industry through participation, that is, in the garb of a nationalized or partly nationalized firm. In reality governments intervene in many other ways. For instance, using their legislative mandate, governments impose taxes, give subsidies, and enforce quotas, licences, and limits on profit rates. There is a considerable literature modeling such interventions (see Schmalensee and Willig, 1989, vol. 2). However, usually in this literature the government has not been treated as a part of the "game." Presumably because of its special legislative powers, it has been treated as an entity controlling the industry from outside.

This is not necessary. Despite its special legislative powers, it is entirely possible to treat it as another "player" in the industrial game. Indeed it is probably more correct to model government as an entity which may have a different objective function from profit but in strategic terms is no different from other agents, especially large ones such as monopoly houses and multinationals. Hence, in analyzing the government's interaction with such agents it may be best to treat the government as just another agent in a strategic environment and analyze the properties of the Nash equilibrium and some of its refinements. This is in fact what is attempted in Anant et al. (1991).

Ours is a model of Pigouvian intervention in which a firm sets price in order to maximize profit and government chooses an *ad valorem* tax rate in order to maximize revenue collection. We characterize the Nash equilibrium of this model and then go on to consider a two-period model in which the firm chooses technology in period 1 and then they play the above game in period 2. Anant et al. (1991) demonstrate that in the subgame perfect equilibrium the firm may adopt an inefficient technology. Moreover, the inefficiency is not of the usual kind of operating at a "wrong" point on the average cost curve but the more fundamental one of being on a "wrong" average cost curve, that is, of choosing a technology which involves a higher cost of production everywhere *vis-à-vis* some other available technology.

Although in this model the inefficiency is of a special kind, inefficiencies in general are a recurring theme in models of industry with Pigouvian interventions. One important class of problems arises from the realistic assumption that the regulator (i.e. in this case the government) has less information about the firms it tries to regulate than the firms themselves have. If the government has knowledge of the types of firms that exist but cannot determine in advance which firm is of which kind then we have a classic asymmetric information model, examples of which were encountered in chapter 5.

If, on the other hand, the information problem takes a form where the government can observe certain characteristics of a firm (such as its capital stock) but not all (for instance, its production function), then the government could try to control by imposing regulations based on the observable characteristics. The model of Averch and Johnson (1962) belongs to this class.[4] In the Averch–Johnson model the regulator can observe the cash flow and capital stock of a firm or a public utility, and it tries to limit the latter's profit by placing a ceiling on the rate of return that the capital is allowed to earn. Hence, the firm can loosen the constraint by using more capital. It is not surprising, therefore, that one of the inefficiencies that occurs in this model takes the form of an excessive use of capital.

16.5   THE STATE AND THE LAW: SOME OPEN ISSUES

The modeling of government behavior is one of the weakest areas of economics. As seen above, in the existing literature the pervasive assumption concerning government (or state-owned enterprises) is that it maximizes social welfare. Now, whereas it would be entirely reasonable to assert that government *ought* to be a maximizer of social welfare, the assumption that it *is* so is tenuous, to say the least. It seems arguable that the widespread use of this assumption is a reflection of the common human tendency to confuse "ought" with "is."

There is, perhaps, also an element of vested interest in the economist's adherence to this assumption. It is the welfare-maximizing government that justifies the existence of the economic adviser. After all, advising consumers is useless because they are maximizers of utility. Telling firms what behavior on their part would be good for the economy would be equally futile because they have their own selfish objectives. If the government were also recognized to be motivated by its own interests – or, more sophisticatedly, by the collective interests of those who govern – then the economist's recommendations, at least in the form in which they are currently made, would have little value, if any.

Realism demands that it is time to take a critical look at the economist's view of government as an agent that pursues social welfare and as a receptacle of autonomous variables. The analysis of the internal structure of government is likely to be a difficult research program, however, and will probably occupy our efforts for a long time to come. But with the development of game theory, there is reason to be more hopeful now than ever before.

With a more sophisticated conceptualization of the state many simple-minded models of industrial regulation would have to be abandoned or fundamentally reconstructed. Consider, for instance, the contemporary view of the role of law in regulating an economy. According to this view what a new law does is alter the pay-off functions of agents. Suppose, for instance, that new legislation says that if a person's car emits pollutants above a certain level the person will have to pay a penalty. At first sight it appears that this *does* change the pay-off functions of the "players" in the economy. After all, if a person's car pollutes more than the cut-off level he has to pay a penalty and therefore gets a smaller total pay-off.

The reason why this seems to be so is that we treat individuals associated with government as agents who habitually enforce the law. Then if we think of the "economy game" as one which is played by only the nongovernmental individuals, of course, the game is altered: if a person chooses to pollute, in the post-law situation his pay-off is lower.

However, once we disabuse ourselves of such a piecemeal view of an economy and think of *all* citizens, including the policeman and the judge, as players, it is not clear that the law does anything to peoples' pay-off functions. After all, a law is some ink smeared on paper. If all players decide to ignore the ink, then the situation after the enactment of the law is no different from the situation before. Hence, it seems to me that a law does not change the *game*. Its influence is instead on the solution. It creates focal points, influences the beliefs of players, especially their beliefs concerning other players' beliefs, and, through these, influences the *outcome* of the game.

The shift in viewpoint that is being urged is by no means innocuous. With the rapid progress of economics over the last decades, the impediment to effectively regulating the economy is no longer solely our knowledge of how an economy works but also our failure to implement what we know. And a principal cause of the latter is our rather inadequate understanding of the state, the law, and their status in the functioning of an economy.

NOTES

1 See Stiglitz (1991) and the other papers that appear in the Symposium section of the same issue of the *Journal of Economic Perspectives*. Barring the brief incursion in chapter 14, the present book has stayed away from this emergent discipline.

2 The subject, however, has been of continuing interest to the political analyst (e.g. Miliband, 1969). Indeed my tendency to equate the state with the government would meet with severe objection from many of these writers (see Miliband, 1969, chapter 3). My defense is that how fine a distinction one draws between different concepts depends on what use one wants to put them to.

3 I confine attention to symmetric Nash equilibria, that is, those equilibria in which all private firms produce identical levels of output.

4 For discussion of the Averch–Johnson model and other related exercises, see Baron (1989).

References

Abreu, D. (1986) "External equilibria of oligopolistic supergames," *Journal of Economic Theory*, 39.

Abreu, D. (1988) "On the theory of infinitely repeated games with discounting," *Econometrica*, 56.

Abreu, D., Pearce, D. and Stacchetti, E. (1986) "Optimal cartel equilibria with imperfect monitoring," *Journal of Economic Theory*, 39.

Adams, W. J. and Yellen, J. L. (1976) "Commodity bundling and the burden of monopoly," *Quarterly Journal of Economics*, 90.

Allen, F. (1985) "On the fixed nature of share-cropping contracts," *Economic Journal*, 95.

Anant, T. C. A., Basu, K. and Mukherji, B. (1991) "A model of monopoly with strategic government intervention," mimeo, Delhi School of Economics.

Areeda, P. and Turner, D. F. (1975) "Predatory pricing and related practices under Section 2 of the Sherman Act," *Harvard Law Review*, 88.

Asch, P. (1983) *Industrial Organization and Antitrust Policy*, New York: Wiley.

Aumann, R. J. (1964) "Markets with a continuum of traders," *Econometrica*, 32.

Averch, H. and Johnson, L. (1962) "Behaviour of the firm under regulatory constraint," *American Economic Review*, 52.

Ayres, I. (1985) "Rationalizing antitrust cluster markets," *Yale Law Journal*, 95.

Bagwell, K. and Ramey, G. (1990) "Capacity, entry and forward induction," mimeo, University of California at San Diego.

Bain, J. S. (1956) *Barriers to New Competition*, Cambridge, MA: Harvard University Press.

Banerjee, A. V. and Cooper, D. J. (1991) "Do quantity setting oligopolists play the Cournot equilibrium?," mimeo, Princeton University.

Bardhan, P. K. (1980) "Interlocking factor markets and agrarian development: a review of the issues," *Oxford Economic Papers*, 32.

Bardhan, P. K. (1984) *Land, Labour and Rural Poverty*, New York: Columbia University Press, Oxford University Press.

Baron, D. (1989) "Design of regulatory mechanisms and institutions." In R. Schmalensee and R. D. Willig (eds), *Handbook of Industrial Organization*, Amsterdam: North-Holland.

Barro, R. J. (1972) "Monopoly and contrived depreciation," *Journal of Political Economy*, 80.

Basu, K. (1987a) "Monopoly, quality uncertainty and 'status' goods," *International Journal of Industrial Organization*, 5.

Basu, K. (1987b) "Disneyland monopoly, interlinkage and usurious interest rates," *Journal of Public Economics*, 34.

Basu, K. (1987c) "Modeling finitely-repeated games with uncertain termination," *Economics Letters*, 23.

Basu, K. (1988) "Why monopolists prefer to make their goods less durable," *Economica*, 55.

Basu, K. (1989a) "A theory of association, social status, prices and markets," *Oxford Economic Papers*, 41.

Basu, K. (1989b) "Technological stagnation, tenurial laws and adverse selection," *American Economic Review*, 79.

Basu, K. (1990a) "On the non-existence of a rationality definition for extensive games," *International Journal of Game Theory*, 19.

Basu, K. (1990b) "Duopoly equilibria when firms can change their decision once," *Economics Letters*, 32.

Basu, K. (1990c) *Agrarian Structure and Economic Underdevelopment*, Chichester: Harwood.

Basu, K. (1991a) "A characterization of the class of rationalizable equilibria of oligopoly games," mimeo, Princeton University.

Basu, K. (1991b) "Strategic incentives and an explanation of Stackelberg equilibria in oligopoly," mimeo, Princeton University.

Basu, K. (1992) "Limited liability and the existence of share tenancy," *Journal of Development Economics*, 38.

Basu, K. (forthcoming) "Collusion in finitely-repeated oligopolies," *International Journal of Industrial Organization*.

Basu, K. and Bell, C. (1991) "Fragmented duopoly: theory and applications to backward agriculture," *Journal of Development Economics*, 36.

Basu, K. and Singh, N. (1990) "Entry-deterrence in Stackelberg perfect equilibria," *International Economic Review*, 31.

Basu, K. and Weibull, J. (1991) "Strategy subsets closed under rational behaviour," *Economics Letters*, 36.

Baumol, W. J., Panzar, J. C. and Willig, R. D. (1982) *Contestable Markets and the Theory of Industry Structure*, New York: Harcourt, Brace, Jovanovich.

Baumol, W. J., Panzar, J. C. and Willig, R. D. (1986) "On the theory of perfectly contestable markets." In J. E. Stiglitz and G. F. Mathewson (eds), *New Developments in the Analysis of Market Structure*, London: Macmillan.

Beato, P. and Mas-Collel, A. (1984) "The marginal cost pricing as a regulation mechanism in mixed markets." In M. Marchand, P. Pestieau, and H. Tulkens (eds), *The Performance of Public Enterprises*, Amsterdam: North-Holland.

Becker, G. S. (1991) "A note on restaurant pricing and other examples of social influences on price," *Journal of Political Economy*, 99.

Bell, C. (1988) "Credit markets, contracts and interlinked transactions." In H. B. Chenery and T. N. Srinivasan (eds), *Handbook of Development Economics*, vol. 1, Amsterdam: North-Holland.

Benoit, J.-P. and Krishna, V. (1985) "Finitely repeated games," *Econometrica*, 53.
Benoit, J.-P. and Krishna, V. (1987) "Dynamic duopoly: prices and quantities," *Review of Economic Studies*, 54.
Benoit, J.-P. and Krishna, V. (1989) "Renegotiation in finitely-repeated games," mimeo, Harvard University.
Berge, C. (1963) *Topological Spaces*, Edinburgh: Oliver and Boyd.
Bernheim, B. D. (1984) "Rationalizable strategic behaviour," *Econometrica*, 52.
Bernheim, B. D. and Ray, D. (1989) "Collective dynamic consistency in repeated games," *Games and Economic Behaviour*, 1.
Bertrand, J. (1883) "Recherches sur la theorie mathematique de la richesse," *Journal des Savants*, 48 (English translation in A. Daughety (ed.) (1988) *Cournot Oligopoly: Characterization and Applications*, Cambridge: Cambridge University Press).
Bhaduri, A. (1983) *The Economic Structure of Backward Agriculture*, New York: Academic Press.
Bhagwati, J. N. (1970) "Oligopoly theory, entry prevention and growth," *Oxford Economic Papers*, 22.
Bhaskar, V. (1988) "The kinked demand curve: a game-theoretic approach," *International Journal of Industrial Organization*, 6.
Bhaskar, V. (1989) "Rational play in a quick response duopoly," *Economics Letters*, 29.
Binmore, K. (1987) "Modeling rational players," *Economics and Philosophy*, 3.
Bond, E. W. and Samuelson, L. (1984) "Durable good monopolies with rational expectations and replacement sales," *Rand Journal of Economics*, 15.
Bowman, W. S. (1957) "Tying arrangements and the leverage problem," *Yale Law Journal*, 67.
Boyer, M. and Moreaux, M. (1987) "Being a leader or a follower: reflections on the distribution of roles in duopoly," *International Journal of Industrial Organization*, 5.
Braverman, A. and Srinivasan, T. N. (1981) "Credit and sharecropping in agrarian societies," *Journal of Development Economics*, 9.
Braverman, A. and Stiglitz, J. (1982) "Sharecropping and the interlinking of agrarian markets," *American Economic Review*, 72.
Braverman, A., Guasch, L. and Salop, S. (1983) "Defects in Disneyland: quality control as a two-part tariff," *Review of Economic Studies*, 50.
Brock, W. A. and Scheinkman, J. A. (1985) "Price setting supergames with capacity constraints," *Review of Economic Studies*, 52.
Bulow, J. I. (1982) "Durable-goods monopolists," *Journal of Political Economy*, 90.
Bulow, J. I., Geanakoplos, J. D. and Klemperer, P. D. (1985) "Multimarket oligopoly: strategic substitutes and complements," *Journal of Political Economy*, 93.
Burstein, M. L. (1960) "The economics of tie-in sales," *Review of Economics and Statistics*, 42.
Carbajo, J., de Meza, D. and Seidmann, D. J. (1990) "A strategic motivation for commodity bundling," *Journal of Industrial Economics*, 38.
Caves, R. E. and Uekusa, M. (1976) *Industrial Organization in Japan*, Washington, DC: Brookings Institution.

Chamberlin, E. H. (1933) *The Theory of Monopolistic Competition*, Cambridge, MA: Harvard University Press (6th edition, 1948; 7th edition, 1956).

Chamberlin, E. H. (1957) *Towards a More General Theory of Value*, Oxford: Oxford University Press.

Chandra, N. K. (1977) "Monopoly legislation and policy in India," *Economic and Political Weekly*, 12, Special issue.

Cho, I.-K. and Kreps, D. (1987) "Signaling games and stable equilibria," *Quarterly Journal of Economics*, 102.

Coase, R. (1972) "Durability and monopoly," *Journal of Law and Economics*, 15.

Cournot, A. A. (1838) *Recherches sur les principes mathématiques de la théorie des riches*, Paris: Hachette (English translation, 1897, Macmillan).

Cremer, H., Marchand, M. and Thisse, J. F. (1989) "The public firm as an instrument for regulating an oligopolistic market," *Oxford Economic Papers*, 41.

Cremer, H., Marchand, M. and Thisse, J. F. (1991) "Mixed oligopoly with differentiated products," *International Journal of Industrial Organization*, 9.

Daripa, A. (1991) "Strategic leadership incentives and profitability in duopoly," mimeo, Princeton University.

Dasgupta, P. and Maskin, E. (1986) "The existence of equilibrium in discontinuous economic games," *Review of Economic Studies*, 53.

D'Aspremont, C. and Gerard-Varet, L. A. (1980) "Stackelberg-solvable games and pre-play communication," *Journal of Economic Theory*, 23.

D'Aspremont, C., Gabszewicz, J. J. and Thisse, J. F. (1979) "On Hotelling's stability in competition," *Econometrica*, 47.

Daughety, A. (ed.) (1988) *Cournot Oligopoly: Characterization and Applications*, Cambridge: Cambridge University Press.

De Fraja, G. and Delbono, F. (1989) "Alternative strategies of a public enterprise in oligopoly," *Oxford Economic Papers*, 41.

Dixit, A. (1979) "A model of duopoly suggesting a theory of entry barriers," *Bell Journal of Economics*, 10.

Dixit, A. (1980) "The role of investment in entry-deterrence," *Economic Journal*, 90.

Dixit, A. and Norman, V. (1978) "Advertising and welfare," *Bell Journal of Economics*, 9.

Dixit, A. and Stern, N. (1982) "Oligopoly and welfare: a unified presentation with applications to trade and development," *European Economic Review*, 19.

Dorfman, R. and Steiner, P. O. (1954) "Optimal advertising and optimal quality," *American Economic Review*, 44.

Dreze, J. (1979) "Demand estimation, risk aversion and sticky prices," *Economics Letters*, 4.

Eaton, B. C. and Lipsey, R. G. (1989) "Product differentiation." In R. Schmalensee and R. D. Willig (eds), *Handbook of Industrial Organization*, Amsterdam: North-Holland.

Edgeworth, F. Y. (1897) "La teoria pura del monopolio," *Giornale Degli Economisti*, 14 (English translation in F. Y. Edgeworth (1925) *Papers Relating to Political Economy*, vol. 1, London: Macmillan).

Edgeworth, F. Y. (1925) *Papers Relating to Political Economy*, vol. 1, London: Macmillan.

Ely, R. T. (1900) *Monopolies and Trusts*, London: Macmillan.

Encaoua, D. and Jacquemin, A. (1980) "Degree of monopoly, indices of concentration and threat of entry," *International Economic Review*, 21.

Encaoua, D., Geroski, P. and Jacquemin, A. (1986) "Strategic competition and the persistence of dominant firms." In J. E. Stiglitz and G. F. Mathewson (eds), *New Developments in the Analysis of Market Structure*, London: Macmillan.

Farm, A. and Weibull, J. (1987) "Perfectly flexible pricing in a homogeneous market," *Scandinavian Journal of Economics*, 89.

Farrell, J. and Maskin, E. (1989) "Renegotiation in repeated games," *Games and Economic Behaviour*, 1.

Farrell, J. and Shapiro, C. (1989) "Optimal contracts with lock-in," *American Economic Review*, 79.

Fellner, W. (1950) "Collusion and its limits under oligopoly," *American Economic Review, Papers and Proceedings*, 40.

Fershtman, C. (1985) "Internal organizations and managerial incentives as strategic variables in competitive environment," *International Journal of Industrial Organization*, 3.

Fershtman, C. (1990) "The interdependence between ownership status and market structure: the case of privatization," *Economica*, 57.

Fershtman, C. and Judd, K. L. (1987) "Equilibrium incentives in oligopoly," *American Economic Review*, 77.

Frank, R. H. (1985) *Choosing the Right Pond: Human Behaviour and the Quest for Status*, Oxford: Oxford University Press.

Friedman, J. (1971) "A non-cooperative equilibrium for supergames," *Review of Economic Studies*, 28.

Friedman, J. (1977) *Oligopoly and the Theory of Games*, Amsterdam: North-Holland.

Friedman, J. (1985) "Cooperative equilibria in infinite horizon noncooperative supergames," *Journal of Economic Theory*, 35.

Friedman, J. (1986) *Game Theory with Applications to Economics*, Oxford: Oxford University Press.

Friedman, M. (1976) *Price Theory*, Hawthorne, NY: Aldine.

Fudenberg, D. and Tirole, J. (1986) *Dynamic Models of Oligopoly*, Chichester: Harwood.

Gabszewicz, J. J. and Thisse, J. F. (1979) "Price competition, quality and income disparities," *Journal of Economic Theory*, 20.

Gabszewicz, J. J. and Thisse, J. F. (1980) "Entry (and exit) in a differentiated industry," *Journal of Economic Theory*, 22.

Gabszewicz, J. J., Thisse, J. F., Fujita, M. and Schweizer, U. (1986) *Location Theory*, Chichester: Harwood.

Gal-Or, E. (1985) "First mover and second mover advantages," *International Economic Review*, 26.

Gilbert, R. and Vives, X. (1986) "Entry-deterrence and the freerider problem," *Review of Economic Studies*, 53.

Glicksberg, I. (1952) "A further generalization of the Kakutani fixed point theorem with application to Nash equilibrium points," *Proceedings of the American Mathematical Society*, 3.

Green, E. J. and Porter, R. H. (1984) "Non-cooperative collusion under imperfect price information," *Econometrica*, 52.

Grossman, S. (1981) "Nash equilibrium and the industrial organization of markets with large fixed costs," *Econometrica*, 49.

Guenault, P. H. and Jackson, J. M. (1960) *Control of Monopoly in the United Kingdom*, Harlow: Longman.

Gul, F., Sonnenschein, H. and Wilson, R. (1986) "Foundations of dynamic monopoly and the Coase conjecture," *Journal of Economic Theory*, 39.

Hadley, E. M. (1970) *Antitrust in Japan*, Princeton, NJ: Princeton University Press.

Hall, R. and Hitch, C. (1939) "Price theory and business behaviour," *Oxford Economic Papers*, 2.

Hart, O. (1985) "Monopolistic competition in the spirit of Chamberlin: a general model," *Review of Economic Studies*, 51.

Hicks, J. (1956) *A Revision of Demand Theory*, Oxford: Clarendon Press.

Hildenbrand, W. and Kirman, A. P. (1976) *Introduction to Equilibrium Analysis*, Amsterdam: North-Holland.

Hiroshi, I. (1986) "Antitrust and industrial policy in Japan: competition and cooperation." In G. R. Saxonhouse and K. Yamamura (eds), *Law and Trade Issues of the Japanese Economy*, Seattle, WA: University of Washington Press.

Holmstrom, B. R. and Tirole, J. (1989) "The theory of the firm," In R. Schmalensee and R. D. Willig (eds), *Handbook of Industrial Organization*, Amsterdam: North-Holland.

Hotelling, H. (1929) "Stability in competition," *Economic Journal*, 39.

Ireland, N. J. (1990) "The mix of social and private provision of goods and services," *Journal of Public Economics*, 43.

Jacquemin, A. (1987) *The New Industrial Organization*, Boston, MA: MIT Press.

Jencks, C., Perman, L. and Rainwater, L. (1988) "What is a good job? A new measure of labour market success," *American Journal of Sociology*, 93.

Judd, K. L. (1990) "Cournot versus Bertrand: a dynamic resolution," mimeo, Hoover Institution.

Kaldor, N. (1934) "Mrs Robinson's 'Economics of imperfect competition'," *Economica*, 1.

Kamien, J. I. and Schwartz, N. L. (1974) "Product durability under monopoly and competition," *Econometrica*, 42.

Katz, M. L. (1986) "Game-playing agents and unobservable contracts," mimeo, Princeton University.

Klemperer, P. D. (1987) "Markets with consumer switching costs," *Quarterly Journal of Economics*, 102.

Klemperer, P. D. and Meyer, M. A. (1989) "Supply functions equilibria in oligopoly under uncertainty," *Econometrica*, 57.

Kohlberg, E. (1989) "Refinement of Nash equilibrium: the main ideas," mimeo, Harvard University.

Kohlberg, E. and Mertens, J. F. (1986) "On the strategic stability of equilibria," *Econometrica*, 54.

Konishi, H., Okuno-Fujiwara, M. and Suzumura, K. (1990) "Oligopolistic competition and economic welfare: a general equilibrium analysis of entry regulation and tax subsidy schemes," *Journal of Public Economics*, 42.

Kreps, D. (1990) *A Course in Microeconomic Theory*, Princeton, NJ: Princeton University Press.

Kreps, D. and Scheinkman, J. (1983) "Quantity precommitment and Bertrand competition yield Cournot outcomes," *Bell Journal of Economics*, 14.

Kreps, D. and Wilson, R. (1982) "Sequential equilibria," *Econometrica*, 50.

Kreps, D., Milgrom, P., Roberts, J. and Wilson, R. (1982) "Rational cooperation in the finitely-repeated Prisoner's Dilemma," *Journal of Economic Theory*, 27.

Kuhn, H. W. (1950) "Extensive games," *Proceedings of the National Academy of Sciences*, 36.

Kuhn, H. W. (1953) "Extensive games and the problem of information." In H. W. Kuhn and A. Tucker (eds), *Contributions to the Theory of Games*, vol. 2, Princeton, NJ: Princeton University Press.

Leibenstein, H. (1950) "Bandwagon, snob and Veblen effects in the theory of consumers' demand," *Quarterly Journal of Economics*, 64.

Leibowitz, S. J. (1982) "Durability, market structure and new–used goods models," *American Economic review*, 72.

Levenstein, M. C. (1989) "The feasibility and stability of collusion: a study of the pre-World War I bromine industry," mimeo, Yale University.

Levhari, D. and Srinivasan, T. N. (1969) "Durability of consumption goods: competition versus monopoly," *American Economic Review*, 59.

Levitan, R. and Shubik, M. (1972) "Price duopoly and capacity constraints," *International Economic Review*, 13.

Luce, R. D. and Raiffa, H. (1957) *Games and Decisions*, New York: Wiley.

Mailath, G. (1988) "Endogenous sequencing of firm decisions," mimeo, University of Pennsylvania.

Mani, S. (1985) "Concentration and market power in the Indian automotive tyre industry," *Economic and Political Weekly*, 20, Review of Management.

Marschak, T. and Selten, R. (1978) "Restabilizing responses, inertia supergames and oligopolistic equilibria," Quarterly Journal of Economics, 92.

Marshall, A. (1890) *Principles of Economics*, London: Macmillan (8th edition, 1920).

Marshall, A. and Marshall, M. P. (1879) *The Economics of Industry*, London: Macmillan.

Martin, S. (1990) "Fringe size and cartel stability," mimeo, European University Institute.

Maskin, E. and Tirole, J. (1988) "A theory of dynamic oligopoly, II: Price competition, kinked demand curves and Edgeworth cycles," *Econometrica*, 56.

Mason, E. (1957) *Economic Concentration and the Monopoly Problem*, Cambridge, MA: Harvard University Press.

Merrill, W. C. and Schneider, N. (1966) "Government firms in oligopoly industries: a short-run analysis," *Quarterly Journal of Economics*, 8.

Milgrom, P. and Roberts, J. (1982) "Predation, reputation and entry deterrence," *Journal of Economic Theory*, 27.

Miliband, R. (1969) *The State in Capitalist Society*, New York: Basic Books.

Mirrlees, J. A. (1971) "An exploration in the theory of optimum income taxation," *Review of Economic Studies*, 38.

Mirrlees, J. A. (1975) "Pure theory of underdeveloped economies." In L. G. Reynolds (ed.), *Agriculture in Development Theory*, New Haven, CT: Yale University Press.

Mishra, A. (1991) "Clientelization and fragmentation in backward agrarian markets," mimeo, Delhi School of Economics.

Modigliani, F. (1958) "New developments on the oligopoly front," *Journal of Political Economy*, 66.

Moulin, H. (1979) "Dominance solvable voting schemes," *Econometrica*, 47.

Mussa, M. and Rosen, S. (1978) "Monopoly and product quality," *Journal of Economic Theory*, 18.

Myerson, R. (1978) "Refinements of the Nash equilibrium concept," *International Journal of Game Theory*, 7.

Nash, J. (1951) "Non-cooperative games," *Annals of Mathematics*, 54.

Newbery, D. M. G. (1977) "Risk-sharing, sharecropping and uncertain labour markets," *Review of Economic Studies*, 44.

O'Brien, D. P. (1990) "Marshall's industrial analysis," *Scottish Journal of Political Economy*, 37.

Oi, W. (1971) "A Disneyland dilemma: two-part tariffs for a Mickey Mouse monopoly," *Quarterly Journal of Economics*, 85.

Ordover, J. and Saloner, G. (1989) "Predation, monopolization and antitrust." In R. Schmalensee and R. D. Willig (eds), *Handbook of Industrial Organization*, Amsterdam: North-Holland.

Osborne, M. and Pitchik, C. (1986) "Prince competition in a capacity constrained duopoly,"*Journal of Economic Theory*, 38.

Pal, D. (1991) "Cournot duopoly with two production periods and cost differentials," *Journal of Economic Theory*, 55.

Paranjape, H. K. (1986) "The Monopolies and Restrictive Trade Practices Act: a review 1970–83." In S. Guhan and M. Shroff (eds), *Essays in Economic Progress and Welfare*, Oxford: Oxford University Press.

Parks, R. W. (1974) "The demand and supply of durable goods and durability," *American Economic Review*, 64.

Pearce, D. (1984) "Rationalizable strategic behaviour and the problem of perfection," *Econometrica*, 52.

Peck, M. J. (1961) *Competition in the Aluminium Industry 1945–1958*, Cambridge, MA: Harvard University Press.

Phlips, L. (1983) *The Economics of Price Discrimination*, Cambridge: Cambridge University Press.

Pigou, A. C. (ed.) (1925) *Memorials of Alfred Marshall*, London: Macmillan.

Porter, R. H. (1983) "A study of cartel stability: the Joint Executive Committee 1880–1886," *Bell Journal of Economics*, 14.

Radner, R. (1980) "Collusive behaviour in non-cooperative epsilon-equilibria of oligopolies with long but finite lives," *Journal of Economic Theory*, 22.

Rappaport, A. and Chammah, A. M. (1965) *Prisoner's Dilemma*, Ann Arbor, MI: University of Michigan Press.

Reny, P. (1986) Rationality, common knowledge and the theory of games, Ph.D. dissertation, Princeton University.

Robinson, J. (1933) *The Economics of Imperfect Competition*, London: Macmillan.

Rosen, J. B. (1965) "Existence and uniqueness of equilibrium points for concave *n*-person games," *Econometrica*, 33.

Rosenthal, R. W. (1981) "Games of perfect information, predatory pricing and the chain store paradox," *Journal of Economic Theory*, 25.

Rotemberg, J. and Saloner, G. (1990) "Collusive price leadership," *Journal of Industrial Economics*, 39.

Rowley, C. K. (1966) *British Monopolies Commission*, London: Allen and Unwin.

Rudra, A. (1982) *Indian Agricultural Economics: Myths and Realities*, Delhi: Allied Publishers.

Saha, B. and Sen, Anindya (1990) "Layoff compensation as commitment for entry-deterrence," Discussion Paper 39, Indira Gandhi Institute of Development Research, Bombay.

Saloner, G. (1987) "Cournot duopoly with two production periods," *Journal of Economic Theory*, 42.

Salop, S. C. (1979) "Monopolistic competition with outside goods," *Bell Journal of Economics*, 10.

Scherer, F. M. (1980) *Industrial Market Structure and Economic Performance*, 2nd edn, Boston, MA: Houghton Mifflin.

Schmalensee, R. (1978) "Entry deterrence in the ready-to-eat breakfast cereal industry," *Bell Journal of Economics*, 25.

Schmalensee, R. (1982) "Commodity bundling by single-product monopolies," *Journal of Law and Economics*, 25.

Schmalensee, R. (1986) "Advertising and market structure." In J. E. Stiglitz and G. F. Mathewson (eds), *New Developments in the Analysis of Market Structure*, London: Macmillan.

Schmalensee, R. and Willig, R. D. (eds) (1989) *Handbook of Industrial Organization*, vols 1 and 2, Amsterdam: North-Holland.

Schydlowsky, D. M. and Siamwalla, A. (1966) "Monopoly under general equilibrium: a geometric exercise," *Quarterly Journal of Economics*, 80.

Scitovsky, T. (1944) "Some consequences of the habit of judging quality by price." In T. Scitovsky, *Papers on Welfare and Growth*, Stanford, CA: Stanford University Press.

Selten, R. (1975) "Reexamination of the perfectness concept for equilibrium points in extensive games," *International Journal of Game Theory*, 4.

Selten, R. (1978) "The chain-store paradox," *Theory and Decision*, 9.

Sen, Amartya (1967) "Isolation, assurance and the social rate of discount," *Quarterly Journal of Economics*, 81.

Sen, Anindya (1990) "Privatisation and social welfare," Discussion Paper 32, Indira Gandhi Institute of Development Reseach, Bombay.

Sertel, M. R. (1988) "Regulation by participation," *Journal of Economics*, 48.

Shaked, A. and Sutton, J. (1983) "Natural oligopolies," *Econometrica*, 51.

Shapiro, C. and Stiglitz, J. E. (1984) "Equilibrium unemployment as a worker discipline device," *American Economic Review*, 74.

Sheshinski, E. (1976) "Price, quality and quantity regulation in monopoly situations," *Economica*, 63.

Shubik, M. (1980) *Market Structure and Behaviour*, Cambridge, MA: Harvard University Press.

Sieper, E. and Swan, P. L. (1973) "Monopoly and competition in the market for durable goods," *Review of Economic Studies*, 40.

Singh, N. (1989) "Theories of share cropping." In P. Bardhan (ed.), *The Economic Theory of Agrarian Institutions*, Oxford: Clarendon Press.

Singh, N. and Vives, X. (1984) "Price and quantity competition in a differentiated duopoly," *Rand Journal of Economics*, 15.

Sklivas, S. D. (1987) "The strategic choice of managerial incentives," *Rand Journal of Economics*, 18.

Slade, M. E. (1987) "Interfirm rivalry in a repeated game: An empirical test of tacit collusion," *Journal of Industrial Economics*, 35.

Smith, A. (1776) *The Wealth of Nations*, Strahan and Cadell (page references are to the Random House edition, 1937).

Spence, A. M. (1974) *Market Signalling*, Cambridge, MA: Harvard University Press.

Spence, A. M. (1977) "Entry, capacity, investment and oligopolistic pricing," *Bell Journal of Economics*, 8.

Spence, A. M. (1980) "Multi-product quantity-dependent prices and profitability constraints," *Review of Economic Studies*, 47.

von Stackelberg, H. (1934) *Marktform and Gleichgewicht*, Berlin: Julius Springer.

Stahl, D. (1986) "Revocable pricing can yield collusive outcomes," *Economics Letters*, 22.

Stern, N. (1987) "The effects of taxation, price control and government contracts in oligopoly and monopolistic competition," *Journal of Public Economics*, 32.

Stigler, G. J. (1947) "The kinky oligopoly demand curve and rigid prices," *Journal of Political Economy*, 55.

Stigler, G. J. (1950) "Monopoly and oligopoly by merger," *American Economic Review*, 23.

Stigler, G. J. (1957) "Perfect competition, historically contemplated," *Journal of Political Economy*, 65.

Stigler, G. J. (1963) "United States v. Loew's Inc.: a note on block-booking," *The Supreme Court Review*, 1.

Stigler, G. J. (1964) "A theory of oligopoly," *Journal of Political Economy*, 72.

Stiglitz, J. E. (1974) "Incentives and risk-sharing in sharecropping," *Review of Economic Studies*, 41.

Stiglitz, J. E. (1990) "The roles of the state and the private sector: roundtable discussion." In *Proceedings of the World Bank Annual Conference on Development Economics*, Washington, DC: World Bank.

Stiglitz, J. E. (1991) "Symposium on organizations and economics," *Journal of Economic Perspectives*, 5.

Stiglitz, J. E. and Mathewson, G. F. (eds) (1986) *New Developments in the Analysis of Market Structure*, London: Macmillan.

Stokey, N. L. (1981) "Rational expectations and durable goods pricing," *Bell Journal of Economics*, 12.

Summers, L. H. (1986) "On frequent-flyer programs and other loyalty-inducing economic arrangements," *Economics Letters*, 21.

Sweezy, P. (1939) "Demand under conditions of oligopoly," *Journal of Political Economy*, 47.

Sylos-Labini, P. (1956) *Oligopolio e progresso tecnico* (English translation,

Cambridge, MA: Harvard University Press, 1962).

Tirole, J. (1988) *The Theory of Industrial Organization*, Boston, MA: MIT Press.

Town, R. J. (1991) "Price wars and demand fluctuations: a re-examination of the Joint Executive Committee," EAG Discussion Paper, US Department of Justice, Washington, DC.

Van Damme, E. E. C. (1987) *Stability and Perfection of Nash Equilibirium*, Berlin: Springer.

Varian, H. R. (1983) *Microeconomic Analysis*, New York: Norton.

Varian, H. R. (1989) "Price discrimination." In R. Schmalensee and R. D. Willig (eds), *Handbook of Industrial Organization*, Amsterdam: North-Holland.

Vickers, J. (1984) "Delegation and the theory of the firm," *Economic Journal*, 95, Supplement.

Waterson, M. (1984) *Economic Theory of the Industry*, Cambridge: Cambridge University Press.

von Weizsacker, C. C. (1984) "The costs of substitution," *Econometrica*, 52.

Whinston, M. D. (1990) "Tying, foreclosure and exclusion," *American Economic Review*, 80.

Whitaker, J. K. (1975) *The Early Economic Writings of Alfred Marshall, 1867–1890*, London: Macmillan.

Williams, P. L. (1978) *The Emergence of the Theory of the Firm: From Adam Smith to Alfred Marshall*, London: Macmillan.

Subject Index

advertising, 99–104
and welfare, 100–3
agent monotonicity, 52, 60
agrarian markets, 196–7, 202–4
airline pricing, 196, 207
aluminum industry, 141
Antimonopoly Law, 47
antitrust legislation, 28, 48–9, 51, 60, 62–3, 97, 150–1, 161, 163–5
arborescence, 106
Assurance Game, 187
asymmetric information, 51, 179, 209, 216
automobiles, 66–7, 71

backward-induction argument, 6, 115, 123, 157, 178, 183–4
barriers to entry, see entry deterrence
Battle of the Sexes, 5–8, 10, 108, 122–3
Bayes consistency, 110–11
behavior strategy, defined, 105
Bertrand equilibrium, 1, 40–2, 64, 68, 70, 136, 147–8, 193
and the nonexistence problem, 41–2, 136
best response function, 9
best response property, 19, 20
block booking, 65
brand differentiation, 42, 67–8, 93, 96–9, 163
breakfast cereal industry, 96
Britain, 49, 65, 96

Calcutta Club, 72
cartels (see also collusion), 2, 149–50

centipede game, 157
Chain Store paradox, 177–8
Clayton Act, 48, 65
cluster markets, 45, 60, 64
Coase conjecture, 80, 88
collusion (see also combination), 2, 13, 96, 98, 114–15, 129, 130, 132, 137, 149–61, 201
combination, 2, 161
commodity bundling, see tie-ins
common knowledge, 18, 19, 121–2, 159–60, 178
competition, 2, 28–30, 49, 80, 86–8, 94, 104, 182–3, 199
competitive equilibrium, see competition
competitive fringe, 33–5, 161
complements 60, 69–71
strategic, 69–71, 206
consumers' surplus, 28, 35, 45, 48, 51, 207, 209
contestability, 186
contract curve, 50, 132
Cournot equilibrium, 31, 33–7, 39, 41–3, 70, 124–7, 135–7, 147–8, 153–6, 161, 192
credible threats, 107–9

disguised unemployment, 203–4
Disneyland monopoly (see also two-part tariffs), 47–8, 50
doctors, 67, 71
dominant firms, 33–5, 161
dominant-strategy equilibrium, 12, 13
Dorfman–Steiner condition, 100
duopoly, see oligopoly

durable goods, 60-1, 66, 80-92
  and competition, 86-8
  and monopoly, 81-6
  renting and selling of, 88-92

East Europe, 209
Edgeworth box, 49, 50
education, 78
efficiency (*see also* Pareto optimality),
  49 51, 59
efficiency wage, 78
entry, sequential, 182-6
entry cost, 172-3
entry deterrence, 35, 96-9, 104, 109, 115,
  163-87, 207, 212-14
epistemology, 121
equity, 49, 51, 59
excess capacity, 163, 170, 176, 186
excess demand, 71-2, 75-7
excess supply, 78

fairness, 49, 51
fashion products, 71
Federal Trade Commission, 49
fixed point theorem, 9, 24
folk theorem, 117, 160
forward induction, 122-3, 167, 204, 207
fragmented markets, 197, 202-3
France, 1
free entry (*see also* entry deterrence), 29,
  30, 182-3
frequent flier programs, 196, 207
fringe, *see* competitive fringe

game, Chain Store, 177-82
  extensive form, defined, 105-7
  with imperfect monitoring, 153
  normal form, defined, 8
  with uncertain termination, 160-1
game tree, 6
gasoline market, 161
Germany, 151
Glicksberg theorem, 12
government intervention, 208-16
  Pigouvian, 209, 215-16

Hollywood, 78-9

imperfect information game, 109
imperfect monitoring, *see* monitoring
incentive equilibrium, 192-3

income tax, 51
India, 49, 161, 165, 212
interlinkage, 45, 51, 60, 64, 203
internal structure of firms (*see also*
  managerial incentives), 26, 133-4,
  142, 195, 209
  of government, 209, 217
interpersonal comparison, 96, 104
inventories (*see also* excess capacity),
  134, 141

Japan, 49, 151-2

kinked demand curve, 140-1

law and the state, 217-18
leverage, 62-3
limit pricing, 164, 167, 172, 186
localized rivalry, 96
location, 42, 66-7, 93-9, 104
lock-ins (*see also* switching costs), 70,
  196-7

managerial incentives, 189-94
managers, 188-95
market share, 68
mixed oligopoly, 209-11
mixed strategy, 10-12, 107, 136, 148-207
  defined, 10, 107
monitoring, perfect and imperfect,
  153-4
Monopolies and Restrictive Practices
  Commission, 49, 65
Monopolies and Restrictive Practices
  (Inquiry and Control) Act, 49, 165
Monopolies and Restrictive Trade Practices Act, 49
monopolistic competition, 30
monopoly, 2, 25-8, 39, 44-65, 71-7,
  80-6, 88-92, 101-3, 137-40, 150-1,
  164, 167, 172-4, 197, 199, 213-14

Nash equilibrium, 6, 8-19, 31, 36, 39,
  68, 70, 87, 94-5, 105, 107-9,
  113-14, 116-17, 120-1, 126-8, 137,
  148, 156, 166-7, 191, 200-1, 203-5,
  207, 211, 215, 218
  defined, 8, 107
  existence of, 8, 9, 94-5
  with mixed strategies, 11, 12, 15
nationalization, 209, 212

nationalized firms, *see* public-sector firms
nonlinear pricing, 44, 51–9, 209
  defined, 52

offer curve, 47
oligopoly, 13, 31–3, 37–42, 87–8, 99–101, 105–6, 114–15, 124–31, 149, 151–6, 160, 165–76, 189–95, 197–202, 209–12
  and brand proliferation, 96–9
  and location, 93–6

Pareto domination, 13, 17, 18
Pareto optimality, 48, 50–1, 120–1
partly state-owned firms, 212–14
pay-off matrix, 5, 8
perfect competition, *see* competition
perfect equilibrium, 13–18, 41, 105, 110–12, 130–2
  defined, 15, 110
  existence of, 15, 16
perfect information game, 109
perfection, *see* perfect equilibrium
perfect monitoring, see monitoring
perfect recall, 106
perturbed game, 14, 15
Pigouvian intervention, *see* government intervention
predatory pricing, 164
pre-play communication, 17, 18, 121
price cycles, 42–3
price discrimination (*see also* nonlinear pricing), 62, 63, 65, 81
price war, 153, 155–6
principal–agent model (*see also* incentive equilibrium), 188
principle of minimum differentiation, 94
Prisoner's Dilemma, 10, 13, 104, 114, 156, 178
  history of, 24
privatization, 209, 212
product differentiation, 42, 66, 70
public-sector firms (*see also* partly state-owned firms) 209–14
public utility, 58
punishment, 118

quality (*see also* product differentiation), 66–8, 71–2, 78, 80
  hierarchies in, 67–8

judged by price, 71–2
quick-response duopoly, 133, 137–41

rational expectations, 74
rationality, the concept of (*see also* common knowledge), 18–19, 156–9, 178–9
rationalizability, 18–23, 37–9, 157
  defined, 19, 20
  existence of, 20, 22
rationing, 135
renegotiation proofness, 120–2
restaurant queues, 71
Robinson–Patman Act, 48, 63, 65

sales, 189
sequential equilibrium, 110–12, 151, 157–8, 180–1
share tenancy, 195
Sherman Act, 48–9, 150, 156, 161
signal, 122, 165–7
simple strategy profiles, 118–19
snob effects (*see also* status goods), 78
social welfare, *see* welfare
solution concept, 7, 120
  set-valued, 24
spatial competition, 94
Stackelberg equilibrium, 32–4, 125–7, 137, 167, 190, 195
  endogenous explanation of, 195
Stackelberg perfect equilibrium, 173–6
state-owned firms, *see* public-sector firms
status goods, 71
strategic complements and substitutes, *see* complements, substitutes
strategic-form game, 6
strict equilibrium, 13
subgame, defined, 107
subgame perfection (*see also* perfect equilibrium), 33, 105, 107–9, 113–14, 117–19, 123, 126, 129–32, 137, 153–5, 160–1, 169–71, 183, 191, 203
  defined, 108
substitutes, 42, 69–71
  strategic, 69–71, 206
supply function as strategy, 133, 141
supply functions equilibria, 141–8
switching costs, 70, 104, 196–202, 203
Switzerland, 150
Sylos postulate, 165, 167–8

tie-ins, 45, 60–3
tit-for-tat, 157
transportation cost, 94
trembling hand perfection, 110, 130, 140
trigger strategy, 114–16, 152, 160
two-part tariff, 45–8, 50–2, 62

United Kingdom, 49, 65, 96
United States, 49, 60, 64, 65, 96, 150

upper semi-continuous function, 79, 84
    defined, 79
used goods, 88

Vancouver gasoline market, 161

wages, 72, 78, 161
welfare, 58, 100–3, 209, 211–12, 216–17

zaibatsus, 151–2

Author Index

Abreu, D., 117–18, 153, 161
Adams, W.J., 65
Allen, F., 195
Anant, T.C.A., 209, 215–16
Areeda, P., 186
Asch, P., 63, 150, 161
Asheim, G., 132
Aumann, R.J., 29
Averch, H., 216
Ayres, I., 64

Bagwell, K., 167, 207
Bain, J.S., 2, 163, 168, 176, 186
Banerjee, A.V., 132
Bardhan, P. K., 64–5, 197
Baron, D., 218
Barro, R.J., 81, 92
Basu, K., 24, 42–3, 46, 65, 71–2, 92, 115,
    129, 132, 160, 162, 164, 170–2, 176,
    178, 195, 196, 202–3, 209, 215–16
Baumol, W.J., 186
Beato, P., 209
Becker, G., 71
Bell, C., 64, 196, 202–3
Benoit, J.-P., 43, 114, 117, 120, 135, 160
Berge, C., 79
Bernheim, B.D., 18, 42, 120, 164, 183–5
Bertrand, J., 1, 37, 40, 132
Bhaduri, A., 197
Bhagwati, J.N., 163
Bhaskar, V., 137, 140–1
Binmore, K., 115
Bond, E.W., 92
Bowman, W.S., 60
Boyer, M., 195

Braverman, A., 45, 65
Brock, W.A., 135, 161
Bulow, J.I., 70–1, 80, 88, 91–2, 204, 206
Burstein, M. L., 60–1, 65

Carbajo, J., 63
Caves, R.E., 49, 152
Chamberlin, E.H., 2, 4, 30, 35, 81
Chammah, A.M., 156
Chandra, N.K., 49
Cho, I.K., 122
Clark, J.B., 3
Coase, R., 80, 88
Cooper, D.J., 132
Cournot, A.A., 1, 25, 28, 132
Cremer, H., 209

Daripa, A., 194
Dasgupta, P., 148
D'Aspremont, C., 94, 96, 188
Daughety, A., 3
De Fraja, G., 209, 211
Delbono, F., 209, 211
Dixit, A., 34, 69–70, 100, 103–4, 162,
    166–72
Dorfman, R., 99
Dreze, J., 141

Eaton, B.C., 66
Edgeworth, F.Y., 26, 37, 41–2
Ely, R.T., 25, 49
Encaoua, D., 34–5

Farm, A., 137
Farrell, J., 120, 196

Fellner, W., 151
Fershtman, C., 188, 193, 195, 212-13
Frank, R., 78
Friedman, J., 9, 39, 114, 117, 152
Friedman, M., 30
Fudenberg, D., 151
Fujita, M., 93

Gabszewicz, J.J., 66, 68, 71, 82, 93-4, 96
Gal-Or, E., 195
Geanakoplos, J.D., 70-1, 204, 206
Gerard-Varet, L. A., 188
Geroski, P., 35
Gilbert, R., 182
Glicksberg, 1., 12
Green, E.J., 153-6, 161
Grossman, S., 142
Guasch, A., 45
Guenault, P.H., 49
Gul, F., 92

Hadley, E.M., 151
Hall, R., 140
Hart, O., 35, 142
Hicks, J., 35, 59
Hildenbrand, W., 29
Hiroshi, I., 49
Hitch, C., 146
Holmstrom, B. R., 26
Hotelling, H., 93, 97

Ireland, N.J., 209

Jackson, J.M., 49
Jacquemin, A., 34-5, 186
Jencks, C., 78
Johnson, L., 216
Judd, K.L., 134, 141, 188, 193, 195

Kaldor, N., 35
Kamien, J.I., 92
Katz, M.L., 185
Kirman, A.P., 29
Klemperer, P.D., 70-1, 134, 142, 144,
    146, 196-7, 204, 206
Kohlberg, E., 122-3
Konishi, H., 209
Kreps, D., 29, 42, 105, 107, 110-11,
    133-7, 148, 156-7, 179
Krishna, V., 43, 114, 117, 120, 135, 160
Kuhn, H., 24, 105, 107

Leibenstein, H., 78
Leibowitz, S.J., 92
Levenstein, M.C., 161
Levhari, D., 92
Levitan, R., 43
Lipsey, R.G., 66
Luce, R.D., 24

Mailath, G., 195
Mani, E., 161
Marchand, M., 209
Marschak, T., 137
Marshall, A., 1-3, 40, 59
Marshall, M.P., 1, 2
Martin, S., 161
Mas-Colell, A., 209
Maskin, E., 43, 120, 148
Mason, E., 161
Merrill, W.C., 209
Mertens, J.F., 122
Meyer, M., 142, 144, 146
de Meza, D., 63
Milgrom, P., 156-7, 179
Milliband, R., 218
Mirrlees, J.A., 65, 78
Mishra, A., 167, 204
Modigliani, F., 163
Moreaux, M., 195
Moulin, H., 24
Mukherji, B., 209, 215-16
Mussa, M., 80, 86
Myerson, R., 16

Nash, J., 9
Newbery, D.M.G., 195
Norman, 100, 103-4

O'Brien, D.P., 3
Oi, W., 45
Okuno-Fujiwara, M., 209
Ordover, J., 179
Osborne, M., 42, 137

Pal, D., 127, 129
Panzar, 186
Paranjape, 49
Parks, R.W., 86
Pearce, D., 18, 161
Peck, M.J., 141
Perman, L., 78
Phlips, L., 52-3

Pigou, A.C., 3
Pitchik, C., 42, 137
Porter, R.H., 153–6, 161

Radner, R., 156
Raiffa, H.D., 24
Rainwater, L., 78
Ramey, G., 167, 207
Rappaport, A., 156
Ray, D., 120
Reny, P., 115
Roberts, J., 156–7, 179
Robinson, J., 2, 35
Rosen, J.B., 9
Rosen, S., 80, 86
Rosenthal, R.W., 115, 156–8
Rotemberg, J., 161
Rowley, C.K., 49, 65
Rudra, A., 197

Saha, B., 187
Saloner, G., 42, 161, 179
Salop, S.C., 45, 93, 186
Samuelson, L., 92
Scheinkman, J.A., 42, 133–7, 148, 161
Scherer, F.M., 161
Schmalensee, R., 26, 61, 93, 96, 96, 100, 103–4, 215
Schneider, 209
Schwartz, N.L., 92
Schweizer, U., 93
Schydlowsky, D.M., 65
Scitovsky, T., 71
Seidmann, D.J., 63
Selten, R., 16, 105, 110, 137, 163, 177–9
Sen, Amartya, 187
Sen, Anindya, 187, 209
Sertel, M.R., 209
Shaked, A., 68
Shapiro, C., 78, 196
Sheshinski, E., 80, 86
Shubik, M., 43
Siamwalla, A., 65
Sieper, E., 92
Singh, N., 70, 164, 170–2, 176, 195
Sklivas, S.D., 188, 195
Slade, M.E., 161

Smith, A., 28, 161
Sonnenschein, H., 92
Spence, A.M., 52–3, 78, 163, 166, 168, 171
Srinivasan, T.N., 65, 78, 92
Stacchetti, E., 161
Stackelberg, H. von, 32
Stahl, D., 137
Steiner, P.O., 99
Stern, N., 34, 209
Stigler, G., 28, 33, 61, 63, 141, 155–6
Stiglitz, J., 63, 193, 209, 218
Stokey, N., 80, 92
Summers, L. H., 196
Sutton, J., 68
Suzumura, K., 209
Swan, P.L., 92
Sweezy, P., 140
Sylos-Labini, P., 2, 165, 176, 186

Thisse, J.F., 66, 68, 71, 82, 93–4, 96, 209
Tirole, J., 26, 43, 88, 90, 136, 161
Town, R.J., 161
Tucker, A.W., 24
Turner, D.F., 186

Uekusa, M., 49, 152
Ullman, L., 78

Van Damme, E.E.C., 16
Varian, H.R., 29, 65
Vickers, J., 188, 195
Vives, X., 70, 182

Waterson, M., 66
Weibull, J., 24, 137
von Weizsacker, C.C., 196
Whinston, M.D., 63
Whitaker, J.K., 3
Williams, P.L., 35
Willig, R.D., 26, 186, 215
Wilson, R., 92, 105, 107, 110–11, 156–7, 179
Wodehouse, P.G., 161

Yellen, J., 65